The KINGDON POCKET GUIDE
AFRICAN

The **KINGDON POCKET GUIDE** to
AFRICAN MAMMALS

JONATHAN KINGDON

RUSSEL FRIEDMAN · SOUTH AFRICA

First published 2004

Copyright © 2004 Jonathan Kingdon

Russel Friedman Books CC
PO Box 73, Halfway House 1685, South Africa
Email: rfbooks@iafrica.com
Website: www.rfbooks.co.za

ISBN 1-875091-14-9

Published in the United Kingdom by A&C Black Publishers Ltd, 37 Soho Square, London W1D 3QZ

A CIP catalogue record for this book is available from the British Library.

All rights reserved. No part of this publication may be reproduced or used in any form or by any means – photographic, electronic or mechanical, including photocopying, recording, taping or information storage and retrieval systems – without permission of the publishers.

Typeset and designed by D & N Publishing, Hungerford, Berkshire

Printed and bound in Italy by G. Canale and C. S.p.a.

10 9 8 7 6 5 4 3 2 1

CONTENTS

Preface	6
Introduction	7
How to Use this Guide	8
The African Environment	9
Evolution in Africa	18
Mammals	20
PRIMATES	**21**
Apes	22
Colobid Monkeys	26
Cheek-pouch Monkeys	34
Lorisids	58
Galagos or Bushbabies	60
BATS	**68**
Fruit Bats	68
Insect Bats	74
INSECTIVORES	**88**
Hedgehogs	88
Shrews	90
HARES	**94**
RODENTS	**98**
Squirrels	98
Anomalures	112
Spring Hare	116
Gundis	116
Dormice	116
Blesmols (Mole-rats)	118
Root-rats	118
Porcupines	120
Cane-rats	120
Dassie Rat	122
Jerboas	122
Specialised Rat-like Rodents	122
Murid Rats and Mice	132
CARNIVORES	**142**
Dogs and Allies	142
Mustelids (Weasels and Allies)	148
Otters	150
Mongooses	152
Hyaenas	162
Genets and Civets	164
African Palm Civet	168
Cats	170
SCALY ANT-EATERS	**176**
AFROTHERIA	**178**
Aardvark	178
Golden Moles	178
Elephant Shrews	182
Otter Shrews	186
Hyraxes	188
Elephants	190
ODD-TOED UNGULATES	**192**
Horses (Zebras and Wild Ass)	192
Rhinoceroses	198
EVEN-TOED UNGULATES	**200**
Hippopotamuses	200
Pigs	202
Chevrotains	206
Deer	206
Giraffes	206
Oxen (Buffalo)	210
Spiral-horned Bovines (Bushbuck and Allies)	212
Duikers	220
Dwarf Antelopes	228
Dikdiks	232
Rhebok	234
Reduncine Antelopes (Reedbucks and Kobs)	234
Gazelles	238
Impala	244
Alcelaphine Antelopes (Wildebeest and Allies)	244
Horse-like Antelopes (Oryx and Allies)	252
Sheep and Goats	256
Further Reading	**258**
Glossary	**259**
Scientific Name Index	**264**
English Name Index	**269**

PREFACE

The larger mammals, particularly those in well-protected national parks, are generally easy to view (sometimes on foot, but more usually from a vehicle or hide). Outside protected areas they can usually only be seen at some distance. The great majority of African mammals are small, very shy, mainly nocturnal species. Scientists employ sophisticated methods to study such species, including tailor-made traps, electronic sensors, radio- and spool-tracking, bat-detectors and hidden recorders. However, for both the amateur naturalist and scientist alike, a good pair of eyes, a pencil and notebook can be all that are required. To augment the naked senses and provide permanent records of momentary events binoculars, a tape-recorder and camera are useful adjuncts.

Anyone interested in mammals should keep notes and records. Every human/animal encounter has some significance, even apparent 'accidents', such as an otter shrew in a fishing net, a Wild Dog killed by a speeding lorry, or a tomb bat drowned in a school cistern. Indeed there are aspects of the biology of such animals that might never have been discovered but for such mishaps.

Most mammals are encountered indirectly, most commonly by their tracks, diggings, excreta and feeding sites. Bones and skulls are occasional finds but, sadly, some of the richest sites for animal remains, often of rare and little-known species, are on town market stalls. This plunder is a growing menace in those African countries that permit the commercial exploitation of 'bushmeat' for urban markets. A campaign against this highly damaging trade is gathering momentum and deserves the widest possible support.

We owe to amateur naturalists most of what we know about mammals in Africa, much of it collected from keen African observers. From the earliest foreign explorers to contemporary civil servants, naturalists have recorded countless interesting details. The collators of this accumulated knowledge have, for the most part, been non-Africans writing for non-African audiences. Today this is changing. Fireside gossip is no longer the preferred medium for communicating indigenous knowledge about local animals. African naturalists and scientists increasingly publish for an international audience and this is the context for a new generation of field guides.

The authority for this book lies in an African childhood and lifetime of research, travel, university teaching and writing on various aspects of evolution in Africa. Most publishing projects rely on author, studio artist and graphic workshop to supply the texts, illustrations and maps for their cooperative enterprise. The dislocations are obvious to any careful analyst of the end result. This book breaks new ground in that the author is also illustrator, cartographer and designer. I trust that the results speak for themselves. My qualifications for the task lie with several previous works, most notably with *East African Mammals: An Atlas of Evolution in Africa*, *Island Africa* and *Self-made Man (a Biologist's Genesis)*. I hope this pocket guide will accompany the solitary naturalist on his or her mammal-watching excursions through the African landscape. I also hope it will reach new potential audiences in schools and cities. Here there are new demands for a working knowledge of wildlife. Rapid growth of economically vital tourist industries (mostly founded on wildlife) ensures that the new enthusiasts and wildlife experts are teachers, rangers, couriers and drivers in schoolrooms and minicabs or on park outings. I hope that my work will help these new persuaders to convince both locals and visitors alike of the enormous value and significance of Africa's natural heritage.

INTRODUCTION

This pocket guide derives from my more extended *Field Guide to African Mammals* which, in turn, owed much of its material to the still earlier volumes of my *East African Mammals: An Atlas of Evolution in Africa*.

African mammals have featured in books for over 500 years and such books have an interesting history that reflects changing ideas and an ever enlarging list of species.

At first, information tended to derive from travellers' tales and these early 'guides' were known as 'bestiaries', volumes in which facts and fables were inextricably mixed. With Europe's global expansion and the rise of colonialism, Africa's mammals, no less than those of other continents, became the playthings of the privileged and guides from this period were 'records of big game', primarily designed for hunters.

In the middle years of the last century there was a change in vocabulary. 'Game' became 'wildlife' as vast urban audiences received natural history stories and vivid images of animals in their homes and schools via books and television. The life histories of some popular species became familiar through the work of talented film-makers, naturalists and scientists. This phase coincided with the growth of mass tourism and the declaration of many magnificent national parks. Most current field guides are oriented to this period of expanding tourism and the growth of natural history as a major form of recreation.

Now we have begun a fourth era, marked by our self-discovery as mammals that have created their own extraordinary niche. It is a niche in which consciousness and technological power have brought responsibility for the fate of our own and all other life on earth. Space travel and satellite photography have given us a new awareness of our cosmic fragility and biological limitations, while problems created by pollution and environmental degradation have led to a new concern for the health of the biosphere. As we are ever more frequently reminded of the finite nature of natural ecosystems and their fragile complexity, Africa's uniquely rich 'biodiversity' has become a byword. That biodiversity happens to include us.

It is with this deeper sense of involvement and intensity of interest that the work of home-grown authors, such as myself, has begun to appear, but our efforts are part of an urgent effort to understand and interpret the richest and most complex array of mammals in the world. Much of this urgency is driven by the need to conserve species and communities that are being needlessly exterminated but there is also a pressing need to include mammals in our view of Africa's past, present and future. For example, the discovery of an ancient and uniquely African radiation of mammals, dubbed the 'Afrotheria', has only just begun to receive the recognition it deserves.

The Afrotheria includes seven very different classes of animals, ranging from the very largest, elephants, to the near smallest, golden moles. That such astonishing contrasts should exist within a single radiation can be partially explained by Afrotheria's near-monopoly of Africa during the earliest years of mammalian evolution and the absence of competing mammal lineages during our continent's prolonged geological isolation.

We live in a time of unprecedented accumulation of knowledge. Each year we learn more about living and extinct animals, about pre-history, human origins and processes that govern our past, present and future. From this cascade of new discovery has come the awareness that the survival of other animals is not entirely detached from our own. As more people gain the ability and leisure to see African wildlife, their pleasure, interest and awe may be heightened by an awareness that what they are seeing would have been a familiar aspect of the existence of their ancestors, from ancient hominids to recent hunter-gatherers. As we come to understand how human beings have evolved within African natural communities we can gain a perspective on ourselves as an inextricable part of mammalian life on earth. This, surely, adds a new incentive to the joys of learning about African mammals.

HOW TO USE THIS GUIDE

This pocket guide is essentially visual in nature, with colour illustrations the primary clues as to what animal you might be seeing.

Plates are labelled with their English common name (as used in the *Kingdon Field Guide*) and face a brief text and coloured map of their distribution. The text provides measurements (HB head and body length; SH shoulder height; T tail; W weight; and FA forearm for bats).

There is a brief DESCRIPTION of each species (or for some small mammals, the genus); this is followed by summaries of HABITAT, FOOD, and BEHAVIOUR.

Correct identification of an animal depends upon the nature of the encounter. In the field the great majority of clues are indirect but, in a guide to a fauna of well over 1,000 species, an inventory of tracks, outlines of burrows, forms of excreta, etc., would be impractical. This guide is therefore limited to concise verbal descriptions and detailed full-colour illustrations.

Mammal books that emulate bird books with an item-by-item enumeration of colour patches, long or short crests, etc., are not well suited to the more subtle variation and complexity of most mammals. Comparisons with familiar animals, such as dogs, cats, sheep, etc., are rendered useless by the sheer diversity of African mammals. Therefore, the colour plates in this guide aim to assist identification by illustrating something of a species' 'jizz'. Jizz is the naturalist's word for the total sum of form, colour, stance, silhouette and movement that allows an accurate assessment of a species-specific shape. Ritualised displays often serve to emphasise a species' peculiarities. Some plates illustrate these postures.

While I hope the 'once-in-a-lifetime' visitor to Africa will find this guide useful, it is intended as a celebration of the great diversity of mammalian forms. The guide includes summary descriptions of behaviour but readers seeking more detail on the behaviour of African mammals should refer to my *Kingdon Field Guide to African Mammals* and to Richard Este's excellent *Behaviour Guide to African Mammals*.

Much mammal life is accessible to quiet observation but any serious contemplation of mammals can only be a humbling experience. In their world we are like deaf-mutes. We can neither register nor interpret the most important dimension of their existence: scent. For a few species (mostly primates like us) scent may be subordinate to vision but for the majority scent is a central regulator of their social life, a major mechanism for orienting themselves and a source of what we would call 'exquisite sensations'.

If mammals have been shaped by the way they make a living they also shape the lives of their prey and of the plants they eat. An example is my own discovery of a unique relationship between bark-eating anomalures and the awoura (*Julbernardia*) trees on which they feed (see p. 112). This interdependence between gigantic, slow-growing forest trees and small, short-lived, gliding rodents is so specific that it must go back millions of years. In keeping their flight paths to the tree trunks clear, the anomalures prune (and eventually kill) the tree's competitors, thereby compensating them for wounding their bark. Mutually beneficial relationships are known among bats and the flowering plants that they pollinate, and among primates and the tree seeds that they disperse, but many, much subtler relationships await discovery and study. The inter-relatedness of mammals and all other organisms in natural communities is a compelling reason why we should strive to conserve ecosystems intact, as well as the entire range of mammal species, not just the ones we find attractive or agreeable.

THE AFRICAN ENVIRONMENT
VEGETATION

African vegetation is dominated by an equatorial belt of rain-fed forest and three principal desert areas: the Sahara, the Horn (Somalia) and SW Africa (Namibia). Between these extremes are moist forest–savannah mosaics, woodlands (dominated by leguminous trees, called Miombo in the south-east and Doka in the north-west), various wooded grasslands or savannahs, often dominated by *Acacia* bush or scrub, and verging on subdesert or semi-desert in places. The desert graduates from bare sand dunes (erg) and rocky pavements or screes (hammada) through various conditions in which ephemeral grasses or herbs, scattered shrubs and small trees modify the desert sufficiently to permit various mammals to survive.

Montane areas also range from nearly bare screes on the top of Mt Kilimanjaro through various Afro-alpine habitats to montane grasslands, moorlands and forests. In the Cape and Karoo there are unique shrublands, moors, grasslands and semi-deserts subject to frequent summer fires and sustained by winter rains. There are few places where these vegetation communities have not been affected by human settlement, felling, frequent fires and large herds of livestock. Nonetheless, national parks have often succeeded in maintaining relatively healthy and representative communities of indigenous animals and plants.

The gross vegetation zones listed above break down into subtypes that often define the habitats of particular mammal species. Some major types and categories are:

A. FOREST
1. Lowland rainforests (wetter and drier types)
2. Dry evergreen forests
3. Swamp forests (palms, mangroves, etc.)
4. Montane forests (Afro-montane, Mediterranean, etc.)
5. Mediterranean oak and conifer forests
6. Various mosaics and transitions

Partially cleared rainforest, Yekepa district, Liberia.
PHOTO M. COE

Afro-montane rainforest, Parinari mist forest, Mount Nimba, Liberia. PHOTO M. COE

Forest–savannah transition, Pare Mountains, Tanzania. PHOTO J. KINGDON

Diagram of forest profile, showing changes in ground cover.

Swamp forest, *Phoenix, Marantocioa, Pseudospondias, Elaeis, Mitragyna, Calamus*

Montane forest, *Podocarpus, Cyathea, Ocotea, Aningeria*

B. WOODLANDS
1. Miombo (*Brachystegia/Julbernardia* dominant)
2. Sudanian Doka (*Isoberlinia* dominant)
3. Mopane (*Colophospermum* dominant)
4. Various mosaics

Mopane woodland, Zimbabwe.
PHOTO M. COE

Woodland, *Brachystegia, Terminalia* spp.

C. SAVANNAHS, BUSHLANDS AND THICKETS
1. Various *Acacia* dominant (evergreen to very dry)
2. Bushlands and thickets (often *Commiphora* dominant)
3. Mosaics (from moist to very dry)

Open *Acacia* savannah, Nyambeni, Kenya.
PHOTO M. COE

Acacia Savannah, *Acacia* spp.

Thicket, *Commiphora, Combretum, Acacia, Teclea, Maba*

D. GRASSLANDS AND MARSHES
1. Fire-induced grasslands (*Themeda*, etc.)
2. Valley-bottom grasslands (some semi-aquatic)
3. Montane grasslands
4. Various mosaics and secondary types

Acacia/Commiphora/Combretum thicket, Mkomazi, Tanzania.
PHOTO J. KINGDON

Fire-induced grassland, Samburu, Kenya. PHOTO B. WHITE

Swamp, *Pistia, Nymphaea, Phragmites, Papyrus, Miscanthidium, Phoenix*

Swamp vegetation, Okavango, Botswana. PHOTO M. COE

Giant Groundsel, Afro-alpine zone, Mount Kenya. PHOTO M. COE

E. MONTANE AND AFRO-ALPINE
1. High-altitude alpine types
2. Bamboo (plus forest/grassland mosaics)
3. Undifferentiated (from arid to humid)

Juniper-Hagenia forest/grassland mosaic, Bale Mountains, Ethiopia.
PHOTO J. KINGDON

Alpine zone, *Lobelia, Carex, Senecio*

Subalpine or Ericaceous zone, *Erica arborea*

Bamboo, *Arundinaria*

F. SHRUB, SCRUB, MOORLAND AND SEMI-DESERT
1. Semi-arid shrublands
2. Succulent Karoo types
3. Cape fynbos
4. Desert margins scrub and mosaics

Cape Fynbos. PHOTO J. KINGDON

G. DESERTIC
1. Absolute desert
2. Sand deserts (ergs)
3. Stone deserts (hammada, reg)
4. Subdeserts (graded or mosaic)
5. Semi-deserts (graded or mosaics)

Subdesert, Namaqualand, South Africa. PHOTO M. COE

Semi-desert, *Aloe, Calotropis, Sansevieria, Commiphora, Balanites, Euphorbia*

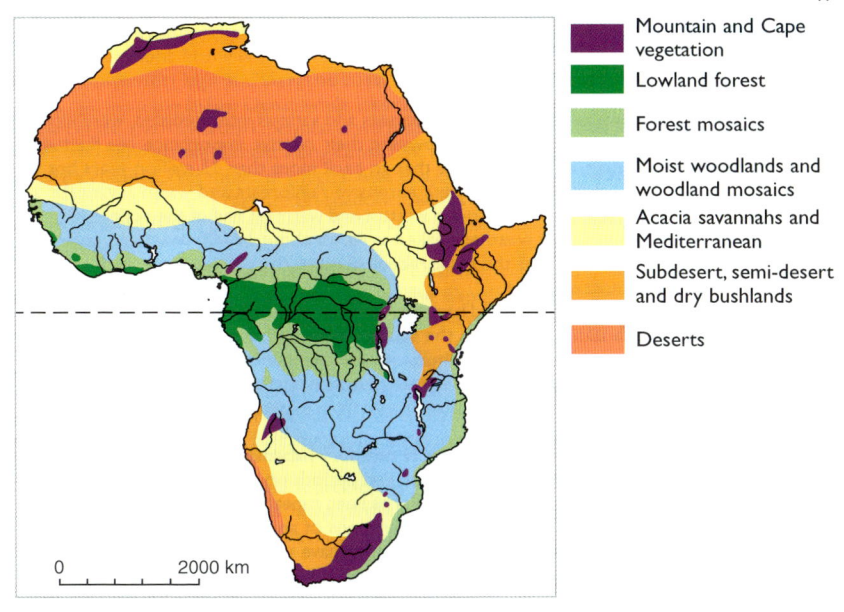

Principal vegetation zones in Africa.

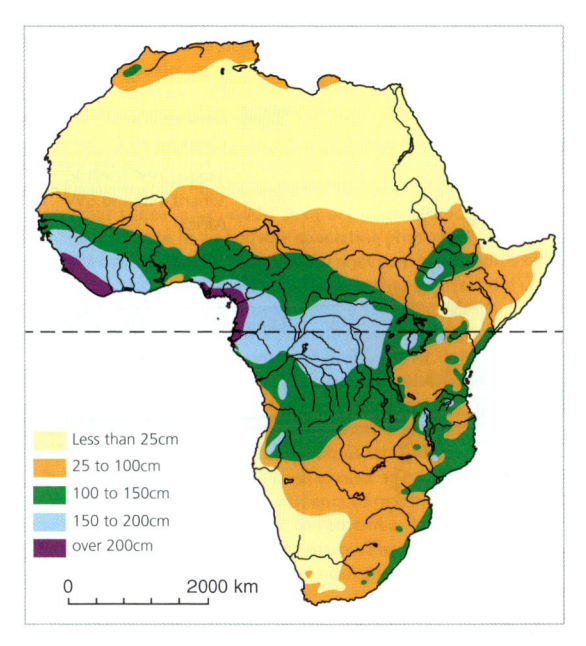

- Mountain and Cape vegetation
- Lowland forest
- Forest mosaics
- Moist woodlands and woodland mosaics
- Acacia savannahs and Mediterranean
- Subdesert, semi-desert and dry bushlands
- Deserts

Annual rainfall.

- Less than 25cm
- 25 to 100cm
- 100 to 150cm
- 150 to 200cm
- over 200cm

MAMMALS

Every user of this pocket guide is a mammal and, as doctors, drug-manufacturers and physiologists have always known, the study of human kinship with other mammals offers us many fundamental truths about ourselves. Take warm blood for example. Internally stable temperatures are central to what mammals are. A naked human freezes to death within hours in a northern winter and, likewise, quickly dies of heatstroke if exposed to a desert midsummer. This is because *biologically* we are still equatorial primates. While we have developed technical solutions to both these extremes of climate (i.e. clothes or air conditioners), other mammals have biological techniques that enable them to survive both extremes, relying on fur for insulation against extremes of temperature, and sweating or panting in order to cool down.

It is glands similar to sweat glands, mammae, which have been modified to produce the milk that give mammals both their common and their scientific name – mammals are animals whose mothers have mammary glands.

Mammal mothers are unique not only in nursing their offspring on milk but in nurturing them *before* birth through a placenta that grows into the wall of the uterus. The placenta allows the foetus to plug into its mother's circulation and so share in her respiratory and excretory systems and in the nutrients carried in her blood. It also stops the mother rejecting the foetus as an alien body.

A mammal is not only sheltered as a foetus in the womb, maternal care also shelters it after birth. Whereas emergence from an egg exposes a newly hatched invertebrate fish or reptile to predators, competitors, changes in climate and the need to find food, newborn mammals escape these rigours through maternal care. Mammals are also relatively independent of the environment for the duration of their infancy and adolescence. This trait is unique to mammals and is most prolonged in primates, especially hominid apes. Among hominids humans have extended this central mammalian characteristic furthest. Not only has our childhood been extended biologically, contemporary humans continue to extend its environmental dimension – detachment from ecological systems. Because much of our technology plays a role analogous to maternal protection we have, in a limited sense, become permanent youngsters, the most mammalian of mammals.

Mothering is also the key to social life in mammals. The physical costs of bearing and suckling offspring are so great for the females that they go to elaborate lengths to fit the timing of reproduction to the best time of year and to ensure access to the best resources both for themselves and for their offspring. To achieve this some species share or enter the territories of prime male land-holders. Others seek out the protection of dominant males at the top of a strict hierarchy while still others choose males that will help raise offspring.

Different patterns of male competition and female choice have dramatic consequences for the external appearance and anatomy of males. Weaponry, in the form of horns, tusks or antlers, has been developed to defend territories or rank. Age-graded gigantism has evolved in the males of hierarchical species, such as gorillas, elands and giraffes. Long-term pair-bonding is usually matched by the sexes being of similar size (typified by wild dogs).

Diversity of size and form is built on those most fundamental of faculties: finding and processing food. Major groupings within the mammals are often named and defined by the shape and form of their teeth (such as ro*dents*, scan*dents*, tubuli*dents*). Furthermore, mammals as a whole have uniquely modifiable teeth and lower jaws. Although these derive from structures similar to those in other vertebrates, the jaw consists of a single mandibular bone anchored in and powerfully hinged onto the skull. Reptiles by contrast have jaws that are a weaker assemblage of bones.

The senses play a very precise role in the life of all mammals. Sight, hearing, scent and touch are balanced in permutations that are unique to each species and that balance finds a gross expression in the shape of animal heads. For example, a Serval Cat's huge ears, a Fishing Genet's moustache of face whiskers, a bushbaby's bulging eyes and an Aardvark's nose tube each manifest unique techniques for finding food. All possess a full set of faculties but the Serval Cat must pick up sound waves from tiny mice in dense grass, the genet senses waves from small fish in water, the bushbaby receives optical wavelengths in near total darkness and the Aardvark locks onto molecular traces of scent emanating from termites hidden deep in the soil. All these faculties had to be developed by stages from the less specialised conditions that preceded them.

The overall shape and proportions of a mammal are therefore the end-products of its lineage and its progressive adaptation to an exact and exacting ecological niche. Much of the fascination of observing animals lies in matching such expressions of form to function. Form is not only anatomical; mammals act, behave, occupy habitats and have habits that are all expressions of their total adaptation. Every species manifests a unique way of making a living.

In this book species have been grouped on the main braches of the mammal tree, these are 'orders' such as primates, bats or carnivores and families such as dogs, cats and mongooses.

In any branching structure that tries to reflect genealogy there are trunks, branches, lesser branches, fronds and twigs, while species can be visualised as leaves.

The condensed format of a pocket guide, where well defined species are the primary subject, necessarily ignores some subdivisions of Linnaean systematics such as suborders, infraorders, superfamilies, subfamilies, tribes and subgenera. However, it should be remembered that nomenclature is actively changing as the system first published by Linnaeus in 1758 is being continuously refined to accommodate new discoveries in genetics and evolutionary genealogy.

Today more and more naturalists and scientists are studying the life histories, genes and fossil antecedents of living animals and plants. We are fortunate to be witness to an explosion of new knowledge about the mammals of Africa. They are proving to be important characters in a central chapter of the evolving story of life on earth.

PRIMATES Primates

All primates derive from, and to some degree retain, a primitive body plan which they share with other unrelated arboreal mammals, such as squirrels, tree shrews and possums. The common arboreal condition is long-backed and short-necked, with five-fingered, clinging hands and feet. The forearms are linked to the chest by collar bones (clavicles) and the compact head has forward-oriented eyes and a short, flexible neck.

A great diversity of anatomical specialisations has developed in primates and these correspond to different climbing or locomotory techniques, e.g. relatively slow, careful climbers have specialised in extreme mobility in their limb joints and a powerful grip in their hands and feet, while fast branch-runners have long tails as balancers, long, flexible backs, limbs with narrow hands and fingers, small thumbs and well-developed bifocal vision to help them assess distance and space.

Judging from tooth structures in fossils, the arboreal mammals that gave rise to primates were mainly insectivorous. Earliest extensions in diet would have been small vertebrates and ripe, soft fruits. Some primates then tackled unripe or hard fruits, resins, flowers, nectar, buds, young leaves and, later, mature leaves. Trends towards consuming larger quantities of abundant but more difficult foods (such as old leaves, resins, hard nuts and seeds) led to early specialisation in lineages.

Powerful big toes are known to have developed in fossil primates by at least 60 million years ago. Thumbs have a less certain ancestry and are less universal (some primates, notably colobus species, have lost them altogether). Naked, padded digits and palms on both hands and feet are universal and clearly represent one of the very earliest adaptations of primates.

The decline of the sense of smell seems to be associated with the superiority of touch and vision as the means of exploring and surviving in a world of three-dimensional space latticed by branches. Fossils reveal that some primates had begun to have a more forward orientation of the eyes by about 60 million years ago. This narrowing of the field of vision seems to have been compensated for by greater ability to rotate the head on a very short neck. Efficient rotation is helped by a compact, round head.

In Africa the Primates order has two major subdivisions: apes and Old World monkeys (Catarrhini) and the prosimian bushbabies and lorisids (Strepsirrhini). The infraorder Catarrhini subdivides into two families: the Hominidae (apes and humans) and the Cercopithecidae (colobid or 'thumb-less' monkeys, and cercopithecids or 'cheek-pouch' monkeys). The Strepsirrhini also subdivides into two families: the Loridae (the Potto and its allies) and the Galagonidae (galagos).

All these and further subdivisions have diagnostic characteristics, but their enumeration would inordinately extend the length of this guide where individual species are our central concern.

APES AND HUMANS Hominidae

CHIMPANZEE *Pan troglodytes*

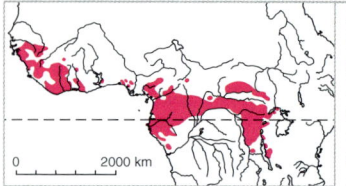

SIZE HB 63.5–90cm. SH 100–179cm. W av. 30kg (female), 35kg (26–40kg) (male).
DESCRIPTION A robust ape with long, somewhat tufted black hair, bare face, bare prominent ears and bare parts of the abdomen. The brows are rounded and the margins of the nostrils are scarcely raised. females slightly lighter than males and develop pink swelling of the ano-genital skin which fluctuates in size according to the phase of their menstrual cycle. Three, perhaps four subspecies.
HABITAT Mainly rainforests and forest galleries extending into savannah woodlands. Chimpanzees also frequent lowland and mountain forests, showing a preference for mixed and colonising communities.
FOOD Highly variable according to individual population and season. Fruit comprises about half the diet but leaves, bark and stems are also important. Animal foods range from termites and other insects to birds, eggs and nestlings; small mammals are taken occasionally. While preferred foods, such as figs, are fruiting, Chimpanzees may spend most of their time feeding on a few species. At other times they may be forced to forage widely and have been recorded as taking up to 300 different food types and as many as 20 in any single day.
BEHAVIOUR Chimpanzees form social communities of 15–20 animals within large territories that are defended by both sexes but mostly by males. Only females cross community boundaries. Groups vary in composition and size according to the seasonal distribution of food. Adult males are fiercely intolerant of their counterparts in neighbouring groups. Immigrant oestrous females are generally accepted into groups but their offspring may be attacked and killed.

Chimpanzees feed most actively during the early morning and evening and rest during the heat of the day. They build individual nests of branches. Adult males co-operate in hunting monkeys. Chimpanzees communicate vocally using more than 30 calls, and have a wide variety of facial expressions, suggesting almost human levels of subtlety, but which may also be part of very loud and active social displays.

BONOBO or PYGMY CHIMPANZEE *Pan paniscus*

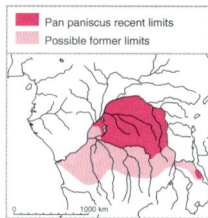

SIZE HB 55–60cm. SH 90–100cm. W 30kg (25–35kg).
DESCRIPTION Looks like a juvenile Chimpanzee. The more obvious of its youthful characteristics are a rounder cranium, less pronounced brow ridges and muzzle and less tendency to go bald. Hair on the scalp is splayed and flat while that on the cheeks and chin is heart-shaped and surrounds a black face with pink-edged eyes and lips. All limbs, especially the legs, are long and fine. The narrow foot opposes an enlarged 'thumb'. Calls are higher and weaker equivalents of those uttered by common Chimpanzees.
HABITAT A mosaic of swamp, primary and secondary forests in a landscape of very mild relief, with a humid, stable climate. It is possible that to the far east of its range the Bonobo occupies montane forest. Leguminous trees are important sources of food.
FOOD More than half the diet comprises fruits and seeds. Leaves, flowers and various other plant parts provide fibre and protein, as do smaller quantities of mushrooms, invertebrates, small vertebrates, honey and eggs. Some 150 foods are currently known but a few species, notably velvet tamarind, a liane and soap-berries, are staple foods for periods of a month or more.
BEHAVIOUR Some differences from common Chimpanzees can be related to the bonobo's greater environmental affluence; for example, male defences are obsolete during frequent gluts of fruits. Other differences derive directly from the extension of juvenile traits in both sexes. Thus males remain close to their mothers up to adulthood. Reproductive behaviour has been diverted to social ends and seduction has overtaken male dominance as the main regulator in Bonobo society.

West African Chimpanzee

Eastern Chimpanzee

Chimpanzee

Central African Chimpanzee

Bonobo

Bonobo

Bonobo

Chimpanzee

GORILLA *Gorilla gorilla*

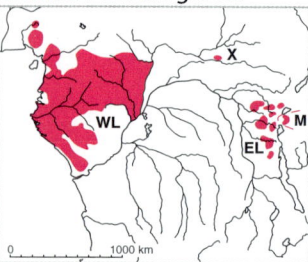

SIZE SH 130–150cm (female), 140–185cm (male). W 68–114kg (female), 160–210kg (male).
DESCRIPTION Very large, barrel-chested ape with relatively even hair, a bare black face and chest, and small ears. The bar-shaped brows are joined and the nostril margins are raised. Females are much smaller than males. The belly of wild gorillas is much more massive than in captive specimens. The long blue-black coat of the Mountain Gorilla contrasts with the shorter and sparser brownish coat of the lowland forms. The small of the back, or 'saddle', of mature males becomes grey or white with age, hence the name 'silverback' for old males.

Subspecies: Western Lowland Gorilla, *G. g. gorilla* (W Nigeria to R. Zaïre/R. Sangha): brownish with a broad face but relatively small jaws. (It is possibly a species, distinct from the eastern form.) Mountain Gorilla, *G. g. beringei* (volcanic slopes of Rwanda and Zaïre): very black and densely furred, with a broad face and massive jaws. Eastern Lowland Gorilla, *G. g. graueri* (Impenetrable forest, Uganda, rift wall and lowlands of E Zaïre): short black fur, narrow face and very large body size. (Uganda gorillas could be a fourth race.)

HABITAT Discontinuous. Lowland populations are found in lowland tropical rainforest; over part of their range in W Africa they inhabit mixed tropical rainforest where fruits play a larger part in the diet and the animals frequently climb trees to feed. The Mountain Gorilla is confined to mountain and subalpine environments. In most areas gorillas prefer open clearings, valley bottoms, landslides, etc., where there is a dense tangle of ground-level herbaceous growth.

FOOD Compared with the Lowland Gorillas, the Mountain Gorilla eats fewer plant species and feeds mainly on leaves, shoots and stems; *Galium* vines, wild celery and three or four other species make up a high proportion of the diet. The Western Lowland Gorilla eats more fruits but also relies on wild ginger (*Afromomum*) for a high proportion of its diet.

BEHAVIOUR Gorillas form small, non-territorial harems dominated by a single, mature male. Male offspring are driven out and females not infrequently change groups. Females gravitate to solitary adult males and such primary pairs display the strongest bonds (adult females do not bond with other females). Whenever established pairs are joined by other adult females the sequence of arrival determines female rank order.

The abundance of fast-growing food permits such large groups to forage together (something physically impossible in most W African habitats). There is no defence of the home range and the ranges of all groups overlap those of their neighbours quite extensively; avoiding action is normally taken during encounters. More than half the day is spent foraging, either on the move or temporarily static. Gorillas tend to behave like ruminants, with very long rest periods. Mutual evasion is facilitated by frequent advertising signals emitted by dominant males. The commonest call bears some structural resemblance to Chimpanzee hooting. It is a crescendo of deep, booming hoots, culminating in a tattoo of chest-beating (this can be heard over 2km away on a clear day). Various degrees and conditions of alarm are signified by barks, roars or screams, almost all made only by the male.

On rare occasions when neighbouring males fail to evade one another, there are displays of roaring, chest-beating, plant-bashing and charging. Very occasionally these culminate in a fight. Similar displays greet human intruders, predators and competing herbivores. In contrast to dominant males, females and young are quiet and retiring. They have a modest repertoire of grunts, burps, growls and whines.

Gorillas reproduce at a very slow rate, on average one young every 4 years (a maximum of about 10 in a female's lifetime). Mothers give continuous care and attention to their young and the dominant male is always alert to the safety and well-being of all members of his group, willing to defend the young against all-comers. Gorillas live for 50–60 years.

Lowland Gorillas

female

male

Mountain Gorilla
silverback male

*sketches of
Mountain Gorillas*

COLOBID MONKEYS Colobinae

These are medium-sized arboreal monkeys with proportionally big bodies and small heads. The thumb is atrophied; the fingers are aligned in a powerful hook, enabling them to swing easily from branches. However, they have to take food directly into the mouth.

OLIVE COLOBUS *Procolobus verus*

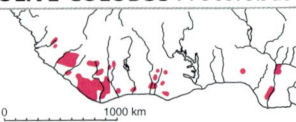

SIZE HB 43–50cm (female and male). T 57–64cm. W 3–4.5kg (female), 3.3–5.7kg (male).
DESCRIPTION The smallest colobus, cryptically coloured, with a dull grey underside and greenish olive upperside, graduating to brown on the back.
HABITAT Secondary growth within high forest; also along the margins of the forest zone, as well as in swamp and palm forests.
FOOD 70% young leaves, buds and flowers, only 10% old leaves. Preference for unripe fruits.
BEHAVIOUR Groups of 5–15 animals tend to contain 1 adult male with several females and their young. Almost exclusively arboreal and extremely shy.

RED COLOBUS *Piliocolobus*

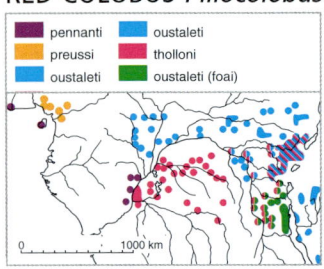

pennanti • oustaleti
preussi • tholloni
oustaleti • oustaleti (foai)

SIZE HB 45–62cm (female), 45–70cm (male). T 42–80cm. W 7–9kg (female), 9–13kg (male).
DESCRIPTION Red colobus occur in numerous populations and species. All tend to be some permutation of red, white, black, brown and grey. They have exceptionally small heads on long-backed, pot-bellied bodies.
HABITAT Only in moist, evergreen forest close to permanent water. Although most red colobus are found in lowland forest, some occur in montane areas up to 1,500m. FOOD Very selective of the plant types and parts that form the principal components of their diet but they eat many species. Groups can have a massive impact on the foliage of their food trees.
BEHAVIOUR Troops number up to 100 animals and reside within a 25–150ha territory. The territory is vigorously defended against intruders and advertised by all group members calling with a variety of barks and chirps. Males remain in the territory throughout their lives but females may move.

TSHUAPA RED COLOBUS *Piliocolobus tholloni*   see map above

DESCRIPTION Of almost uniform foxy-red colouring, darkening to a deep brown on the shoulders and lighter on the underside. Long face, square muzzle.

PENNANT'S RED COLOBUS *Piliocolobus pennanti*   see map above

DESCRIPTION Reddish above and paler red below, with forequarters and crown verging towards black, and a white ruff.

PREUSS'S RED COLOBUS *Piliocolobus preussi*   see map above

DESCRIPTION Tentatively treated as a distinct species, this colobus shares some features (colour) with *P. pennanti* while others (such as hair-growth patterns on the head and nose shape) are typical of the western *P. badius* group.

WESTERN RED COLOBUS *Piliocolobus badius*

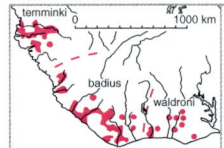

SIZE HB 47–63cm. T 52–75cm. W 5.5–10kg.
DESCRIPTION Black or dark grey upperparts with lower limbs and underparts ranging from rich red to light orange.

Olive Colobus

Tshuapa Red Colobus

Preuss's Red Colobus

Western Red Colobus

Pennant's Red Colobus

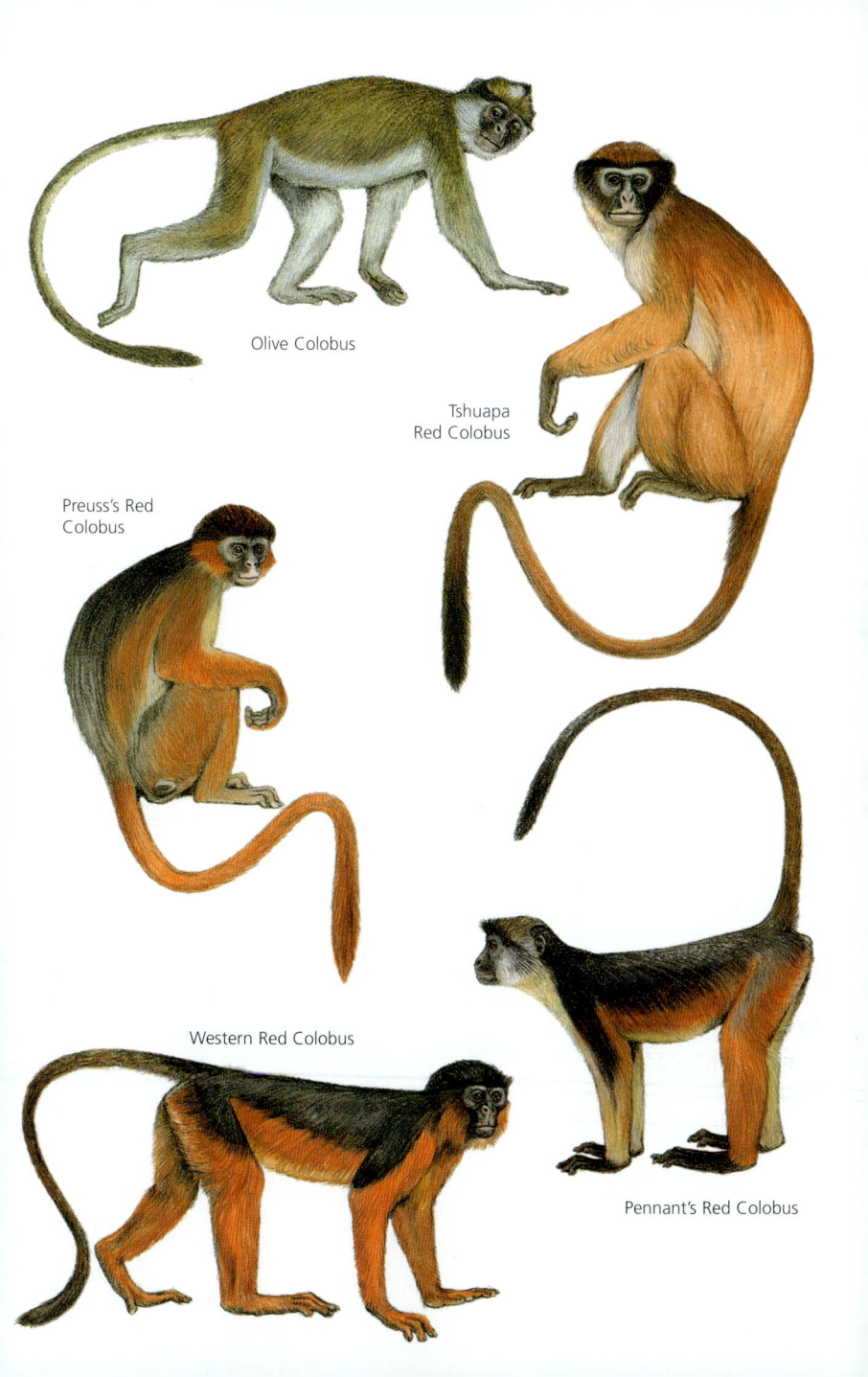

ZANZIBAR RED COLOBUS *Piliocolobus kirkii*

- Central African Red Colobus
- Iringa Red Colobus
- Zanzibar Red Colobus
- Tana River Red Colobus

SIZE See lower range of measurements.

DESCRIPTION Has a ragged, tesselated coat of three colours: red, black and white, individually very variable. The vocalisations of this species are different from any other species.

HABITAT Occurs in relict patches throughout Zanzibar I., but found mainly in the southern part of the island and also in scrub forest growing on waterless coral rag on the eastern side of the island. A small population has been translocated to Pemba I.

FOOD Some groups feed almost exclusively on mangrove leaves and the populations on coral rag appear to subsist on a drier, coarser diet than any recorded for red colobus. More than 60 food plants.

IRINGA RED COLOBUS *Piliocolobus gordonorum*

SIZE See lower range of measurements.

DESCRIPTION A dark, tricoloured species (red, black and white) with a thin, shaggy coat, less tesselated than the Zanzibar species and with a tendency to darker tones.

HABITAT Restricted to a few small forests on the Uzungwa Mts, where it survives in riverine and montane forest patches between 550 and 6,000m. The range is shared by Angola Pied Colobus and other monkeys.

FOOD About two-thirds leaf stems (petioles) from some 35 tree species. Both ripe and unripe fruits make up nearly 20% of the diet, with buds, flowers, new leaves and very small quantities of older leaves making up the balance.

TANA RIVER RED COLOBUS *Piliocolobus rufomitratus* see map above

SIZE See lower range of measurements.

DESCRIPTION Colobus with a dull, greyish brown back, paler greyish limbs and a grey-white underside. Head pattern is distinctive. In spite of resembling some *P. tephrosceles* in colour, it differs in size and skull shape.

HABITAT Frequenting riverine and gallery forest, only on the levees of the R. Tana between Kipendi village and the mouth of the river, notably the Mnazini and Kinyadu forests. These forests are dominated by *Pachystela* and *Barringtonia*.

FOOD On the R. Tana only 22 food trees are used by red colobus, fewer than in any other area where red colobus monkeys have been studied. Diet comprises a quarter fruits and seeds, two-thirds buds, flowers and young leaves, and just over 10% of old mature leaves. Dependent on the leaves and fruit of *Ficus sycomorus*.

CENTRAL AFRICAN RED COLOBUS *Piliocolobus oustaleti*

see map on p.26 and above

SIZE See upper range of measurements.

DESCRIPTION Some populations are relatively uniform and others are highly variable at the individual level. Most have dark extremities to the limbs (often black hands and feet), with red markings especially on the cap.

HABITAT Ranges between 300 and 2,500m, spanning a wide range of forest types from levee, swamp, lowland and mixed to montane forests.

FOOD In Kibale (Uganda) young leaves and buds comprise nearly half and mature leaves a quarter of the annual diet. At Gombe, in Tanzania (a more markedly seasonal forest), these proportions are inverted. At both sites intense competition from frugivorous primates probably helps to explain their very minor consumption of fruits and seeds.

Zanzibar Red Colobus
Piliocolobus kirkii

Tana River Red Colobus
Piliocolobus rufomitratus

Iringa Red Colobus
Piliocolobus gordonorum

Central African Red Colobus
Piliocolobus oustaleti tephrosceles

PIED COLOBUS *Colobus*

Pied colobus are long-fingered, agile monkeys. Each species has a distinctively shaped face but they are best distinguished by their colouring. Territories are smaller than those of red colobus. They can subsist on material that is older and less palatable to the red colobus and tend to feed from fewer tree species.

BLACK COLOBUS *Colobus satanus*

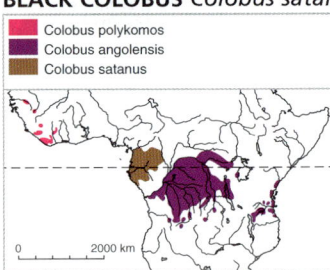

Colobus polykomos
Colobus angolensis
Colobus satanus

SIZE HB 50–77cm. W 9–15kg.
DESCRIPTION All-black, without tassels or a tufted tail, and most like the Angola Colobus in general morphology. It has a shorter nose, thicker incisors and lacks the loud, reverberating calls of other species.
HABITAT Limited to high-canopy forests between SW Cameroon, Bioko I. (formerly Fernando Po) and the R. Zaïre.
FOOD A very high proportion of seeds and unripe fruits. Shows a marked preference for the leaves of lianes. In sand-dune forest young and old leaves are eaten equally. In the Ogooué basin it scarcely eats old leaves at all but takes a larger proportion of fruits and seeds.
BEHAVIOUR Exists at lower densities and is quieter than pied colobus.

WESTERN PIED COLOBUS *Colobus polykomos*   see map above

SIZE HB 50–61cm (female), 50–67cm (male). T 63–90cm. W 6.6–10kg (female), 8–11.7kg (male).
DESCRIPTION Black body and legs, tail wholly white, bonnet of straggly silver hair and long white epaulettes.
HABITAT Rainforest and forest galleries are preferred.
FOOD Selective in their feeding habits, taking only about one-third of their total diet from the 20 dominant species of trees and lianes available.

ANGOLA PIED COLOBUS *Colobus angolensis*   see map above

SIZE HB 50–61cm (female), 50–67cm (male). T 63–90cm. W 9–20kg.
DESCRIPTION Black bodied with a white ruff and long epaulettes. Tail varies from all-white to black.
HABITAT Montane and lowland forests.
FOOD Diet combines about two-thirds of leaves with one-third fruits and seeds.

GEOFFROY'S PIED COLOBUS *Colobus vellerosus*

Colobus vellerosus
Colobus guereza (lowland)
Colobus guereza (eastern highlands)

SIZE HB 50–67cm. T 63–90cm. W 8–15kg.
DESCRIPTION Black with a broad white ruff which completely encircles the face and is reminiscent of a nun's wimple.
HABITAT Ranges between the R. Bandama to Dahomey and Togo in lowland rainforest and gallery forests.
FOOD Tends to feed in more shaded, middle layers of the forest when mixed with red colobus.

GUEREZA COLOBUS *Colobus guereza* (syn. *C. abyssinicus*)   see map above

SIZE HB 48–65cm (female); 54–75cm (male). T 65–90. W 10–23kg.
DESCRIPTION Black and white with shorter, thinner fur in lowland forests but very long and thick fur in mountain areas.
HABITAT Wide ranging, from lowland tropical rainforest to the upper reaches of montane forest.
FOOD In all areas where they have been studied, Guerezas have been found to be the most folivorous colobus species except for the Olive Colobus. About three-quarters of the diet consists of leaves.
BEHAVIOUR Inhabit small territories where several related offspring live with 1 or more hierarchically ranked males. Mutual male intolerance forces males to disperse and promotes female cohesion.

Black Colobus

Western Pied Colobus

Black Colobus *facial details*

Angola Pied Colobus *Southern highlands form*

Geoffroy's Pied Colobus

Guereza Colobus *East African highland form*

Guereza Colobus *Central African lowland form*

CHEEK-POUCH MONKEYS Cercopithecinae

BABOONS *Papio*

Large, terrrestrial, predominantly quadrupedal, monkeys of open country. Adult males bigger and longer muzzled than females. Live in harems of a single male with one or more females.

- Papio papio
- Papio hamadryas
- Papio anubis
- Papio cynocephalus
- Papio ursinus

SACRED BABOON *Papio hamadryas*

SIZE HB 50–65cm (female), 70–95cm (male). T 40–60cm. SH 40–50cm (female), 50–65cm (male). W 10–15kg (female), 15–20kg (male).
DESCRIPTION Grizzled, greenish brown. Active harem males dove-grey, with lighter cheek ruffs, tail tip and callosity margins.
HABITAT Arid subdesert, steppe, hillsides, escarpments and mountains bordering the Red Sea.
FOOD Opportunistic omnivore.
BEHAVIOUR Blood-related harems sleep together.

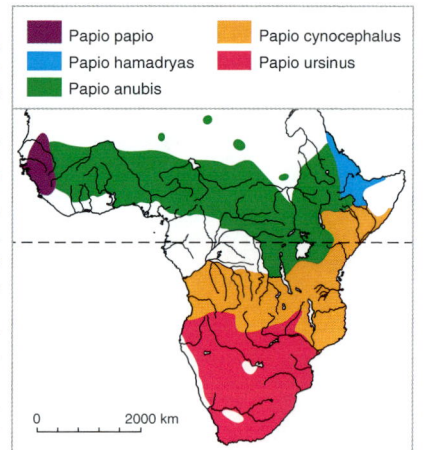

GUINEA BABOON *Papio papio*

SIZE HB 55cm (female), 75cm (male). T 35–60cm. SH 45cm (female), 60cm (male). W est. 12kg (female), est. 19kg (male).
DESCRIPTION Grizzled, reddish brown with a sharply defined cape on adult males.
HABITAT Woodlands, savannah and steppe within reach of water; gallery forests in south of range.
FOOD Seeds, shoots, roots, fruits, fungi, invertebrates, small vertebrates and eggs.
BEHAVIOUR Large aggregations of harem groups, numbering 10–200 (sometimes exceeding 500) individuals, may forage together.

OLIVE BABOON *Papio anubis*   see map above

SIZE HB 50–114cm; est. 75cm (female), est. 100cm (male). T 45–71cm. SH est. 55cm (female), est. 70cm (male). W 11–30kg (female), 22–50kg (male).
DESCRIPTION Grizzled, olive-brown. Adult males have cape over neck and shoulders.
HABITAT Ranging throughout Sahelian woodland and forest-mosaic habitats.
FOOD Grass is a principal food in open areas, and fruits in forests.
BEHAVIOUR Males may co-operate in some feeding situations.

YELLOW BABOON *Papio cynocephalus*   see map above

SIZE HB est. 65cm (female), est. 98cm (male). T 45–68cm. SH est. 50cm (female), est. 66cm (male). W 11–15kg (female), 22–30kg (male).
DESCRIPTION Slender, with brindled yellow-brown upperparts. Paler below, it lacks cape or mane.
HABITAT Over a great part of its range it is specific to fire-climax Miombo (*Brachystegia*) woodland. It also occupies dry bushland, thickets, steppes and the coastal littoral.
FOOD The seeds, flesh and pods of leguminous trees are seasonal staples but Miombo fauna, such as mopane worms and various insects, are equally important. Young antelopes and hares are caught.
BEHAVIOUR Forages in extended, well-spaced troops.

CHACMA BABOON *Papio ursinus*   see map above

SIZE HB 50–80cm (female), 80–110cm (male). T 50–85cm. SH 40–60cm (female), 50–75cm (male). W 12–30kg (female), 25–45kg (male).
DESCRIPTION Grizzled khaki or grey to dark brown and black. Males have very long, narrow muzzles.
HABITAT All types of woodland, savannah, steppes and subdesert, montane, Cape and Karoo flora.
FOOD Omnivorous.
BEHAVIOUR Troops average 20–50 animals but up to 100 is possible. Multi-male hierarchies normal.

Guinea Baboon

Sacred Baboon

Olive Baboon

Yellow Baboon

Chacma Baboon

GELADA *Theropithecus gelada*

Theropithecus gelada gelada
T. g. obscurus

SIZE HB 50–65cm (female), 68–75cm (male). T 32–50cm (female), 45–55cm (male). SH 40–50cm (female), 55–65cm (male). W 13kg (10–15kg) (female), 20kg (15–22kg) (male).

DESCRIPTION Brown terrestrial monkey with thick fur, giving the impression of a heavy body on short limbs. Outer fur tassels of adult males often have a bleached appearance, especially on the head, chest, tufted tail and lower hindlimbs.

HABITAT Feeds mainly on the flat margins of high grass plateaus. Bands keep within 2km of the escarpment edges, where they retreat at night or at the least alarm.

FOOD Almost entirely leaves of grasses, which are plucked blade by blade with strong, opposable thumb and fingers.

BEHAVIOUR Gelada bands are social units, numbering between 50 and 250 animals, which consist of 2–30 harems (each led and controlled by a single adult male) and 1 or more bachelor groups. Bands cluster together on sleeping-cliffs and often feed and move in a single, dispersed scatter.

MANDRILL *Mandrillus sphinx*

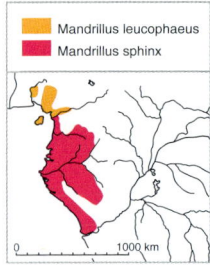

Mandrillus leucophaeus
Mandrillus sphinx

SIZE HB 55–70cm (female), 70–95cm (male). T 7–10cm. SH 45–50cm (female), 55–60cm (male). W 10–15kg (female), 19–30kg (male).

DESCRIPTION A heavily built baboon with a grizzled olive-brown coat, pointed orange beard, crested crown and dull white to grey underside. In males the bare face and posterior are bright red, white and blue. Males have two swollen nasal ridges, which are electric blue and grooved, giving the impression of a permanent snarl. White fur surrounds the red-lipped mouth and forms leaf-shaped flashes behind the flesh-coloured ears.

HABITAT Primary evergreen rainforest, stretching between 100 and 300km inland from the Atlantic coast. In this forest the fruiting of trees and lianes is irregular, resulting in periodic shortages of fruits.

FOOD Omnivorous, with fruits preferred whenever they are available. In the course of a year groups of Mandrills are thought to range over an area of about 50km^2. They forage very intensively in a succession of small subsections, exhausting local resources over variable amounts of time (but on average moving on about once a month).

BEHAVIOUR The smallest social unit is the extended harem led by a single dominant male. In groups with two or more males subordinate individuals establish size hierarchies. The mandrill can walk 5–15km in the course of a day and densities in undisturbed areas have been estimated at 5 to 7 animals per km^2. Single animals are uncommon, often old males presumably displaced by fighting. Small groups of Mandrills may forage silently but bands or clans are very noisy and emit a continuous chorus of two-phase barks, frequent 'crowing', grunts and squeals. The Mandrill sleeps in trees but always travels on the ground.

DRILL *Mandrillus leucophaeus* *see map above*

SIZE HB 45–60cm (female), 75–90cm (male). T 6–12cm. SH 45–50cm (female), 55–60cm (male). W 10–15kg (female), 15–20kg (male).

DESCRIPTION A stocky, large-headed olive-brown baboon with an off-white underside and a broad, leaf-shaped white ruff surrounding a naked black face. A dense neck-cape serves to greatly enlarge the visual impact of the adult male's head and chest.

HABITAT Evergreen forest on littoral and in Cameroun mountains up to 1,000m; also forest–savannah mosaics. Drills have also been noted in rocky areas within the forest.

FOOD Omnivorous with reliance on fruit staple; also much herbaceous growth, roots, mushrooms, invertebrates (notably worms, termites, ants and spiders) and small vertebrates.

BEHAVIOUR Social structure resembles that of the Mandrill. Groups travel on the ground but forage and sleep in the trees.

Gelada

Gelada *male demonstrating 'Gelada grin' display*

Gelada *female from the front*

Gelada *female showing sexual swellings*

Mandrill *male*

Mandrill *female*

Drill

Drill *head tilt*

Mandrill *grimace*

DRILL-MANGABEYS *Cercocebus*
Sometimes known as 'eyelid monkeys', because of their white upper eyelids, these are large monkeys from riverine habitats. Live in multi-male, multi-female groups. Relatively terrestrial but able to swim.

RED-CAPPED MANGABEY *Cercocebus torquatus*

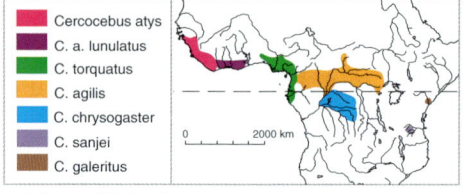

- Cercocebus atys
- C. a. lunulatus
- C. torquatus
- C. agilis
- C. chrysogaster
- C. sanjei
- C. galeritus

SIZE HB 45–60cm (female), 47–67cm (male). T 60–75cm. SH 38–42cm (female), 40–45cm (male). W 5–8kg (female), 7–12.5kg (male).
DESCRIPTION The dark grey tail frequently held with white tip over the head.
HABITAT Seldom far from swamp or valley forest. Occupies region between Cross R. to Ubangui/Zaïre rivers.
FOOD Mainly fruits and nuts, supplemented by the stems and roots of undergrowth plants.

SOOTY MANGABEY *Cercocebus atys*   *see* map above
SIZE HB 45–60cm (female), 47–67cm (male). T 40–80cm. SH 38–42cm (female), 40–45cm (male). W 4.5–7kg (female), 7–12kg (male).
DESCRIPTION Smoky- or slate-grey. Orbits and muzzle rectangular in outline.
HABITAT Restricted to Upper Guinea. Commonest close to swamp and palm forests.
FOOD Fruits, including the flesh and kernels of very hard fruits and nuts, are the main staple.

AGILE MANGABEY *Cercocebus agilis*   *see* map above
SIZE HB 44–55cm (female), 51–65cm (male). T 45–79cm. SH 37–42cm (female), 40–45cm (male). W 5–7kg (female), 7–13kg (male).
DESCRIPTION Drab, speckled olive colour with short, fine fur.
HABITAT Endemic to regions north of the R. Zaïre, especially extensive equatorial swamp forests from Atlantic to eastern Zaïre. Seldom moves out of seasonally flooded swamp forest.
FOOD Almost entirely certain dominant swamp-forest trees (notably dika nuts or Gabon chocolate, *Irvingia*, and sugar plums, *Uapaca*), but some 42 species of fruits have been recorded.

TANA MANGABEY *Cercocebus galeritus*   *see also* map above

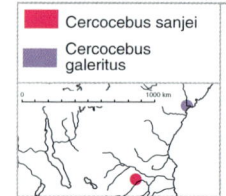

- Cercocebus sanjei
- Cercocebus galeritus

SIZE HB est. 42–53cm (female), est. 50–63cm (male). T 45–77cm. SH est. 35–41cm (female), est. 40–44cm (male). W est. 5–6.5kg (female), est. 8–10kg (male).
DESCRIPTION Grizzled ash-coloured, limp, shaggy fur, prominent white eyelids, flash of paler fur on temples, white borders to the black face.
HABITAT Restricted to gallery forests along the floodplain of the R. Tana in Kenya. Prefers levee forest.
FOOD Mainly fruits; figs are especially important.

SANJE MANGABEY *Cercocebus sanjei*   *see* maps above
SIZE HB est. 50–65cm. T est. 55–65cm. SH est. 40–50cm. W est. 7–9kg.
DESCRIPTON Fine ash-grey grizzle colour, with limp crown hair.
HABITAT Valley forests on the Uzungwa massif.
FOOD Fruits, mostly ripe, comprise 70% of the diet; foliage makes up most of the balance.

GOLDEN-BELLIED MANGABEY *Cercocebus chrysogaster*   *see* map above
SIZE HB 45–55cm (female), 52–66cm (male). T est. 50–75cm. SH 38–42cm (female), 42–46cm (male). W 6–8kg (female), 10–14kg (male).
DESCRIPTION The most drill-like species, with a naked violet rump, bright fur and robust build.
HABITAT The southern section of the Zaïre depression swamp complex.
FOOD Presumed to be mainly fruits.

Red-capped Mangabey

Sooty Mangabey

Agile Mangabey

Tana Mangabey

Golden-bellied Mangabey

Sanje Mangabey

BABOON-MANGABEYS *Lophocebus*

These are large, black or brown monkeys with very long tails and rather 'ragged', tesselated fur with tufts on the crown or brows. Less riverine specialists than drill-mangabeys.

GREY-CHEEKED MANGABEY *Lophocebus albigena*

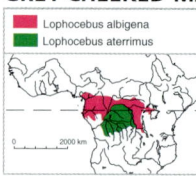

SIZE HB 43–61cm (female), 54–73cm (male). T 73–100cm. SH 38–43cm (female), 40–45cm (male). W 4–7kg (female), 6–11kg (male).
DESCRIPTION Dark brown with long, ragged tail and tufted crown. Male loud call a very distinctive 'whoop gobble'.
HABITAT Rainforest, both primary and secondary but with a strong preference for swamp forest.
FOOD Mainly fruits and nuts.
BEHAVIOUR Groups of 5 or 6 females and young with several adult males, one of which is dominant.

BLACK MANGABEY *Lophocebus aterrimus*   *see* map above

SIZE HB 45–65cm. T 80–85cm. SH 40–45cm. W 4–7kg (female), 6–11kg (male).
DESCRIPTION Long-limbed, all-black monkey with slightly prehensile tail.
HABITAT Moist rainforest but especially swamp forests. Seldom descends to the ground.
FOOD Mainly fruits.
BEHAVIOUR Multi-male groups numbering 14–20 animals break down into smaller units while feeding.

BARBARY MACAQUE *Macaca sylvanus*

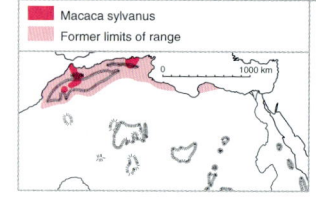

SIZE HB 55–65cm (female), 65–75cm (male). SH 45cm (female), 50cm (male). W 4–7kg (female), 7–10kg (male).
DESCRIPTION Dull ochre-grey with variable intensities of orange tinting the crown, hands and feet.
HABITAT Cedar forests at higher altitudes are preferred.
FOOD Grass and cedar leaves are winter and spring staples.
BEHAVIOUR 7–40 individuals (usually 10–30) maintain contact with one another by means of a wide range of vocalisations.

ALLEN'S SWAMP MONKEY *Allenopithecus nigroviridis*

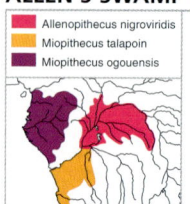

SIZE HB 40–45cm (female), 45–50cm (male). T 45–55cm. SH est. 30cm (female), est. 35cm (male). W 3.6kg (female), 6.2kg (male).
DESCRIPTION Stocky, khaki-coloured, with shortish tail.
HABITAT Swamp and levee forest bordering rivers and lakes.
FOOD Omnivorous, taking fruits, leaves and invertebrates (including crabs).
BEHAVIOUR Small groups of 2 to 8 individuals feed together.

NORTHERN TALAPOIN *Miopithecus ogouensis*

SIZE HB 25–37cm (female), 30–40cm (male). T 26–53cm. SH est. 19cm (female), est. 22cm (male). W 0.8–1.2kg (female), 1.2–1.9kg (male).
DESCRIPTION Large-headed with a bright, grizzled yellow-olive crown and back.
HABITAT Strictly equatorial, never far from a watercourse. Lives in very dense undergrowth.
FOOD Nearly 80% of the diet consists of fruits.
BEHAVIOUR Lives in groups of 12–20 which join other groups at night-roosts of up to 125 animals.

SOUTHERN TALAPOIN *Miopithecus talapoin*   *see* map above

SIZE HB est. 26–45cm. T est. 25–50cm. SH est. 25cm. W est. 1–2kg.
DESCRIPTION Grizzled, yellowish olive. Black face and ears.
HABITAT Dense evergreen vegetation on the banks of rivers.
FOOD Mainly fruits.
BEHAVIOUR Continuous pigeon-like contact calls while moving or foraging.

Grey-cheeked Mangabey

Black Mangabey

Barbary Macaque

Southern Talapoin *facial detail*

Southern Talapoin *male*

Allen's Swamp Monkey *male*

Northern Talapoin *male*

Northern Talapoin *facial detail*

GUENON MONKEYS *Cercopithecus*

SAVANNAH MONKEYS *Cercopithecus aethiops* superspecies

Small, grizzled, grey, brownish or greenish monkeys with a black face mask and white ruff. They live in groups numbering 5–76 animals (mean 25). Both females and males follow a rank hierarchy but female coalitions modify the pecking order and deter male aggression towards the young.

All young males leave their natal group (usually joining nearest neighbours) whereas females remain with their maternal group. Males only concert their actions during confrontations with other groups.

GRIVET MONKEY *Cercopithecus (a.) aethiops*

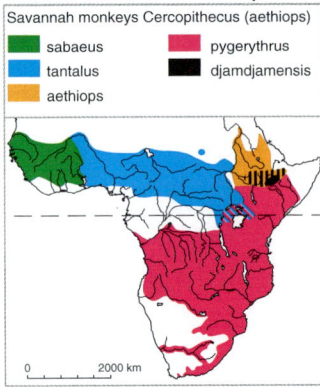

Savannah monkeys *Cercopithecus* (aethiops)
- sabaeus
- tantalus
- aethiops
- pygerythrus
- djamdjamensis

SIZE HB est. 40–60cm. T est. 42–70cm. W est. 5–8kg.
DESCRIPTION Prominent cheek fur laterally elongated; narrow white band above brows. Often a fine white moustache.
HABITAT Savannahs, woodlands, riverine strips and cultivation mosaics.
FOOD Heavily dependent on *Acacia* seeds, flowers, foliage and gum.

TANTALUS MONKEY *Cercopithecus (a.) tantalus*

SIZE HB est. 45–56cm. T est. 45–72cm. W est. 5.5–9kg.
DESCRIPTION Largest of the savannah monkeys.
HABITAT A most diverse range of woodlands, savannahs and forest mosaics.
FOOD Fruits, buds, seeds, roots, bark, gum and many cultivated plants. Insects, small vertebrates and eggs are also taken.

VERVET MONKEY *Cercopithecus (a.) pygerythrus*   *see* map above

SIZE HB 38–62cm (female), 50–65cm (male). T 48–75cm. W 3.5–5kg (female), 4–8kg (male).
DESCRIPTION Dark tip to the tail. Tufts at the base of the tail are red. The white brow and cheeks join to frame the black face.
HABITAT A wide variety of lightly wooded habitats A significant part of the total range consists of Miombo (*Brachystegia*) fire-climax woodlands.
FOOD Especially important are the seeds, flowers, foliage and gum of *Acacia* and *Albizia*, as well as the fruits of figs and buffalo thorn (*Ziziphus*).

CALLITHRIX MONKEY *Cercopithecus (a.) sabaeus*   *see* map above

SIZE HB est. 38–60cm. T est. 42–72cm. W est. 3.8–7.7kg.
DESCRIPTION Long-legged. The tip of the tail is pale orange. Yellowish cheek ruffs are deflected by a cow-lick which begins below the prominent black ears and sweeps up over the temples. There is barely a trace of light brow band.
HABITAT Wide range of ecotypes, including dry Sahelian woodlands, rainforest margins and mangroves.
FOOD One local peculiarity is reliance on crabs and other seafoods, taken on mudflats at low tide.

BALE MONKEY *Cercopithecus (a.) djamdjamensis*

SIZE HB est. 38–62cm. T est. 38–58cm. W est. 4–8kg.
DESCRIPTION Relatively short-tailed with thick, long fur. The black face, brows and temples show no trace of white except for a fine white moustache. The short white chin and cheek ruff leave the ears exposed.
HABITAT Has been recorded from the bamboo zone (between about 2,200 and 3,200m) and is known to be a generally scarce forest-edge species.
FOOD Not known but *Podocarpus*, *Hagenia* and many other montane trees produce edible fruits. *Acacia* and *Albizia* are likely staples in the lower reaches of the range.

Grivet Monkey

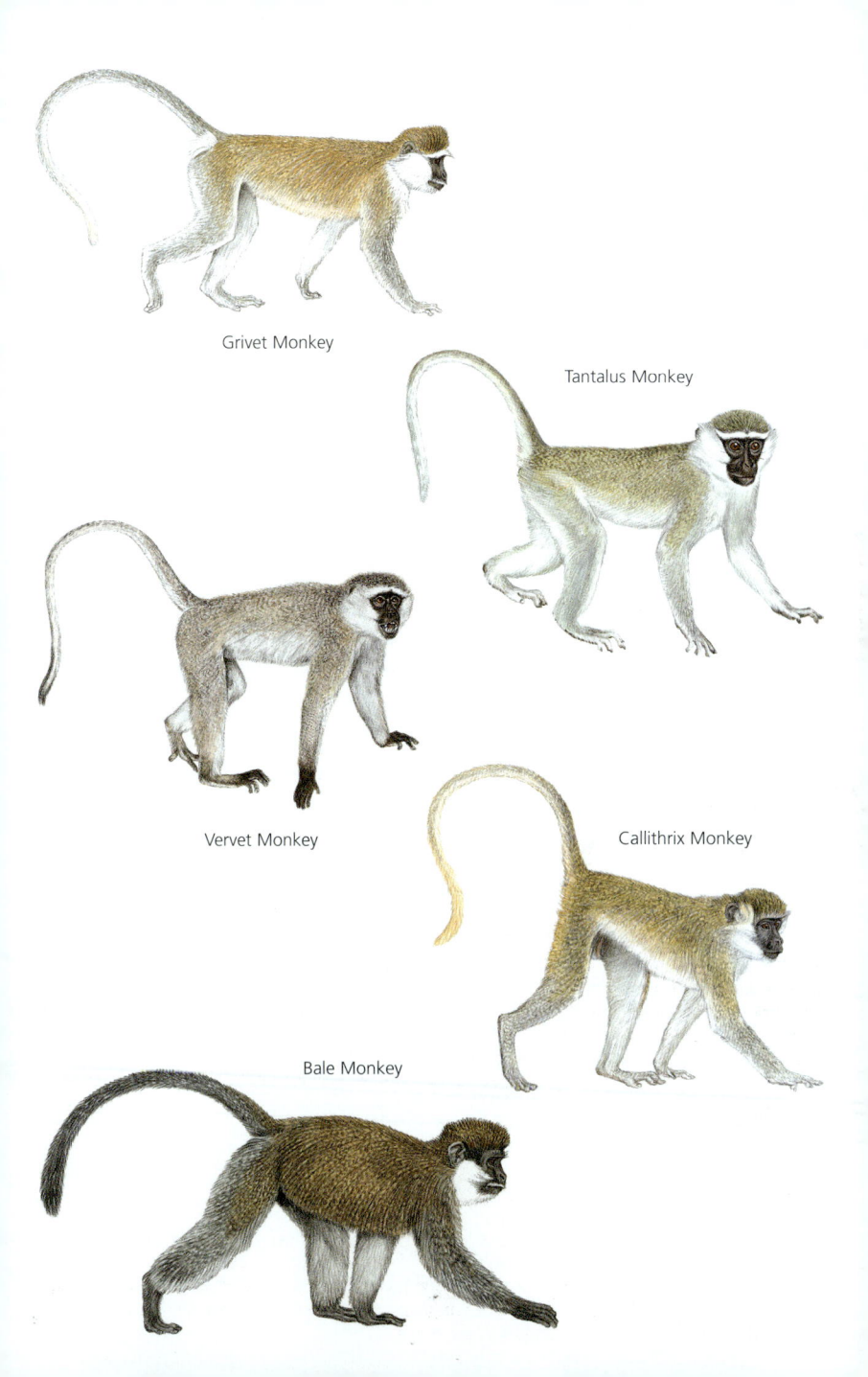

Tantalus Monkey

Vervet Monkey

Callithrix Monkey

Bale Monkey

PATAS MONKEY *Cercopithecus (Erythrocebus) patas*

SIZE HB 48–77cm (female), 60–87cm (male). T 54–74cm. SH 28–45cm (female), 34–50cm (male). W 7–14kg (female), 10–25kg (male).
DESCRIPTION Highly distinctive with long limbs and slender build. Females and young are the colour of dry grass, with shades of fawn, russet and grey. Males are larger and have russet tails, hindquarters and crowns.
HABITAT Vegetation types ranging from open grassland to dry woodland; commonest in thinly bushed *Acacia*-wooded grassland.
FOOD Especially dependent on the pods, seeds, galls, young leaves, gum and flowers of *Acacia* and the fruits of common savannah trees and shrubs, such as torchwood (*Balanites*), *Euclea* and num-num (*Carissa*).
BEHAVIOUR In confrontations between Patas groups all members of a troop display aggression towards the other troop (or solitary individual).

L'HOEST'S MONKEY *Cercopithecus (l'h.) l'hoesti*

Cercopithecus (lhoesti)
C.(l.) preussi
C.(l.) solatus

SIZE HB 45–55cm (female), 54–70cm (male). T 46–80cm. SH est. 29–36cm (female), est. 34–46cm (male). W 3–4.5kg (female), 6–10kg (male).
DESCRIPTION Long-legged, black-bodied with a brilliant white ruff and a russet 'saddle'. Tail is grey at its base and tapers to a black brush.
HABITAT Montane and intermediate forest up to 2,500m from Itombwe to the Ruwenzori Mts. It always travels on the ground but will climb to any level to feed.
FOOD Fruits of yellow wood (*Podocarpus*), koso (*Hagenia*), parasol trees (*Polyscias*), wild custard apple (*Myrianthus*), *Maesa* and the young leaves and shoots of various trees, shrubs and herbs.
BEHAVIOUR Groups consist of a single male and a very variable number of females and their young. Groups form a close association reinforced by much mutual grooming.

PREUSS'S MONKEY *Cercopithecus (l'h.) preussi*   see map above

SIZE HB est. 45–66cm. T 53–61cm. W est. 3.5–7kg.
DESCRIPTION Long-tailed, long-legged dark monkey with grizzled grey crown, cheeks, shoulder and flanks. A mahogany-red streak extends from the shoulders to the root of the tail.
HABITAT Now found in the Oban hills and Obudu but mainly on the north-western flank of Mt Cameroon between 1,000 and 1,800m. Also occurs in some isolated patches of forest in the Cameroon grasslands.
FOOD Fruits, seeds, leaves and flowers.
BEHAVIOUR Groups of 2 to 12 animals consist of a single adult male and one or more females with their young. Males utter a deep, 2-part booming in the morning and early evening.

SUN-TAILED MONKEY *Cercopithecus (l'h.) solatus*   see map above

SIZE HB est. 47–68cm. T est. 48–80cm. W est. 4–9kg.
DESCRIPTION Limbs are long and black, the back grizzled brown and the grey and white tail tipped with bright orange. Prominent muffs over the ears.
HABITAT Moist evergreen forest in a hilly area of approximately 10,000km^2 typified by very frequent rivers and streams that dissect the terrain.
FOOD Fruits that are abundant throughout the year.
BEHAVIOUR Small single-male, multi-female groups travelling on the ground. The forest in the Sun-tailed Monkey's area is inhabited by 13 other species. This is a measure of the food resources but also suggests that the Sun-tail is not in direct competition with other species.

L'Hoest's Monkey

Patas Monkey *male*

Preuss's Monkey

Sun-tailed Monkey

SALONGA MONKEY *Cercopithecus dryas*

SIZE HB est. 37–39cm (female), est. 38–40cm (male). T est. 48–52cm. W est. 2–2.5kg (female), est. 2.5–3.3kg (male).

DESCRIPTION Greyish brown back and upper limbs, black lower limbs, white chest, belly and inner thighs and forearms. Tail grey and white with a black tip and spot near base.

HABITAT Thickets within secondary forest and swamp forest along small rivers. The lower levels are preferred.

FOOD Has been reported to feed on the fruits, young leaves and shoots of monocot gingers and arrowroots.

BEHAVIOUR Local hunters describe groups of up to 30 animals in which more than one adult male is present.

DIANA MONKEY *Cercopithecus diana*

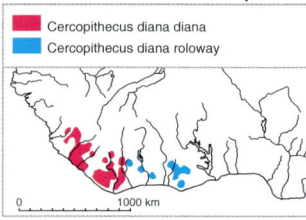

Cercopithecus diana diana
Cercopithecus diana roloway

SIZE HB 40–48cm (female), 50–60cm (male). T 52–82cm. W 2.2–3.5kg (female), 3.5–7.5kg (male).

DESCRIPTION Agile, long-limbed with strongly contrasting colours and pattern. Loud call of male is a volley of reverberating hacks ending in an explosive 'pyow'. Roloway race may be a full species.

HABITAT Dependent on continuous canopy and with a strong preference for high-canopy primary rainforest.

FOOD Primarily fruits and seeds.

BEHAVIOUR Groups of about 6 to 8 females and their young are accompanied by 1 adult territorial male, total 14 (10–50). Groups rally to male's loud calls, typically uttered in the morning, after resting and at any disturbance.

DE BRAZZA'S MONKEY *Cercopithecus neglectus*

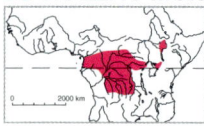

SIZE HB 40–50cm (female), 50–60cm (male). T 53–85cm. W 4–5kg (female), 5–8kg (male).

DESCRIPTION Grey-backed with orange brow and white beard. Habitually retreats at the least disturbance. Undisturbed, it is a quiet, exceptionally slow, deliberate and intensely observant monkey.

HABITAT River-oriented, only moving more than 200m away from the river to visit a major food source.

FOOD Half to three-quarters of diet is fruits and seeds. Shortfalls offset by taking leaves.

BEHAVIOUR One or more females are accompanied by an adult male. The male utters a deep, humming boom most frequently in the early morning, after any disturbance and whenever there is any change in the direction of travel. Its effect is to draw the group together.

OWL-FACED MONKEY *Cercopithecus hamlyni*

SIZE HB est. 40–55cm (female), est. 50–65cm (male). T 50–65cm. W est. 4.5–6kg (female), est. 7–10kg (male).

DESCRIPTION Grizzled grey with black arms, feet, underside and tail tip. Face black or marked with white nose stripe and pale cream brow ridge. Male substantially larger than female. His loud call is a deep boom.

HABITAT Primary habitat is dense montane forests, especially bamboo.

FOOD Bamboo leaves are known to be eaten. The leaves, shoots, pith and stems of several other trees, shrubs and herbs are available all year. Fruits tend to be more restricted.

BEHAVIOUR If social groups are small, dense cover and abundant food permit very small home ranges. Diurnal. Lives in single-male groups numbering less than 10. Very wary. Travels and feeds on the ground. The massive and impressive-looking males are intensely protective. Communication is vocal and olfactory.

Salonga Monkey
facial details

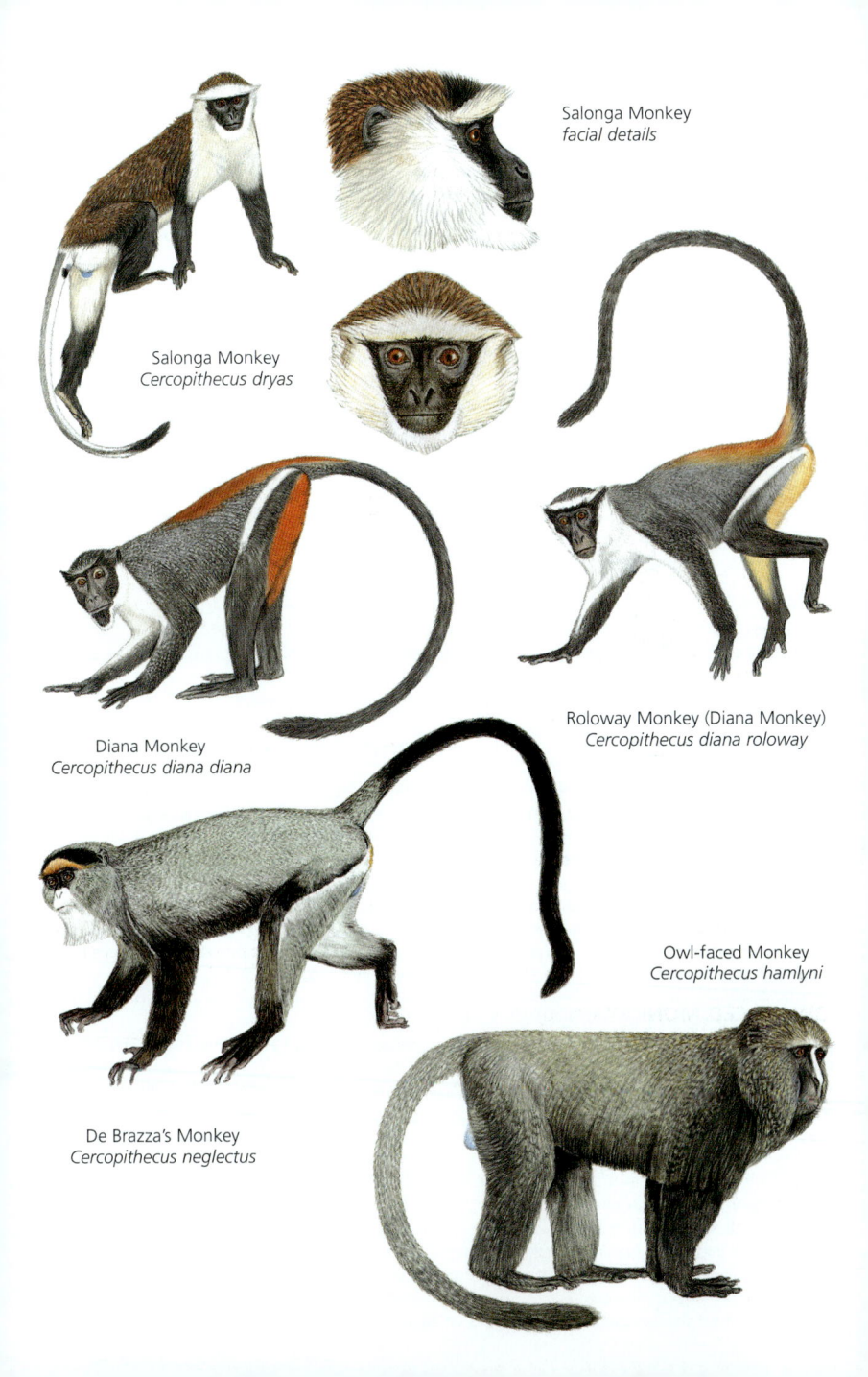

Salonga Monkey
Cercopithecus dryas

Roloway Monkey (Diana Monkey)
Cercopithecus diana roloway

Diana Monkey
Cercopithecus diana diana

Owl-faced Monkey
Cercopithecus hamlyni

De Brazza's Monkey
Cercopithecus neglectus

MONA MONKEYS *Cercopithecus* (*mona*) superspecies

Medium-sized to small, arboreal monkeys with a grizzled back and small dark hands and feet. They rely on dense, relatively unbroken canopy in primary, secondary or well-developed gallery forests.

MONA MONKEY *Cercopithecus* (*m.*) *mona*
SIZE HB 40–50cm (female), 48–60cm (male). T 45–80cm. W 4kg (3–4.5kg) (female), 5kg (4–6kg) (male).
DESCRIPTION Two oval patches of white fur on the hips are unique to this species and noticeable from a distance.
HABITAT Lowland forest. Commonest monkey in mangrove forests of R. Niger delta.
FOOD Fruit, and also invertebrates.
BEHAVIOUR Groups averaging 12 animals are accompanied by a single adult male.

LOWE'S MONKEY *Cercopithecus* (*m.*) *lowei*   *see* map above
SIZE HB est. 40–58cm. T 54–75cm. W 3–5.8kg.
DESCRIPTION Finely grizzled cheek fur contrasts sharply with eye mask.
HABITAT Most forest types, but not common in marshy areas or mangroves. Less wholly arboreal.
FOOD Mainly fruit.
BEHAVIOUR Home ranges extend from about 1.5 to 3ha.

CAMPBELL'S MONKEY *Cercopithecus* (*m.*) *campbelli*   *see* map above
SIZE HB est. 40–58cm. T 54–75cm. W est. 3–5.8kg.
DESCRIPTION Broad, circular, pale cheek ruffs, separated from white brow diadem by the narrowest of temporal streaks.
HABITAT Wide range of forests. Also secondary growth fringing gardens and fields.
FOOD Mainly fruits with flowers and insects.
BEHAVIOUR Resembles other mona species in having small, single-male groups and small ranges.

CROWNED MONKEY *Cercopithecus* (*m.*) *pogonias*   *see* map above
SIZE HB 45 (40–46cm) (female), 50cm (45–58cm) (male). T 50–87cm. W 3kg (2.8–3.6kg) (female), 4.5kg (3.6–4.8kg) (male).
DESCRIPTION Black crest along centre of crown; ear tufts prominent. Exceptionally agile and vocal.
HABITAT Commonest in mature forests and in upper strata.
FOOD Fruits (80%) and invertebrates. Rarely leaves or buds.
BEHAVIOUR The dominant male's booming call rallies group members after dispersal or a disturbance. Both sexes make the strange miaow that is the typical cohesion call.

WOLF'S MONKEY *Cercopithecus* (*m.*) *wolfi*   *see* map above
SIZE HB est. 40–68cm. T 60–75cm. W est. 2–6kg.
DESCRIPTION Hindquarters sharply differentiated (reddish or orange). Ears brightly coloured.
HABITAT Lowland rainforests, with a preference for high-canopy primary and secondary forests.
FOOD Fruits, flowers and invertebrates.
BEHAVIOUR Typical stiff-legged, raised-rump posture forms an eye-catching angle with tail and lowered torso. It would appear that ear movements are important in communication.

DENT'S MONKEY *Cercopithecus* (*m.*) *denti*   *see* map above
SIZE HB 40–70cm. T 70–90cm. W 3–6kg.
DESCRIPTION Brilliant contrast between white belly and dark back. White inner limbs contrast strongly with black arms and grizzled brown legs.
HABITAT Lowland forests with a preference for high-canopy mixed forest.
FOOD Fruits, flowers and invertebrates (especially caterpillars).
BEHAVIOUR When alarmed, will freeze in knots of vegetation for long periods.

Mona Monkey

Lowe's Monkey

Campbell's Monkey

Crowned Monkey

Wolf's Monkey *(facial detail on left)*

Dent's Monkey

GENTLE MONKEYS *Cercopithecus* (*nictitans*) superspecies

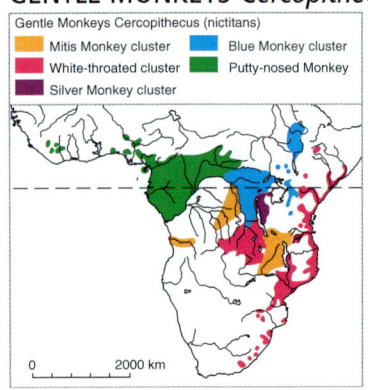

Gentle Monkeys Cercopithecus (nictitans)
- Mitis Monkey cluster
- White-throated cluster
- Silver Monkey cluster
- Blue Monkey cluster
- Putty-nosed Monkey

Large, long-tailed arboreal monkeys with a grizzled back and crown. Coat patterns often have yellowish or reddish zones. Adult males of all species make very loud and distinctive, explosive 'pyows'.

PUTTY-NOSED MONKEY
Cercopithecus (n.) nictitans

SIZE HB 43–53cm (female), 55–70cm (male). T 56–100cm. W 4.2kg (2.7–5kg) (female), 6.6kg (5.5–8kg) (male).
DESCRIPTION Dark, grizzled olive fur on the back, crown, cheeks and base of the tail. The limbs and distal half of the tail are black or dark grey. A brilliant white nose spot is the most striking peculiarity. Two subspecies: *nictitans* (Central Africa), *martini* (West Africa).
HABITAT Evergreen forests from lowland to montane, primary, secondary, narrow galleries and patches; not common in swamp or mangrove forests.
FOOD Fruits, seeds, flowers, foliage and invertebrates. In Gabon 58% of the male's year-round diet consists of fruits, but 76% in females. Both sexes take insects but males take a higher proportion of foliage (30% to the female's 12%).
BEHAVIOUR Groups of 12–30 females defend a territory and are accompanied by a single adult male.

GENTLE MONKEY *Cercopithecus (n.) mitis* (inc. *albogularis*)   see map above
SIZE HB 43–52cm (female), 48–70cm (male). T 55–109cm. W 5kg (3.5–5.5kg) (female), 7kg (5.5–12kg) (male).
DESCRIPTION Similar to Putty-nosed Monkey but without distinctive nose patch. Back and thighs grizzled, forearms, hands, feet and terminal half of tail are black. Underside relatively dark. Cheek fur grizzled. A grizzled brow patch in some species but undifferentiated in others.
SUBSPECIES: Commonly split into two geographic divisions (*mitis* and *albogularis*), but also divisible into 4 'clusters' (each a potential species), and each embracing more than one subspecies.
1. Mitis Monkey cluster (*mitis, maesi, pluto, heymansi, moloneyi, francescae*). Widely separated, central African relict populations. Dark, grizzled backs, dark caps with pallid diadems, pale chins, broad and low, grizzled cheek patches. Moloney's Monkey (*moloneyi*) is illustrated opposite.
2. White-throated Monkey cluster (*albogularis, opistosticus(?), samango, erythrarchus, nyasae, monoides, kibonotensis, kolbi, albotorquatus, phylax, zammaranoi*). Indian Ocean river basin distribution from Cape Province to Somalia. Boundary between white or pale chin fur and grizzled cheek fur very variable.
3. Silver Monkey cluster (*dogetti, kandti, schoutedeni*). Isolated populations associated with the Western Rift Valley. The Golden Monkey, *kandti*, is a high-altitude colonist on volcanic mountains near L. Kivu. Schouteden's Monkey, *schoutedeni*, exists as a tiny population on Shushu I. in L. Kivu. Silver Monkey, *dogetti*, on eastern margins of range.
4. Blue Monkey cluster (*stuhlmanni, elgonis, boutourlinii*). Expansive range in E Zaïre, Ethiopia and E Africa to Great Rift Valley. Very dark, grizzled back, black cap with sharply defined blue-grey grizzled diadem.
HABITAT All types of evergreen forest from riverine, delta, gallery, secondary, primary and montane, including bamboo.
FOOD Diet varies greatly by region and season and between the sexes (males eating less fruit). Prefer fruits wherever possible. Insects form a significant part of diet and are gathered by slow, systematic searching through bark, lichen, moss and rotten wood.
BEHAVIOUR Groups average 10 breeding females and offspring, and a single male. Territories, average 60–70ha, defended by all group members. The male's calls primarily advertise his association with a group of breeding females.

Moloney's Monkey

Martin's Putty-nosed Monkey

Golden Monkey

Blue Monkey

White-throated or Sykes's Monkey

Below: face details of gentle monkeys. Top row, from left: Central African Putty-nosed Monkey, Pluto Monkey, Moloney's Monkey, Stuhlman's Blue Monkey, Mount Kenya Sykes's Monkey. Below, from left: Martin's Putty-nosed Monkey, Zaïre Basin Gentle Monkey, Mbele Gentle Monkey, Silver Monkey, Tanganyika Sykes's Monkey

CEPHUS MONKEYS *Cercopithecus* (*cephus*) superspecies

Long-tailed, arboreal monkeys with grizzled brownish backs and crowns and very diverse and brightly coloured face patterns. Tails are red in several populations and bicoloured in others. Very lively, active monkeys, they make jerky movements of the head and forequarters. Very staccato, chirping alarm calls are made by all species. Uttered in prolonged series by several or all members of a group, these volleys of sound are often a first indication of their presence. Found in equatorial forests from Sierra Leone to W Kenya and about 10° latitude north and south. Absent from colder latitudes and higher altitudes, and from strongly seasonal forests of SE Africa. *Cephus* monkeys favour lowland and medium-altitude forests. They traverse a very wide range of branches, lianas and tangles at all but the very lowest levels of the forest. Individuals forage in a wide scatter, covering up to 1.5km per day in a territory of about 35ha.

The *cephus* group appears in several respects to be a neotenous (juvenilised) form of gentle monkey (the two groups are known to be very closely related). In addition to being smaller and having a more juvenile-looking skull, these monkeys have a faster metabolism and are more active for a longer day than gentle monkeys. They are also highly visually oriented and in polyspecific groups often warn other species of danger. This visual specialisation is corroborated by optical physiology (their eyes have more short-wave cones, which are especially sensitive to both space and colour perception). In contrast to gentle monkeys, which forage in groups for hidden insects, *cephus* monkeys are visual hunters which independently scan foliage and branches for exposed insects. This visual bias is clearly linked with greater use of visual signals. All species have evolved striking facial patterns which correlate with ritualised head-flagging displays performed during courtship and appeasement. Sharp head movements are also typical of this species and include contact and greeting gestures.

At first sight the diversity of guenon facial patterns betrays little sense of a relationship between the different species. However, comparable elements can be established (see diagrams opposite below). Thus, for species that have developed facial signals an elaborate set of light and dark patches expands or contracts to generate an extraordinary array of signal patterns.

In spite of their apparent diversity, all face patterns in the *cephus* group are permutations and elaborations of a single facial format of the gentle monkey type. These patterns can be seen to arise through facial fur developing various pleats, deflections or tufts, through colour tinting of skin and fur, and through 'expansion' and 'contraction' of a limited number of dark or light patches (see figs on page 53). The radiation of *cephus* monkeys is likely to have started in W Africa (*erythrogaster* and *petaurista* as modern derivatives) with an initial eastward expansion no further than the R. Ogooué basin (*cephus* and *sclateri* as modern derivatives), and a later further eastward expansion (*erythrotis* and *ascanius* as derivatives).

SPECIES:

Moustached Monkey, *C.* (*c.*) *cephus* (between R. Sanaga, R. Zaïre and R. Ubangi): red or bicoloured tail, bright blue face, broad yellow cheek ruffs, black and white 'moustache'.

Sclater's Monkey, *C.* (*c.*) *sclateri* (eastern margins of R. Niger delta): off-white tail, blue face, yellowish cheek fur with sinuous border, pale muzzle.

Red-eared Monkey, *C.* (*c.*) *erythrotis* (between R. Cross and R. Sanaga): red tail, purplish face, cream cheek ruff with linear black border, red nose and ears.

Red-tailed Monkey, *C.* (*c.*) *ascanius* (from R. Zaïre/R. Ubangi east to Uganda and W Kenya, S Sudan to Angola and N Zambia): partly or wholly red tail, dark blue face, white or grizzled cheeks and temporal region with variable margins, colour of nose spot shows regional variation.

Lesser Spot-nosed Monkey, *C.* (*c.*) *petaurista* (NW Sierra Leone to Benin): bicoloured khaki/white tail, black face framed by a white ruff, white nose spot.

Nigerian White-throated Monkey, *C.* (*c.*) *erythrogaster* (SW Nigeria): bicoloured khaki/white tail, dark grey face, very attenuated grizzled cheek patches, broad and conspicuous white ruff framing the face, black or white nose, red or slate-grey belly.

Opposite right: Guenon cheek-hair arrangement (left a–g) and tonal contrasts on facial masks (right 1–7) of *cephus* monkeys. Sclater's (b, 4), Lesser Spot-nosed (*buettikoferi*, c, 2) (*petaurista*, 1), Moustached (d, 6), Red-eared (e, 3), Red-tailed (*schmidti*, f, 5), Red-tailed (*atrinasus*, g, 7), generalised guenon (a).

Left: Lesser
Spot-nosed
(*petaurista*)
Right: Nigerian
White-throated

Left: Lesser
Spot-nosed
(*buettikoferi*)
Right:
Red-tailed
(*schmidti*)

Left: Sclater's
Right:
Red-tailed
(*whitesidei*)

Left:
Red-eared
Right:
Red-tailed
(*atrinasus*)

Left:
Moustached
Right:
generalised
guenon

Guenon facial patterns

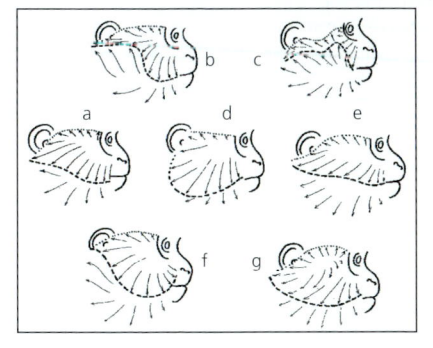

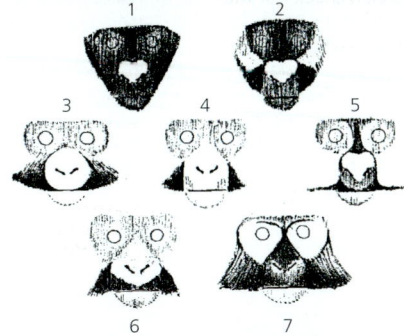

MOUSTACHED MONKEY *Cercopithecus (c.) cephus*

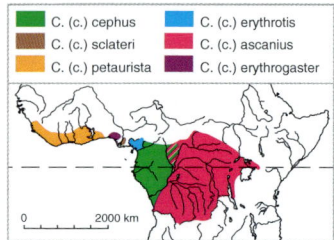

- C. (c.) cephus
- C. (c.) erythrotis
- C. (c.) sclateri
- C. (c.) ascanius
- C. (c.) petaurista
- C. (c.) erythrogaster

SIZE HB 44–50cm (female), 50–58cm (male). T 66–99cm. W 3kg (2–4kg) (female), 4kg (3.8–5kg) (male).
DESCRIPTION The facial skin is bright blue, with broad yellow cheek ruffs and a vivid white 'moustache' of very variable shape above the jet-black lips and very bristly black fur at the corners of the mouth.
HABITAT Lowland rainforest between the R. Sanaga and R. Zaïre/R. Ubangi. Prefers dense foliage and liane tangles and will make use of all forest levels except the lowest. Their distribution between that of Red-eared and Yellow-nosed Monkeys (very similar forms) suggests that they may have recently expanded their range out of an Ogooué basin heartland.
FOOD Mainly fruits (and about 10% leaves, stems and shoots). Adult males have been found to eat much fewer insects than females, which suggests that social monitoring may be at the expense of time spent searching for insects.

SCLATER'S MONKEY *Cercopithecus (c.) sclateri*

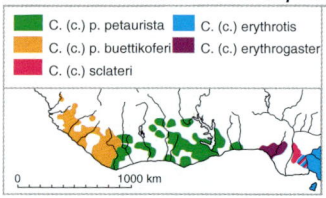

- C. (c.) p. petaurista
- C. (c.) erythrotis
- C. (c.) p. buettikoferi
- C. (c.) erythrogaster
- C. (c.) sclateri

SIZE HB est. 40–45cm (female), est. 45–55cm (male). T est. 45–75cm. W est. 2.5–3.5kg (female), est. 3–4.5kg (male).
DESCRIPTION The tail graduates from light olive to off-white, with a deep russet suffusion on the underside close to the anus. The cap is peaked and encircled by a black margin. The facial skin is blue and there is yellowish cheek fur, with a sinuous dark-tipped border above the white throat and chin fur. Muzzle and ears are usually pallid but animals from towards R. Cross valley have varying tints of red on the nose and ears. Putative hybrids with the Red-eared Guenon have led to it being classified with that species. Aside from this hybrid influence, Sclater's Monkey combines features characteristic of Moustached, Red-tailed and Lesser Spot-nosed Monkeys, suggesting that it is a conservative species illustrative of earlier forms of cephus monkeys.
HABITAT Relict forests and swamps between the R. Niger delta and the Cross River south of Enugu.
FOOD Likely to resemble that of other cephus group monkeys.

RED-EARED MONKEY *Cercopithecus (c.) erythrotis*   see map above

SIZE HB 40–45cm (female), 45–55cm (male). T 53–77cm. W 2.25–3.5kg (female), 3.5–4.5kg (male).
DESCRIPTION Grizzled brown back, shoulders and crown, red tail and rump, and grey forearms, hindlegs, hands and feet. Underparts and inner limbs are white. The face is purplish blue, with cream cheek fur tapered to a point below the ear and with bold black margins. Nose and ears are red. The monkeys on Bioko I. (formerly Fernando Po) belong to a smaller, darker island race. Mainland population larger and less melanic.
HABITAT Lowland rainforests between the R. Cross and R. Sanaga and Bioko I. Today the Moustached Monkey inhabits the intervening country between the very small range of the Red-eared Monkeys and that of the Yellow-nosed Red-tail (some specimens of which resemble it very closely). It seems likely that the range of the Red-eared Monkeys has contracted. Their ecological niche resembles that of other cephus monkeys but they are reported to live mainly in lower forest strata and in regenerating secondary forest. Putty-nosed and mona monkeys frequently follow and associate with Red-eared Monkeys. Deforestation has destroyed a large part of this species' range and remaining populations are heavily hunted. It is common in Korup National Park and Douala Edea Reserve. Although it occurs in many smaller forest reserves it enjoys no practical protection and is in decline everywhere.
FOOD Fruits and insects.

Moustached Monkey

Red-eared Monkey

Sclater's Monkey

RED-TAILED MONKEY *Cercopithecus (c.) ascanius* see map on p.54

SIZE HB 34–48cm (female), 48–52cm (male). T 54–92cm. W 3.5kg (1.8–4kg) (female), 4.5kg (3–6kg) (male).

DESCRIPTION The tail is partly or wholly red and the face is dark blue. Cheeks and temporal region are white or grizzled, with variable margins above the off-white throat and chin. There are several subspecies and intermediate forms. The nose spot varies in colour and shape by region and subspecies.

HABITAT Lowland and submontane forests, riverine galleries and most stages of colonising, secondary or regenerating forest (except for those on poor soils). Red-tailed Monkeys also occur in forest mosaics with a high preponderance of single-stand species, such as ironwood.

FOOD Fruits make up half or more of the diet while insects make up a quarter. Flowers and flower buds are also important. Leaves and leaf buds become a significant part of the diet during seasons of shortage. The flowers of *Markhamia* and *Millettia* (two common colonist trees) and the fruits of false nutmeg (*Pycnanthus*), false figs (*Trilepisium*) and red milkwood (*Mimusops*) are especially favoured and are stored in the cheek pouches until the flesh and flavour have dissipated (a habit that ensures wide dispersal of the seeds). Feeding on fruits close to the sleeping-site begins at dawn (sometimes just before) and is often followed by displacement by larger monkeys. Except for the midday rest, the monkeys are often occupied hunting insects in the late morning and especially the afternoon. Feeding on fruits may then be resumed in the evening, as other monkeys retire, and continues up to nightfall. Major super-abundant food sources (especially those near the borders of 2 or more territories) may draw in temporary aggregations numbering more than 100 red-tails. Such groups are temporary and typically fraught with aggression.

BEHAVIOUR During feeding and especially while hunting insects, disperse individually or in small family clusters.

LESSER SPOT-NOSED MONKEY *Cercopithecus (c.) petaurista* see map on p.54

SIZE HB 40–44cm (female), 44–48cm (male). T 57–68cm. W 2–3.5kg (female), 2.5–4kg (male).

DESCRIPTION The face is black and the tail is bicoloured. Adult males utter a peculiar grating hack and a high-pitched whistle of alarm. Two subspecies: *C. (c.) p. petaurista* (Benin–R Cavally, white cheek stripe only below ear); *C. (c.) p. buettikoferi* (R Cavally west to Guinea, white stripe from temple to ear).

HABITAT Lowland primary and secondary forests, riverine and gallery forests, secondary regeneration and coastal bush.

FOOD Highly frugivorous and may eat less insects than other species in the cephus group. Flowers, flower buds and leaf buds are important while leaves and stems are minor items.

NIGERIAN WHITE-THROATED MONKEY *Cercopithecus (c.) erythrogaster*
see map on p.54

SIZE HB est. 40–45cm (female), est. 45–50cm (male). T est. 60–70cm. W est. 2–4kg (female), est. 3.5–4.5kg (male).

DESCRIPTION Grizzled khaki-coloured back, shoulders and thighs, dark grey outer limbs, lighter inner limbs and a bicoloured tail. The very prominent white ruff frames the dark face, which has narrow, grizzled cheek patches. The cap is black with a broad triangle of pale grizzled fawn. The belly is grey or russet (the latter mostly towards the west of its range) and the nose is either black or white. The distinctive loud call of the male most resembles the grating hack of the Lesser Spot-nosed Monkey.

HABITAT Widespread but very scattered in remaining lowland rainforests of SW Nigeria and S Benin. Also in secondary bush and old farmland, usually in dense vegetation between 2 and 15m. Foraging parties number about 5 but groups of up to 30 have been recorded. At the heart of its remaining range a spacing of 1 group per km^2 has been estimated. All forests in SW Nigeria are subject to intensive logging, clearing and hunting. This species is currently unprotected but a 67km^2 wildlife sanctuary has been declared in the Okomu Forest Reserve. This species also occurs in the Ilfon and Omo Forest Reserves.

FOOD Fruits and insects.

Red-tailed Monkey

Nigerian White-throated Monkey

Lesser Spot-nosed Monkey *facial details*
(left, petaurista; right, buettikoferi)

Lesser Spot-nosed Monkey

LORISIDS Loridae

Pottos and angwantibos are woolly-coated, nocturnal, arboreal prosimians. They are slow-moving with very short tails.

POTTO *Perodicticus potto*

- potto
- ju-ju
- edwardsi
- faustus
- ibeanus

SIZE HB 30–40cm. T 5–10cm. W 0.8–1.6kg.
DESCRIPTION Head round, with small, naked ears and protuberant golden-brown eyes. Hands have a rudimentary knob for an index finger. The spines of the neck vertebrae, enclosed in sleeves of skin, project from the surrounding tissue. Five subspecies (see map); some may be distinct species.
HABITAT Lowland, swamp and lower montane forests; commonest in secondary and colonising forests and along margins.
FOOD Gums are dominant during drier periods, and insects, snails and fruits during the rains.
BEHAVIOUR Solitary. Females range over 3–9ha while males have a 9–40ha range overlapping that of one or more females.

MARTIN'S POTTO *Psuedopotto martini*   no map

SIZE HB est 27–30cm. T est 8–12cm. W est 400–650g.
DESCRIPTION Resembles a long-tailed Common Potto but smaller with less prominent muzzle and relatively long, tapered tail.
HABITAT Uncertain. Possibly restricted to montane forests in the Cameroon highlands and, perhaps, to lower lying forests in the immediate vicinity.
FOOD Its teeth imply a more insectivorous diet than the Potto.
BEHAVIOUR Climbs vertically when disturbed, sometimes fleeing at quite a fast pace, in bursts of action.

CALABAR ANGWANTIBO *Arctocebus calabarensis*

- Arctocebus calabarensis
- Arctocebus aureus

SIZE HB 22.4–26.3cm. T (vestigial). W 230–465g.
DESCRIPTION Almost tail-less, very slender wrists, and tiny hands and feet. Rounded head has short, naked ears, large eyes and a pointed muzzle. Differs from golden species in colour, minor teeth, skull and anatomical structures. In both species the hands, in which the second finger is lost and the third is reduced to a stump, are unique.
HABITAT Confined to areas of very dense, low undergrowth with abundant lianes and vines within primary, secondary and coastal rainforest. Particularly favours the leafy growth that occurs in clearings.
FOOD Mainly caterpillars; also beetles and fruits. Also snails and small lizards. Caterpillars are found by smell in the course of carefully combing through liane tangles.
BEHAVIOUR Solitary; young accompany their mothers for some months after weaning. When caught or attacked they growl.

GOLDEN ANGWANTIBO *Arctocebus aureus*   see map above

SIZE HB 22–26cm. T (vestigial). W 200–270g.
DESCRIPTION Golden or russet-tinted upperside and creamy underside. Fine guard hairs on the back, shoulders and haunches have glistening, crinkled tips which give a 'frosted', form-dissolving appearance to the hunched body.
HABITAT Confined to vine tangles and areas with abundant young (or slow-growing) leafy stems in moist evergreen, lowland rainforests.
FOOD Caterpillars of all species, including hairy and distasteful species that are avoided by other insect-predators. Some of these caterpillars are colonial and many are abundant, especially on rank growth in clearings and on forest edges.
BEHAVIOUR Defensive reaction is unique. The animal stands on widely spaced and fully extended limbs, the head tucked back on the chest. The hindquarters become the obvious focus for attack. If touched, however, the animal lunges at its attacker from between its legs with a quick, slashing bite.

Potto

Martin's Potto

Golden Angwantibo

Calabar Angwantibo

NOTE: not to scale

GALAGOS or BUSHBABIES Galagonidae

Long-tailed, woolly, nocturnal primates, currently divided into four groups. The head is rounded, with large, forward-facing eyes. The naked ears are huge, highly sensitive and very mobile – they can retract into compact, folded structures. Many species are best identified by vocalisations, which differ more than their relative sizes or colours. Some species are exceptionally agile leapers, thanks to the structure of their limbs and the spatulate ends of their fingers and toes. Grooming is a particularly important to galagos, facilitated by modifications to teeth, tongue and claws; the fur diffuses a range of scents secreted by the animal's various scent glands.

GREATER GALAGOS *Otolemur*

The largest and among the most primitive of living galagos. Generally move on all fours and resort to springing leaps only when alarmed or in order to get from one tree to another. Live at very variable densities strung out along river courses in the drier, more open savannahs but continuously in coastal thickets and forests, where they have been estimated to number up to 125 per km². Ranges are shared and defended by related females. Dominant males also permit a small number of subordinate males within their ranges during the dry (non-breeding) season. Subordinate and peripheral individuals rely on scent-marks and loud calls to avoid face-to-face meetings with dominant animals; juveniles may accompany their mothers to form small groups.

GREATER GALAGO *Otolemur crassicaudatus* — see plate 21

SIZE HB 32cm (26–46.5cm). T 41cm (29–55cm). W 1,100g (567–2,000g).
DESCRIPTION A large, brown or grey galago with exceptionally long ears (5–7.2cm), a broad muzzle, large canines and relatively small eyes. There is a dense covering of long guard hairs on the lower back. The Greater Galago walks and runs in preference to leaping. Three subspecies are recognised: *crassicaudatus*, *montieri* and *badius*.
HABITAT Dense vegetation in miombo (*Brachystegia*), coastal and montane areas. This is the common greater bushbaby of S and E Africa.
FOOD *Acacia* gums, flowers and seeds; figs, ebony and other fruits; snails, slugs, insects, reptiles and birds.

SILVER GALAGO *Otolemur argentatus* — see plate 21 and map on p.62
(possibly a form of Greater Galago)

SIZE HB 39cm (35–40cm). T 41cm (34–43cm). W 1100g (730–1814g).
DESCRIPTION Silvery grey with a very pale tail (sometimes black). Face is long and broad muzzled.
HABITAT Woodlands and montane forest to the south-east of the Kavirondo Gulf.
FOOD *Acacia* gum, flowers and fruits; various invertebrates and occasional vertebrates.

SMALL-EARED GALAGO *Otolemur garnettii* — see plate 21 and map on p.62

SIZE HB 26cm (23–34cm). T 36cm (30–44cm). W 760g (550–1200g).
DESCRIPTION Relatively short ears, a pointed muzzle and relatively large eyes. The fingernails are unique in growing sharp, thickened points at their outer margins, which come into play when the galago climbs over large trunks. They are more active leapers. Three subspecies are recognised: *garnettii*, *hindei* and *panganiensis*.
HABITAT Coastal and montane forests (often dry, low-canopy and florally impoverished) but also riverine galleries with numerous *Acacia*; also various cultivation mosaics and urban suburbs.
FOOD Gums, flowers and seeds of *Acacia*; fruits and invertebrates.

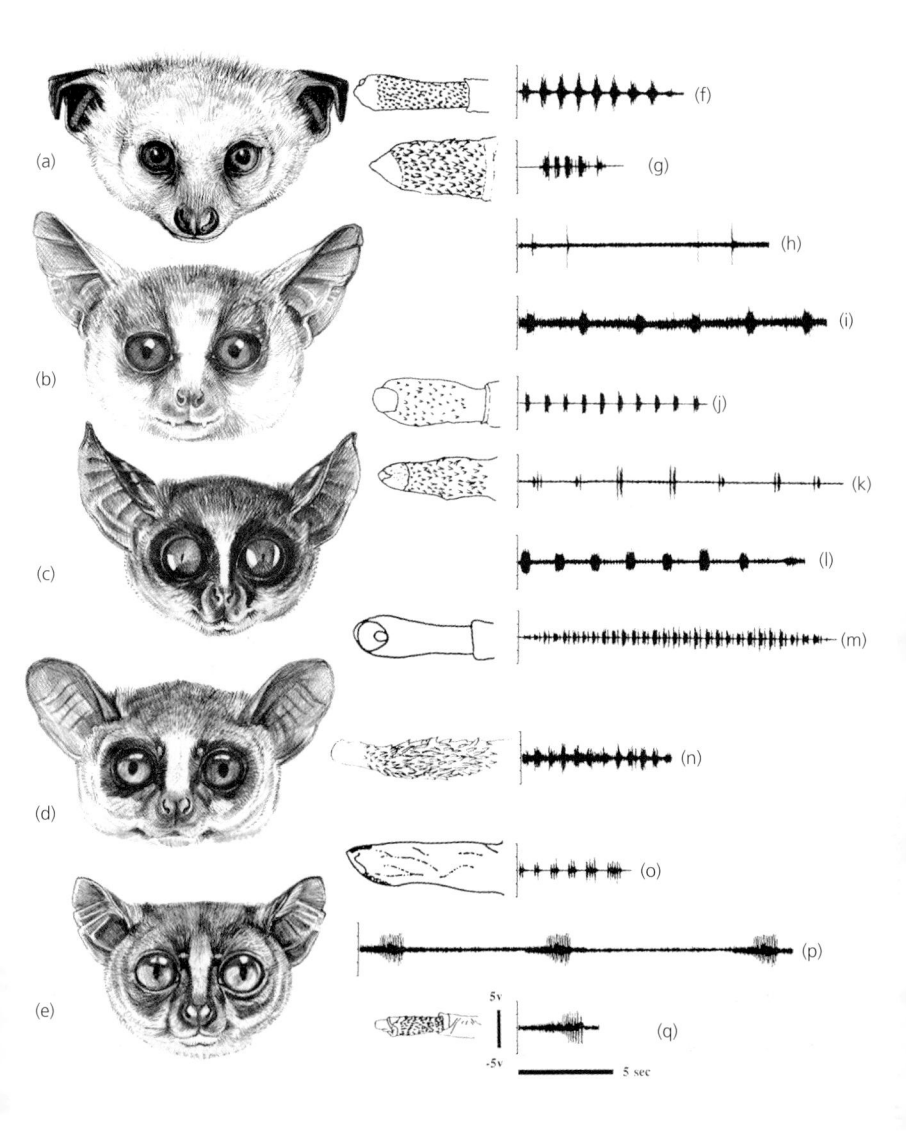

Faces, penile shapes and oscillograms of loud calls for some galagos.
(Courtesy of S. Bearder, L. Ambrose, M. J. Anderson and P. Honess.)

(a) Greater. (b) South African. (c) Spectacled. (d) Zanzibar. (e) Thomas's.

(f) Greater Galago. (g) Small-eared Galago. (h) Pallid Needle-clawed Galago.
(i) Allen's Galago. (j) Senegal Galago. (k) South African Galago.
(l) Spectacled Galago. (m) Rondo Galago. (n) Zanzibar Galago.
(o) Mozambique Galago. (p) Thomas's Galago. (q) Demidoff's Galago.

MWERA GALAGO *Otolemur* sp. nov.?

- Otolemur garnettii
- Otolemur argentatus
- Otolemur sp. nov.?

SIZE HB est. 21cm. T 30cm. W est. 300g.
DESCRIPTION A small, fawnish grey galago with off-white underparts and dark brown hands and feet. Poorly defined brownish patches surround the eyes. The tail is evenly haired, somewhat gingery fawn and may have a white tip. Its calls resemble those of the Greater Galago but are weaker. It may be a dwarfed subspecies.
HABITAT Known from exotic plantations and secondary growth in coastal valleys close to Lindi but likely to be more widespread. This small galago may range well down into Mozambique in relict patches of coastal forest. It occurs within a few kilometres of the much larger Greater Galago.
FOOD Recorded in mango and cashew-nut plantations but nothing known.

NEEDLE-CLAWED GALAGOS *Euoticus*

The sharp nails from which these galagos get their name, and the exceptionally broad span of their hands and feet, enable them to get a firm grip on tree trunks while feeding.

ELEGANT NEEDLE-CLAWED GALAGO *Euoticus elegantulus*

- Euoticus elegantulus
- Euoticus pallidus

SIZE HB 21cm (18–33cm). T 29cm (28–31cm). W 300g (270–360g).
DESCRIPTION Brightly coloured, very agile, long-limbed with white underparts sharply divided from the foxy-red back by an undulating border. Limbs tawny; face and tail ashy grey or brown. Pale, very prominent eyes. The voice is rather bird-like.
HABITAT Between the R. Sanaga and R. Zaïre in both primary and secondary forests but more common in the latter.
FOOD Gum of rain trees (*Albizia*) and other Mimosaceae and insects. About 5% of the annual diet consists of fruits.

PALLID NEEDLE-CLAWED GALAGO *Euoticus pallidus*   see map above

SIZE HB 19 (17–20cm). T 28–33cm. W 200–260g.
DESCRIPTION A small, very agile dull-coloured galago with yellowish grey underparts, grey shoulders, arms and tail. The back is brownish with a chocolate-brown dorsal stripe. Both needle-clawed species have similar vocal repertoires but the calls of the Pallid Needle-clawed Galago may be slightly higher in pitch.
HABITAT Patchily distributed between the R. Cross and R. Sanaga, mainly in secondary forests; also on Bioko I. (formerly Fernando Po).
FOOD Both needle-clawed species are thought to share a similar dependence on gums and insects.

SQUIRREL GALAGOS *Galago (Sciurocheirus)*

Differ from most galagos by landing 'hands first' rather than 'feet first' or with all limbs simultaneously.

ALLEN'S SQUIRREL GALAGO *Galago alleni*

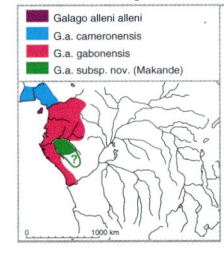

- Galago alleni alleni
- G.a. cameronensis
- G.a. gabonensis
- G.a. subsp. nov. (Makande)

SIZE HB 20cm (15–24cm). T 26cm (20–30cm). W 314g (200–445g).
DESCRIPTION There are three or four regional forms of Allen's Galago, which differ in colour but are all medium-sized with narrow heads and rounded ears (3–4cm long). All have a boldly marked face mask around the eyes and pale nose stripes. The tail is long, bushy and of even thickness. All forms make a repetitive croaking loud call similar to that of the lesser galagos of the savannahs but their whistles are very distinctive.
HABITAT Found between R. Niger and R. Zaïre but may have a wider distribution; lives in the lowest levels of mature primary forest.
FOOD Mainly fruits but insects also important.

Greater Galago (p.60)

Silver Galago (p.60)

Small-eared Galago (p.60)

Silver Galago (p.60)

Pallid Needle-clawed Galago

Mwera Galago

Elegant Needle-clawed Galago

Allen's Squirrel Galago

LESSER GALAGOS *Galago*

Medium-sized, mostly savannah galagos with a grey or brownish back and a round head with large eyes and a short muzzle. All utter short phrases or single cries that have a regular timing repeated many times. They are agile bounders, landing feet first.

SENEGAL GALAGO *Galago senegalensis*

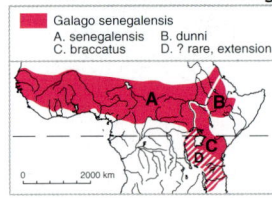

Galago senegalensis
A. senegalensis   B. dunni
C. braccatus   D. ? rare, extension

SIZE HB 16.5cm (13.2–21cm). T 26cm (19.5–30)cm). W 206g (112–300g).
DESCRIPTION Long-limbed with a long, short-haired tail. Back is grey or brown-grey and underparts are yellowish (particularly where the two colours meet). Ears 2.5–5.5cm long. At least 3 races (see map).
HABITAT Woodlands dominated by *Acacia*, *Isoberlinia* and *Julbernardia* between Senegal and E Africa; montane forest margins elsewhere. Densely grassed areas are avoided.
FOOD Gums, invertebrates and fruits (seasonally).
BEHAVIOUR The loud advertising call consists of a single, low-pitched note uttered persistently at a regular tempo. Insects are caught with great dexterity on the ground, in flight and on vegetation.

SPECTACLED GALAGO *Galago matschiei* (syn. *G. inustus*)   see map below

SIZE HB 16cm (14.7–20cm). T 25cm (19–27.9cm). W 210g (170–250g).
DESCRIPTION Dark brown with very large amber eyes surrounded by almost black eye-mask patches. Well-defined ridge borders the eyes, especially at the brows. Lower incisors are sharply protuberant. Nails of hands and feet are keeled and sharply pointed.
HABITAT Primary and secondary lowland forest and lower montane forests where *Parinari excelsa* is a dominant tree.
FOOD Insects, fruits and gums with seasonal changes in preference. Fruits may be a prime choice when available. Caterpillars and beetles are taken during rainy seasons while gums appear to be a dry-season food.
BEHAVIOUR Loud calls are repetitive barks, 'grunt-yaps' and a long, yapping screech.

SOMALI GALAGO *Galago gallarum*   see map below

SIZE HB 17cm (13–20cm). T 25cm (20.5–30cm). W 250g.
DESCRIPTION Sandy-coloured with a broad, round head, medium-sized ears (3–4cm), and large eyes only partially surrounded by narrow brown eye mask.
HABITAT *Acacia*, *Commiphora* and *Combretum* deciduous bushlands and thickets; known from between the valleys of the R. Webe Shebelle and R. Tana.
FOOD Presumed to be mainly gum and invertebrates.
BEHAVIOUR Scattered bush may require this galago to spend more time on the ground. Has been observed feeding and moving over the ground with long, high bounds.

SOUTH AFRICAN GALAGO *Galago moholi*

Galago moholi
Galago matschiei (inustus)
Galago gallarum

SIZE HB 15cm (8.8–20.5cm). T 23cm (11–28cm). W 160g (95–245g).
DESCRIPTION Relatively large ears (2–5cm) and large orange eyes. Eye mask and tail are dark brownish grey. Legs, feet, forearms and hands have a strong yellowish suffusion. (The eye-shine is red.) The loud advertising call differs from that of the Senegal Galago in being single-, double- and triple-unit cries of high pitch, mixed into series and repeated over long periods.
HABITAT Miombo belt from Angola to W Tanzania, Zimbabwe and the Transvaal. Within this zone inhabits Miombo (*Brachystegia*), *Combretum*, *Acacia* and Mopane (*Colophospermum*) woodlands, riverine galleries and forest margins.
FOOD *Acacia* and other gums, invertebrates. Fruits are only occasionally taken.

Senegal Galago

Spectacled Galago

Somali Galago

South African Galago

DWARF GALAGOS *Galagoides*
Diminutive galagos with greenish grey-brown coats, yellowish underparts and elongated, upturned noses. Primarily quadrupedal, they make short leaps rather than long hops.

RONDO GALAGO *Galagoides rondoensis*

Galagoides rondoensis
Possible range

SIZE HB 12cm. T 16cm. W 50g.
DESCRIPTION Warm brown, with a long, dark reddish brown tail which becomes thicker towards its tip.
HABITAT Known from remnant forest patches.
FOOD Insects.
BEHAVIOUR Main vocalisation is rather insect-like: a sustained vibrating call that rises in volume and is sustained for about 10 seconds.

ZANZIBAR GALAGO *Galagoides zanzibaricus*

Galagoides zanzibaricus
Galagoides granti

Includes Matundu Galago '*G. udzungwensis*'.
SIZE HB 15.3cm (12–16.5cm). T 20cm (17–23cm). W 145g (104–203g).
DESCRIPTION Dark brown with warm reddish tints on the crown, shoulders, back and thighs. Lower jaw is shallow and long.
HABITAT Coastal lowland rainforests and thickets, riverine forests and secondary growth, including cultivation mosaics and gardens.
FOOD Invertebrates, mainly insects (moths and beetles) and fruits.
BEHAVIOUR Individual home ranges of about 2–5ha may be wholly or partially shared. Females are intolerant of other neighbouring females.

MOZAMBIQUE GALAGO *Galagoides granti*

SIZE HB 15.5cm (14–19cm). T 22cm (20–26.5cm). W 139–178g.
DESCRIPTION Soft brown suffused with ochre on the shoulders, back and thighs. Yellowish brown extends down the tail, the terminal third of which becomes very dark.
HABITAT Forest mosaics and coastal forests between the R. Zambezi and R. Rufiji.
FOOD Insects and fruits.

DEMIDOFF'S GALAGO *Galagoides demidoff*

demidoff | phasma
murinus | poensis
anomurus | uncertain

SIZE HB 12cm (7.3–15.5cm). T 18cm (11–21.5cm). Ear ave. 24mm. W 60g (44–97g).
DESCRIPTION The smallest primate in Africa. Body colour is brown with paler yellowish underparts. Loud calls are very distinctive; a series of sharp chips that gather in speed and pitch to reach a crescendo in 2–4-second bouts. They also make an insect-like buzzing alarm call. At least five subspecies recognised (see map).
HABITAT Strong preference for dense growth on forest and road margins.
FOOD Mainly beetles, moths, caterpillars and crickets. Fruits also eaten.
BEHAVIOUR Overlapping home ranges of about 1ha. Often sleep in huddles.

THOMAS'S GALAGO *Galagoides thomasi*

SIZE HB 14cm (12.3–16.6cm). T 26cm (15–24cm). Ear ave. 27mm. W 100g (55–149g).
DESCRIPTION Closely resembles Demidoff's Galago. Ashy brown with paler underparts. Call is a repetitive, shrill, rasping chink which increases in pitch and speed and lasts about 4 seconds.
HABITAT High-canopy in primary forest in the regions shared with Demidoff's Galago. Where Demidoff's is absent Thomas's is also found in undergrowth and in secondary forests.
FOOD Mainly insects, beetles, caterpillars, ants and termites, with some fruits and gum.
BEHAVIOUR Thought to form localised populations with little contact with neighbouring groups.

Rondo Galago

Zanzibar Galago

Mozambique Galago

Thomas's Galago

Demidoff's Galago

FRUIT BATS Megachiroptera, Pteropodidae

Large brown eyes in a long, lemur-like head, with funnel-shaped ears and broad, crepe-textured wings (with claws on the first and second digits) are the most notable peculiarities of fruit bats. Entirely dependent on a year-long supply of fruits and flowers. Almost all disperse seeds by picking fruit in one tree and excreting its seeds in another.

FLYING FOXES *Pteropus* (2 species) see map below
SIZE HB 220–265mm. FA 150–161mm. W 400–650g
DESCRIPTION Large, dark-winged fruit bats with yellowish or red heads and 'fox-like' faces.
HABITAT Off Africa, restricted to Pemba I. (*P. voeltzkowi*) and Mafia I. (*P. comorensis*).
FOOD Fruits and flowers.
BEHAVIOUR Roost exposed in large trees, usually in large colonies.

MOUNTAIN FRUIT BAT *Stenonycteris lanosus*
SIZE HB 1,300–1,550mm. FA 850–950mm. W 120–165g.
DESCRIPTION Large with black wings, shaggy, dark grey fur, pointed ears and a long but blunt-ended muzzle.
HABITAT Montane forest areas in E Africa, Ethiopia and Madagascar.
FOOD Fruits, nectar and pollen.
BEHAVIOUR A colonial cave-dweller in montane areas.

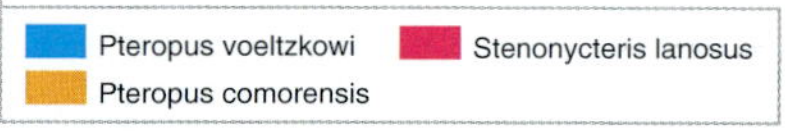

Pteropus voeltzkowi — Stenonycteris lanosus
Pteropus comorensis

STRAW-COLOURED FRUIT BAT *Eidolon helvum*
SIZE HB 150–195mm. FA 110–135mm. W 250–311g. 
DESCRIPTION Large, black-winged with pale tawny fur on the back, shoulders and underside.
HABITAT Breeds in equatorial Africa but ranges all over sub-Saharan Africa outside the breeding season. Roosts typically sited near noise.
FOOD Fruits, flowers, nectar, pollen, buds.
BEHAVIOUR Roosts mainly in large groups in open trees.

Home zone
Migratory range

EGYPTIAN FRUIT BAT (ROUSETTE BAT) *Rousettus aegyptiacus*
SIZE HB 1,300–1,555mm. FA 850–1,060mm. W 110–170g.
DESCRIPTION Large, black-winged with brownish grey fur, dark crown, rounded ears. Vestigial webbing between fifth toe and heel-spur.
HABITAT Sub-Saharan Africa, E Mediterranean and S Arabia. From cave flies long distances to sources of fruits.
FOOD Fruits, flowers, nectar and pollen; occasionally leaves and buds.
BEHAVIOUR A cave-dweller, often very vocal.

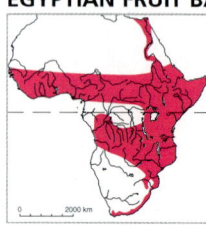

ANGOLA FRUIT BAT *Lissonycteris angolensis*
SIZE HB 105–135mm. FA 65–91mm. W 65–91g.
DESCRIPTION Plain brown fruit bat with oval ears. Patagium is attached to second toe.
HABITAT Tropical Africa, mainly in forests at low and higher altitudes.
FOOD Fruits and flowers.
BEHAVIOUR Roosts singly or in small groups in low, thick vegetation, in hollow trees or near the mouths of caves, and is quiet and cryptic.

Pemba Island Flying Fox

Straw-coloured Fruit Bat

Egyptian Fruit Bat

Mountain Fruit Bat

Angola Fruit Bat

Angola Fruit Bat

NOTE: not to scale

COLLARED FRUIT BATS *Myonycteris* (3 species)

SIZE FA 55–70mm. W 35–80g.
DESCRIPTION Brown or buff with broad shoulder ruffs, or 'collars', in males. Pointed ears resemble those of the Angolan Fruit Bat but are smaller. Species: *M. torquata* (Guinea–Uganda), *M. relicta* (coastal E Africa), *M. brachycephala* (São Tomé and Principe).
HABITAT In or close to rainforest, including savannah/forest mosaics.
FOOD Fruits and nectar.
BEHAVIOUR Roost singly or in small groups in dense, low vegetation.

EPAULETTED FRUIT BATS *Epomophorus* (6 species)

SIZE FA 54–90mm. W 40–120g.
DESCRIPTION Variably tinted, brown fruit bats of differing sizes. All have tufts of white fur at the base of the ears. Males have white 'epaulettes' on their shoulders. Utter chinking, frog-like calls. Species: *E. gambianus*, *E. labiatus*, *E. minimus*, *E. angolensis*, *E. grandis*, *E. wahlbergi*.
HABITAT Mainly savannahs, woodlands and forest mosaics. Some species occur in main forest zones.
FOOD Fruits, flowers, nectar, pollen.

HAMMER BAT *Hypsignathus monstrosus*

SIZE HB 195–200mm (female), 220–275mm (male). FA 118–128mm (female), 125–137mm (male). W 250g (218–377g) (female), 425g (228–450g) (male).
DESCRIPTION The largest continental African fruit bat, with brown fur and membranes and a yellowish brown skin colour on the muzzle, ears and digits. Males are almost twice the weight of females and have inflatable sacs over the raised ridge of the nose and on each side of the neck. The male's lips are also modified to control sound. Both sexes have tubular nostrils and white tufts at the base of the ears. Males make a very loud, explosive, blaring honk. The call carries several kilometres on a still night.
HABITAT Roosts at low levels in heavily shaded forests of almost all types, including mangroves and swamp forest but not montane areas. Seasonal movements poorly known.
FOOD Soft fruits, especially wild figs and the fruit of cabbage trees or forest fever trees (*Anthocleista*). Males may fly up to 10km in search of concentrations of ripe fruits; females forage within a much more localised area.
BEHAVIOUR Competitive assemblies of calling males, or 'leks', provide a point of reference for all Hammer Bats within an 8–10km radius and attract females.

SINGING FRUIT BATS *Epomops* (3 species)

SIZE FA 80–100mm. W 65–158g.
DESCRIPTION Medium-sized brown with white tufts at the base of the ears. Vocalisations very loud and 'musical'. Species: *E. franqueti* (common and widespread), *E. buettikoferi*, *E. dobsoni*.
HABITAT Forests and forest–woodland mosaics.
FOOD Fruits and nectar.

DWARF EPAULETTED FRUIT BATS *Micropteropus* (2 species)

SIZE FA 480–600mm. W 25–40g.
DESCRIPTION Small tawny fruit bats with white tufts at the base of the ears and white 'epaulettes' on adult males. The short muzzle has prominent nostrils. Males make a shrill, chinking call which they repeat monotonously. Species: *M. pusillus* (W & C Africa), *M. intermedius* (Angola and Zaïre).
HABITAT Woodlands, savannahs and forest mosaics outside the main lowland forest blocks.
FOOD Fruits, nectar and pollen.
BEHAVIOUR Roost singly or in small groups in shady vegetation.

Ethiopian Epauletted Fruit Bat
Epomophorus labiatus

Little Collared Fruit Bat
Myonycteris torquata

Hammer Bat
Hypsignathus monstrosus

Franquet's Singing Fruit Bat
Epomops franqueti, female

Franquet's Singing Fruit Bat
male

Peters' Dwarf Epauletted Fruit Bat
Micropteropus pusillus

NOTE: not to scale

TEAR-DROP FRUIT BATS *Scotonycteris* (2 species)

SIZE FA 47–78mm. W est. 35–60g.
DESCRIPTION Both species are rare and little known. Prominent, tear-like white spots occur on either side of the eyes and others over the upper lip. Fur is variably tinted and wings are dark brown. Roost singly in vegetation. Species: *S. ophiodon* (Liberia to R. Zaïre west): FA 74–78mm.
S. zenkeri (Liberia to E Zaïre): FA 47–53mm.
HABITAT Lowland rainforests of W and C Africa; mostly at lowest levels in undergrowth.
FOOD Fruits and flowers. Fruits are possibly gathered from the forest floor.

GOLDEN FRUIT BAT *Casinycteris argynnis*

Casinycteris argynnis
Plerotes anchietae

SIZE HB 90–95mm. FA 50–63mm. W 26–33g.
DESCRIPTION Golden-coloured fruit bat with bold white margins to the mouth, eye and ear base. The hard palate is unlike other fruit bats' in not extending back behind the tooth row, implying that the fruit-squeezing action of the tongue and palate is modified in this species. Roosts singly or in pairs.
HABITAT Known from the main lowland forest block between Cameroon and E Zaïre. Recorded from low dense undergrowth.
FOOD Specialised feeding habits, in which fruits are processed mainly at the front of the mouth, would seem likely.

FLYING CALF *Nanonycteris veldkampi*

SIZE HB 65–75mm. FA 45–50mm. W est. 30g.
DESCRIPTION Very small fawn-brown fruit bat with a slender muzzle and large eyes. Thick, soft fur covers the back and legs and extends onto the membranes. There is a short white 'moustache' and white tufts of fur at the base of the ears. Males have white 'epaulettes'. May congregate at feeding sites.
HABITAT Senegal to E Zaïre in lowland rainforest and forest mosaics.
FOOD Nectar and pollen.

BENGUELA FRUIT BAT *Plerotes anchietae*   *see* map above

SIZE HB 87mm. FA 48–53mm. W est. 38g.
DESCRIPTION Greyish brown fruit bat with rather long, crinkled fur on the lower back and legs. There are white spots at the base of the ears and it lacks a cartilaginous spur on the heel. The muzzle is unusually broad but flat and shallow with very rudimentary teeth. Special sound-amplifying pouches around the eyes of males suggest an unusual loud call.
HABITAT Southern margins of the Zaïre basin between the Atlantic and L. Tanganyika. Probably forest mosaics and riverine strips.
FOOD Nectar and pollen.

NECTAR BAT *Megaloglossus woermanni*

SIZE HB 64–82mm. FA 40–46.5mm. W 12–20g.
DESCRIPTION A very small fruit bat with an extremely fine-pointed muzzle and a very long, thin, brush-textured tongue. The soft pale fur appears to be 'smoked' with brown or sepia. Males have a ruff of stiff, pure white hair, apparently growing from a glandular patch. It is apparently not very vocal. Two races have been described.
HABITAT Main forest blocks from Guinea to Uganda. Roosts in dense forest foliage and has been caught under banana fronds and in huts or houses within the forest. Has been netted flying along forest tracks bordered by flowering trees (*Spathodea*).
FOOD Nectar.

Pohle's Tear-drop Fruit Bat
Scotonycteris ophiodon

Golden Fruit Bat
Casinycteris argynnis

Benguela Fruit Bat
Plerotes anchietae

Flying Calf
Nanonycteris veldkampi

Nectar bat
Megaloglossus woermanni

SLIT-FACED BATS Nycteridae

Immediately recognisable by their long ears and the foliated trench which runs from the forehead to the nostrils and upper lip. The tail terminates in a cartilaginous T- or Y-shape that is unique to this group. These bats are slow foragers, with a moth-like flight

SLIT-FACED BATS *Nycteris* (10 species)

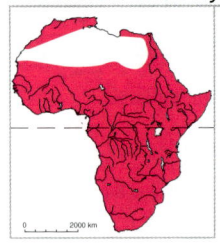

SIZE FA 32–66mm. W 5–36g.

DESCRIPTION Large-eared, broad-winged bats with long, silky fur and a long tail fully enclosed in membrane with a T- or Y-shaped tip. The nose trench, or slit, is surrounded by a series of lobes and flanges, which probably modulate and control their high-frequency 'whispers'. Prefer to roost in cool, dark and, ideally, moist retreats within caves, holes, hollow trees, buildings or culverts but some species will tolerate dense, dark foliage or tangled, shady thickets (notably on termitaries). Roost individually or in groups of up to many thousands. Flight is very acrobatic; if they meet an obstacle in dense vegetation they momentarily perch before taking off again.

HABITAT Found in a wide range of vegetation types but forage at low levels in areas of dense undergrowth, reeds, thickets, mangroves, etc., all over Africa except open desert.
FOOD Crickets, grasshoppers, moths, flies, cicadas, flying termites. Various larger insects, spiders and scorpions are plucked off vegetation, the ground, or caught in flight.
BEHAVIOUR Slit-faced bats emerge late and retire early.

LARGE-WINGED BATS Megadermatidae

Broad-winged, large-eared, large-headed bats with ornate nose-leaves, thin, strut-like legs and long, silky fur. Restricted to Old World tropics and Australasia, these are large-eyed bats that often emerge before dark to hunt invertebrates from perches where they may be relatively conspicuous.

HEART-NOSED BAT *Cardioderma cor*

SIZE HB 70–77mm. FA 54–59mm. W 21–35g.

DESCRIPTION Relatively large bat with long, pale fur and joined ears bearing sharp, two-pointed ear tragi. The prominent muzzle is surrounded by a heart-shaped nose-leaf.
HABITAT Restricted to NE Africa from Eritrea to central Tanzania. The Rift Valley, dry *Acacia* bush and the coastal littoral are preferred habitats. Uses houses for shelter but is shy and prefers dry caves. Roosts in groups of 3–100 or more.
FOOD Invertebrates and, more occasionally, vertebrates (including other bat species), hunted from a limited number of lookout posts on the lower, outer margins of trees or bushes.

BEHAVIOUR After forays, prey is brought back to be eaten at the perch or even to the day-time shelter where debris collects below the roost.

YELLOW-WINGED BAT *Lavia frons*

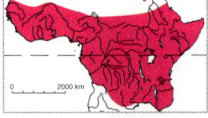

SIZE HB 63–83mm. FA 55–64mm. W 28–36g.

DESCRIPTION Very colourful bat with large black eyes, pale blue-grey fur and bright yellow-orange membranes and ears. The wings are exceptionally broad and the ears are long, with a spiky tragus. The elongated nose-leaf also encloses a pointed sella, or spike, that runs down its centre. Often to be seen roosting in light shade in large savannah trees (especially *Euphorbia* in the dry season). It makes a bird-like contact call.

HABITAT Low-lying savannahs, open woodlands and narrow forest galleries in tropical Africa.
FOOD Invertebrates, occasionally vertebrates; known to chase other bat species.
BEHAVIOUR Apparently able to startle potential predators with its brilliant colouring. When hanging quite still it resembles a dead leaf.

Egyptian Slit-faced Bat
Nycteris thebaica

Heart-nosed Bat
Cardioderma cor

Yellow-winged Bat
Lavia frons

HORSESHOE BATS Rhinolophinae

Elaborate nose-leaves and broad, leaf-shaped ears directed towards effective type of CF sonar.

HORSESHOE BATS *Rhinolophus* (21 species)

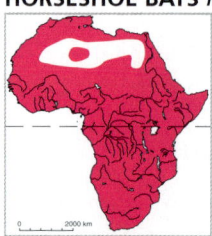

SIZE FA 38–68mm.
DESCRIPTION All horseshoe bats have nose-leaves of a similar structure but the proportions and shapes are distinctive in each species.
HABITAT All vegetation types.
FOOD Varies from species to species. Mosquitoes, moths, beetles, spiders and scorpions are caught in flight, by foraging at low levels or by ambush on the ground.
BEHAVIOUR Roost in caves, holes, buildings, hollow trees. Temperate species choose warm roosts when active but retreat to cool sites when torpid.

LEAF-NOSED BATS Hipposiderinae

Predominantly tropical, close relatives of the horseshoe bats but with more diverse nose-leaves.

LEAF-NOSED BATS *Hipposideros* (13 species)

SIZE FA 28–116mm.
DESCRIPTION Very diverse group with leaf-shaped ears and less elevated nose-leaves than horseshoe bats. Many have scroll-like folds and flanges above the eyes. Sides of the muzzle often bear shallow lappets 'stacked' outside rim of the main 'horseshoe'.
HABITAT Forests, woodlands and savannahs at low and medium altitudes.
FOOD Beetles, cicadas, termites, moths, crickets, ants and woodlice.
BEHAVIOUR Prey is caught in flight or is snatched off leaves or litter by quartering in slow, wavering flight close to the ground.

TRIDENT LEAF-NOSED BATS *Asellia* (2 species)

SIZE HB 50–62mm. FA 45–60mm.
DESCRIPTION Pale with broad, pointed ears and a squat nose-leaf with three very blunt protuberances on its posterior margin. Species: *A. tridens* (Sahara to Pakistan), *A. patrizii* (S Red Sea).
HABITAT Deserts and Sahelian subdeserts.
FOOD Desert insects and scorpions.
BEHAVIOUR Roosts in dark ruins, wells and caves, often in many hundreds.

PERCIVAL'S TRIDENT BAT *Cloeotis percivali*

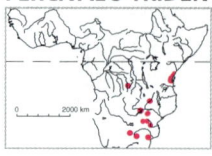

SIZE HB 33–50mm. FA 30–36mm. W est. 4–6g.
DESCRIPTION Pale with orange and buff morphs. Ears very small and rounded. Nose-leaf has 3 prominent points on posterior margin.
HABITAT Patchily distributed in SE Africa, often coastal.
FOOD Small insects.
BEHAVIOUR Roosts in the darkest recesses of caves and mines.

PERSIAN LEAF-NOSED BAT *Triaenops persicus*

SIZE HB 50–57mm. FA 50–55mm. W 8–15g.
DESCRIPTION Rounded ears half-buried in fur. Back of nose-leaf has 3 spear-shaped leaves. Deepset nostrils. Long, narrow head disguised by long, dense fur which may be grey, brown or a rich russet red. Wings dark brown.
HABITAT Mainly coastal species of NW Indian Ocean littoral but ranges up large river valleys inland to uplands.
FOOD Small insects caught in slow, moth-like flight.
BEHAVIOUR Often found in large colonies where individuals hang close together.

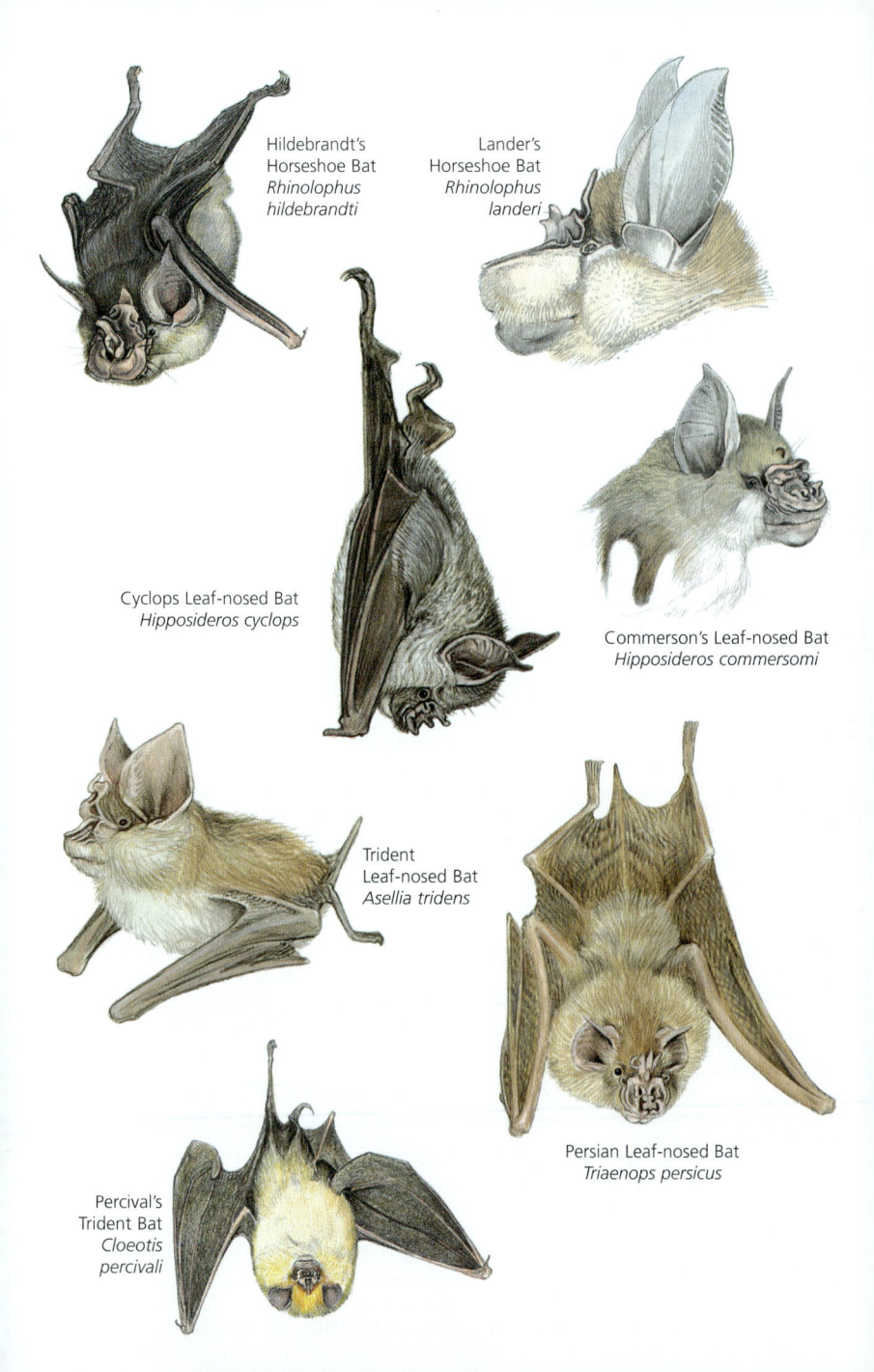

Hildebrandt's Horseshoe Bat
Rhinolophus hildebrandti

Lander's Horseshoe Bat
Rhinolophus landeri

Cyclops Leaf-nosed Bat
Hipposideros cyclops

Commerson's Leaf-nosed Bat
Hipposideros commersomi

Trident Leaf-nosed Bat
Asellia tridens

Persian Leaf-nosed Bat
Triaenops persicus

Percival's Trident Bat
Cloeotis percivali

VESPER BATS Vespertilionidae

A very large and successful family of simple-nosed bats. At a casual glance most vesper bats look bewilderingly alike. Dental patterns and skull structures must be examined in order to distinguish some genera and species. The most obvious characteristics of this family are small eyes, separate ears, with noticeable tragi, and long tails enclosed in membrane. Most species have glands on the muzzle (which may swell and shrink in size).

Primitive bat dentition is characterised by 38 teeth (2-1-3-3: 3-1-3-3) set in a long, slender snout. This formula occurs in the modern hairy bats, *Myotis*. Pipistrelles and twilight bats are thought to have derived from a *Myotis*-like stem while woolly bats and long-fingered bats branched off at a very early stage. In the more advanced genera faces are shorter and the teeth have become reduced in number. The family has a worldwide distribution and occupies all but the very coldest regions and habitats.

HAIRY BATS *Myotis* (12 species)

SIZE FA 31–40mm.

DESCRIPTION Long, hairy muzzles and narrow ears with spike-shaped tragi. Species: *M. blythii, M. bocagei, M. capaccinii, M. emarginatus, M. lesueuri, M. morrisi, M. mystacinus, M. nattereri, M. scotti, M. seabrai, M. tricolor, M. welwitschii*.

HABITAT A wide range of vegetation types and altitudes. Some species may be scattered, roosting singly or in small groups, while others form larger colonies.

FOOD Small insects caught in slow flight within 5m of the ground.

BEHAVIOUR Roost in hollow trees, deep caves or vegetation.

WOOLLY BATS *Kerivoula* (8 species)

Kerivoula
Barbastella

SIZE FA 36–48mm.

DESCRIPTION The woolly fur has a frizzled, frosty or 'crinkly' appearance. The funnel-shaped ears have a long, pointed tragus. The long, sharp muzzle and domed cranium are generally concealed by dense fur, as are the minute eyes. The membrane bears a fine fringe of short hair. Roost among dead leaves, in lichen, old birds' nests, thatch or hollow branches. Species: *K. aerosa, K. africana, K. argentata, K. cuprosa, K. eriophora, K. lanosa, K. phalaena, K. smithi*.

HABITAT Well-watered but otherwise diverse habitats. Woolly bats emerge late and retire early.

FOOD Very small insects caught at low levels in slow, dancing flight.

BEHAVIOUR Roost among dead leaves, in lichen, old birds' nests, thatch or hollow branches.

BARBASTELLE BATS *Barbastella* (2 species)   *see* map above

SIZE FA 35–45mm.

DESCRIPTION Very dark bats with blunt noses and upward-facing nostrils. The forward edges of the large, emarginated ears join forward of the eyes to give a very pinched, pug-nosed appearance. The tragus is triangular. All naked skin is black or deep brown. Utter audible chirps and hums. Species: *B. barbastellus* (Morocco to Senegal), *B. leucomelas* (Egypt).

HABITAT Dry, open woodlands and temperate mountains. Occasional migrants (NW Africa and Egypt).

FOOD Small, soft insects often caught over water or off foliage in slow but well-controlled flight.

BEHAVIOUR Form small summer groups of 10–100, but roost in larger numbers in winter; known to travel nearly 300km.

Sub-Saharan vesper bat heads

Hairy bat sp.
Myotis

Woolly bat sp.
Kerivoula

Butterfly bat sp.
Chalinolobus

Serotine bat sp.
Eptesicus

Moloney's Flat-headed Bat
Mimetillus moloneyi

Pipistrelle sp.
Pipistrellus

Tropical Long-eared bat sp.
Laephotis

Schlieffen's Twilight Bat
Nycteceius schlieffeni

House bat sp.
Scotophilus

Long-fingered bat sp.
Miniopterus

Evening bat sp.
Scotoecus

Welwitsch's Hairy Bat
Myotis welwitschii

Damara Woolly Bat
Kerivoula argentata

Western Barbastelle Bat
Barbastella barbastellus

PLATE 31 VESPER BATS

BUTTERFLY BATS *Chalinolobus* (syn. *Glauconycteris*) (9 species)

SIZE FA 36–50mm.
DESCRIPTION Marked wings, broad, blunt faces, widely spaced nostrils, rounded ears. Often reluctant to fly from day perches.
HABITAT Woodlands, forests and moist savannahs. May roost in clusters under large leaves or in thatch.
FOOD Moths and other small, soft-bodied insects caught early in evening.
BEHAVIOUR Roost in trees or buildings, often attracted to lights, make audible squeaks.

SEROTINE BATS *Eptesicus* (13 species)

SIZE FA 25–55mm.
DESCRIPTION Relatively short ears and blunt tragi. Almost flat top to the skull. Flight resembles that of pipistrelles: erratic fluttering punctuated by fast swoops and dives. Tail membrane appears blunt and rounded. May make audible clicks in flight.
HABITAT Both forest and non-forest species, low and high fliers.
FOOD Small insects caught in flight.
BEHAVIOUR Roost in vegetation, caves and houses.

MOLONEY'S FLAT-HEADED BAT *Mimetillus moloneyi*

SIZE HB 50–60mm. FA 26.5–30mm. W 6–11.5g.
DESCRIPTION Fast, short-winged, whirring flight; very direct with no sharp turns. Head and body flattened, forearms and wings short and compact.
HABITAT Forest and moist forest–savannah mosaics in equatorial Africa.
FOOD Flying termites and ants.
BEHAVIOUR Roost under bark.

NOCTULES *Nyctalus* (3 species)

Nyctecius schlieffeni
Nyctalus

SIZE FA 38–69mm.
DESCRIPTION Pug-nosed, long, narrow wings. Flight fast, on angled wings. Metallic calls are very audible.
HABITAT Temperate and migratory bats with marginal extensions of range into N Africa.
FOOD Large insects.

SCHLIEFFEN'S TWILIGHT BAT *Nyctecius schlieffeni*

SIZE HB 40–56mm. FA 29–35mm. W 6–9g.
DESCRIPTION Variably coloured with dark membranes and bare, swollen muzzle. Emerges early. Erratic flight.
HABITAT Very widespread in savannahs and relatively arid habitats.
FOOD Small insects.
BEHAVIOUR Roosts alone in crevices in trees and buildings.

PIPISTRELLES *Pipistrellus* (16 species)

SIZE FA 20–38mm.
DESCRIPTION Very small bats of variable colouring. Prominent nostrils bring the nose to a sharp point behind the swollen muzzle. The tragus shape is distinctive for most species. Flight is fluttering, with frequent angular turns and swoops.
HABITAT All habitats.
FOOD Insects.

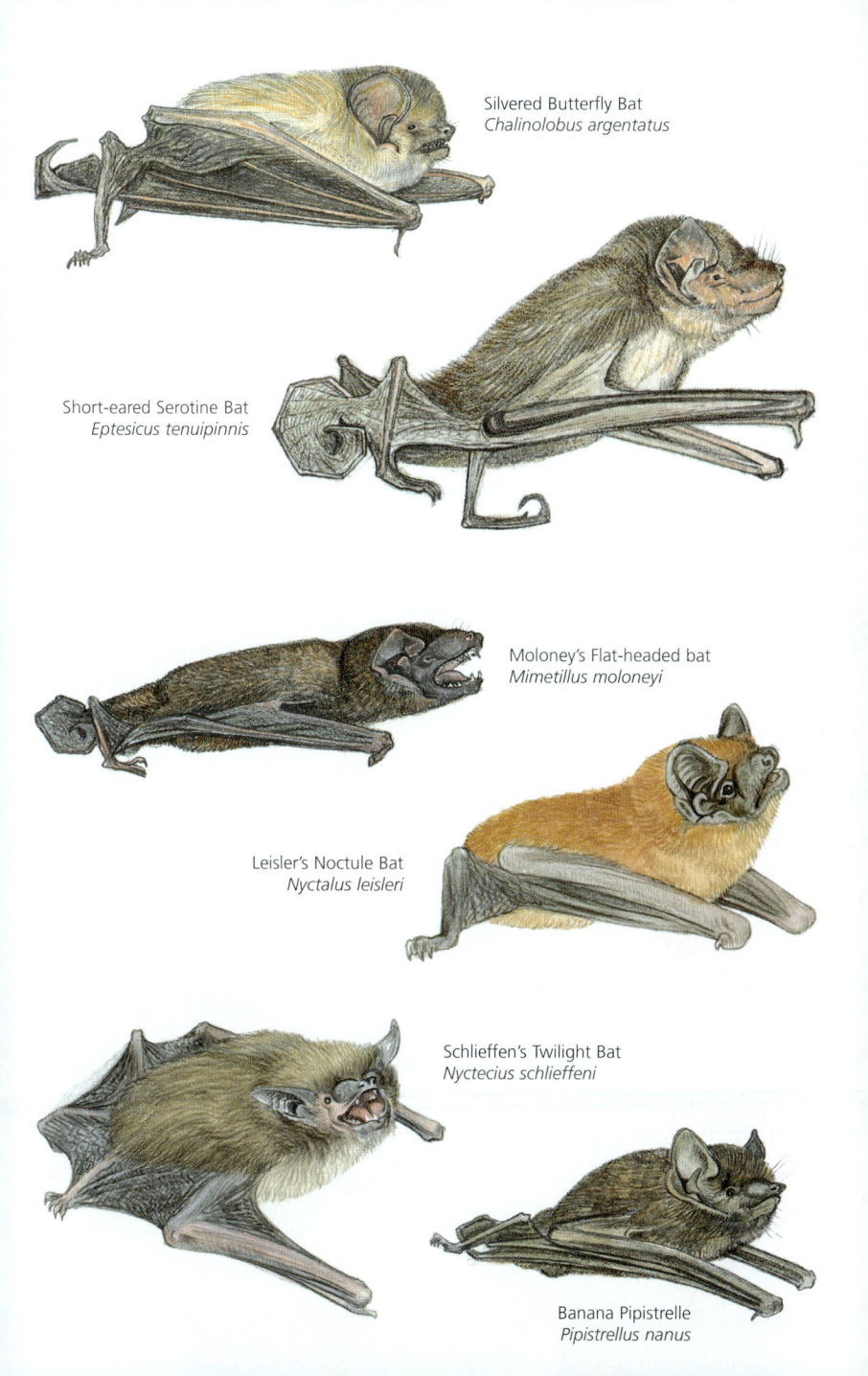

Silvered Butterfly Bat
Chalinolobus argentatus

Short-eared Serotine Bat
Eptesicus tenuipinnis

Moloney's Flat-headed bat
Mimetillus moloneyi

Leisler's Noctule Bat
Nyctalus leisleri

Schlieffen's Twilight Bat
Nyctecius schlieffeni

Banana Pipistrelle
Pipistrellus nanus

HEMPRICH'S LONG-EARED BAT *Otonycteris hemprichii*

SIZE HB 70–130mm. FA 60–66mm.
DESCRIPTION A widespread, large-eared, long-headed desert bat with long, silky pale fur and semi-translucent membranes. Flight is slow and erratic. Emits a buzz call when disturbed in roost.
HABITAT Desert and subdesert steppe environments.
FOOD Desert insects.
BEHAVIOUR Roosts in rock crevices, cliffs or buildings.

TROPICAL LONG-EARED BATS *Laephotis* (4 species)

SIZE FA 35–39mm.
DESCRIPTION The long ears have very large, curved tragi.
HABITAT Rare bats found in dry woodlands and savannahs of S and E Africa. *L. wintoni* has the widest distribution.
FOOD Insects.
BEHAVIOUR Roost in day-time under dead bark.

NORTHERN LONG-EARED BAT *Plecotus austriacus*

Plecotus austriacus
Scotoecus

SIZE HB 40–58mm. FA 37–45mm. W 7–14g.
DESCRIPTION Very long-eared, woolly bats with large, tapered tragi and a blunt face. The long fur has a dark base and a grey-brown surface tint. Claws and feet are small.
HABITAT Dry, open Mediterranean landscapes. Roosts alone or twos and threes in caves, mines or buildings.
FOOD Moths, beetles and other insects taken off foliage or in flight.
BEHAVIOUR Chirps or hums if disturbed. Peripheral range in N Africa.

EVENING BATS *Scotoecus* (2 species)

SIZE FA 29–39mm.
DESCRIPTION Broad-faced brown bats with a blunt tragus in the round ears. Teeth are robust, the canines flat-fronted. Males have an exceptionally long penis. Variable in colour.
HABITAT Tropical bats inhabiting woodlands, savannahs and dry *Acacia* country.
FOOD Insects.

HOUSE BATS *Scotophilus* (5 species)

SIZE FA 42–80mm.
DESCRIPTION Robust bats with blunt heads and long, tapering tragi. There are swollen glands in the corner of the mouth. Colouring varies from greenish olive and yellow to dark brown and off-white.
HABITAT Very varied ecotypes, including uplands, forests and scrub-desert in Africa and Asia.
FOOD Hard-bodied insects.
BEHAVIOUR Emerge early for fast, sweeping flights along habitual flyways.

LONG-FINGERED BATS *Miniopterus* (4 species)

SIZE FA 35–50mm.
DESCRIPTION Double folding of the wing digits (which are exceptionally long) is a distinctive feature. These bats have a high-domed cranium, a very small, pointed muzzle and are dark in colour.
HABITAT Very varied habitats in Africa, Eurasia and Australia.
FOOD Insects.

Hemprich's Long-eared Bat
Otonycteris hemprichii

De Winton's Long-eared Bat
Laephotis wintoni

Northern Long-eared Bat
Plecotus austriacus

Dark-winged Evening Bat
Scotoecus hirundo

Schreiber's Long-fingered Bat
Miniopterus schriebersi

Schreiber's House Bat
Scotophilus nigrita

INSECTIVORES Insectivora

Of the 4 or 5 groups that traditionally occupy this order the elephant shrews, golden moles and tenrecs are now accepted as totally separate and distinct. Shrews and hedgehogs remain in a single order, if only for the sake of convenience.

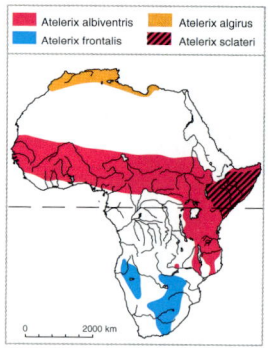

HEDGEHOGS Erinaceidae

■ Atelerix albiventris ■ Atelerix algirus
■ Atelerix frontalis ▨ Atelerix sclateri

DESCRIPTION Hedgehogs are successful and widespread modern survivors of a very ancient group. The evolution of spiny armour has been a major factor in their survival. They have relatively short legs and tail, a sharply pointed face, small eyes and prominent ears. They are nocturnal insect-eaters.

AFRICAN HEDGEHOGS *Atelerix* (4 species)

SIZE HB 14–25cm. T 1.5–5cm. W 250–1,600g.

DESCRIPTION Small, spiny animals with short tails, pointed muzzles and short hairy legs with clawed, well-padded toes. Only active in evenings or at night, they make a sniffing call. They trot with fast leg movements but hunch or roll into a prickly ball at any disturbance.

Species: *A. albiventris* (sub-Saharan non-forest habitats to R. Zambezi), *A. algirus* (Libya to W Sahara), *A. frontalis* (S Africa), *A. sclateri* (Somalia). *A. sclateri* is of uncertain taxonomic status and may be a race of *A. albiventris*.

HABITAT Very widespread but sporadic in drier regions of Africa. A marked preference for relatively open, dry or seasonal habitats with sparse or patchy grass cover, especially overgrazed regions.

FOOD Invertebrates, notably termites, beetles, earthworms, millipedes, small vertebrates, fungi and fallen fruits. African hedgehogs can locate hidden prey by scent and sound, and can dig in soft, loose soils.

BEHAVIOUR Nocturnal or crepuscular animals, they are solitary except females with young. They hibernate in temperate regions and may also aestivate in tropical dry seasons. Various vocalisations including a sniff, growl, twitter, spit, chatter and scream. They travel over a home range, sleeping in changing (but sometimes habitual) day-shelters. One to nine young are born seasonally. The most striking adaptation of hedgehogs is their ability to curl up into a spiny ball. Correlated with this are short blunt ridges on the vertebrae and a wide pelvis, but the main modification is the hemispherical muscle in which the spines are embedded. When this muscle (which is anchored to the forehead) contracts it becomes a bag into which body, head and legs are withdrawn. The spines are an effective protection, although eagle owls and some hungry carnivores appear to have little difficulty in killing and eating hedgehogs.

LONG-EARED HEDGEHOGS *Hemiechinus* (2 species)

■ Hemiechinus aethiopicus
▨ Hemiechinus auritus

SIZE HB 14–27cm. T 1.3–5cm. W est. 150–250g.

DESCRIPTION Variably coloured desert hedgehogs with shorter spines, longer limbs and larger ears than *Atelerix*.

Species: Long-eared Hedgehog *H. auritus* (Egypt–Asiatic species), Desert Hedgehog *H. aethiopicus* (N Africa, Sahara).

HABITAT Deserts. *H. auritus* is a moisture-dependent hibernator preferring cool deserts. *H. aethiopicus* is a drought-adapted aestivator, preferring hot, dry deserts.

FOOD Invertebrates and small vertebrates.

BEHAVIOUR Only active at night (or on overcast, cool mornings or evenings), they sleep in self-dug burrows during the day. Females are known to squeal in defence of their young and butt with their head spines.

White-bellied Hedgehog
Atelerix albiventris

Long-eared Hedgehog
Hemiechinus auritus

SHREWS Soricidae

Mouse-sized mammals with a long, mobile nose and stout, cylindrical skull. Bulldoze insects out of plant debris. Bodies powerful and tubular. Sensitive vibrissae detect invertebrate prey.

MOUSE SHREWS *Myosorex* (12 species)   see map

- Congosorex
- Ruwenzorisorex
- Paracrocidura
- Myosorex

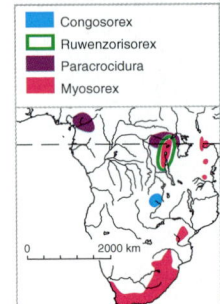

SIZE HB ave. 50–100mm.
DESCRIPTION Small, dark shrews, with reduced eyes and ears, a short tail and well-clawed, slender toes.
HABITAT Mostly temperate or high-altitude regions, often in swampy conditions. Most species are localised endemics. All are very poorly known.

MOLE SHREWS *Surdisorex* (2 species)   no map

SIZE HB 89–108mm. T 24–34mm. W est. 8–10g.
DESCRIPTION Small, brown shrews with dense short fur and no trace of external eyes or ears. Species: *S. novae* (Aberdare Mts), *S. polulus* (Mt Kenya).
HABITAT Surface runways and subterranean tunnels in Afro-alpine and upper montane forest.

CONGO SHREW *Congosorex polli*   see map above

SIZE HB est. 90mm. T est. 60mm.
DESCRIPTION Small brown shrew with a long tail and large ears.
HABITAT Only known from Kasai, S Zaïre (fire-climax Miombo [*Brachystegia*] woodlands).

MUSK SHREWS *Suncus* (4 species)   no map

SIZE HB 50–125mm. T 30–85mm. W 3.5–9.5g.
DESCRIPTION Various shades of brown or grey, with a paler underside.
HABITAT Very patchy distributions. Apparently more common in S Africa than tropical Africa.

CLIMBING SHREWS *Sylvisorex* (10 species)

SIZE HB 45–85mm. T 45–90mm. W 3–12g.
DESCRIPTION Arboreal shrews with long tail, mobile hands and feet and long nose.
HABITAT Predominantly forest or riverine habitats from sea-level up to 4,000m.

RUWENZORI SHREW *Ruwenzorisorex suncoides*   see map above

SIZE HB 92–95mm. T 61–62mm. W est. 18g.
DESCRIPTION Greyish-black with rounded head, short snout and small (but protruding) ears.
HABITAT Montane forests in central Africa (E Zaïre, Rwanda, Burundi and W Uganda).

HERO SHREW *Scutisorex somereni*

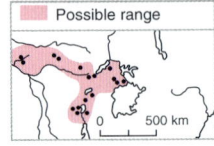

Possible range

SIZE HB 105–150mm. T 70–109mm. W 70–113g.
DESCRIPTION A large grey shrew with a long, tapered nose, shallow ears and thick woolly fur. Distinguished by its 'trotting', rather than 'crawling', gait and complex backbones.
HABITAT Seasonally swampy forests between the R. Itimbiri, R. Lualaba and R. Nile; low and medium altitudes.

Montane Mouse Shrew
Myosorex blarina

Mount Kenya Mole Shrew
Surdisorex polulus

Congo Shrew
Congosorex polli

Greater Musk Shrew
Suncus lixus

Grant's Climbing Shrew
Sylvisorex granti

Ruwenzori Shrew
Ruwenzorisorex suncoides

Hero Shrew
Scutisorex somereni

92 — PLATE 36 SHREWS

RODENT SHREWS *Paracrocidura* (3 species)   *see* map on p.90

SIZE HB ave. 65mm. T ave. 34.5mm.
DESCRIPTION Dark shrews with thin, short fur, dark skin and a short, broad muzzle. Limbs are short with miniscule claws.
HABITAT Montane and lowland forests from Cameroon to W Uganda.

WHITE-TOOTHED SHREWS *Crocidura* (103 species)

SIZE HB 45–140mm. T 45–90mm. W 11–40g.
DESCRIPTION The commonest and most diverse group of African shrews. All have a long, whiskery nose, visible ears and small eyes. Most have some long, fine hairs growing very sparsely on the tail. The group can be divided into 3 subdivisions on the basis of tooth reduction (especially of the last molar). Further clustering into species groups is also possible on the basis of variations in size, colour, length of the hindfeet, and length and hairing of the tail. Certain identification requires close inspection of the teeth but the plate opposite illustrates 14 common species that can be identified according to external characteristics, notably colour, the proportions of hind feet, length and shape of snout, tail length and the pattern of hairs or vibrissae on the tail or rump.
HABITAT All vegetation types at all altitudes, mainly terrestrial, but able to climb and swim. Some species are highly restricted (particularly those in the 'primitive' category); others range very widely (notably some of the 'advanced' groups).
FOOD A very wide range of invertebrates and small vertebrates.

Schouteden's Rodent Shrew
Paracrocidura schoutedeni

Greater White-toothed Shrew
Crocidura flavescens

White-toothed shrews

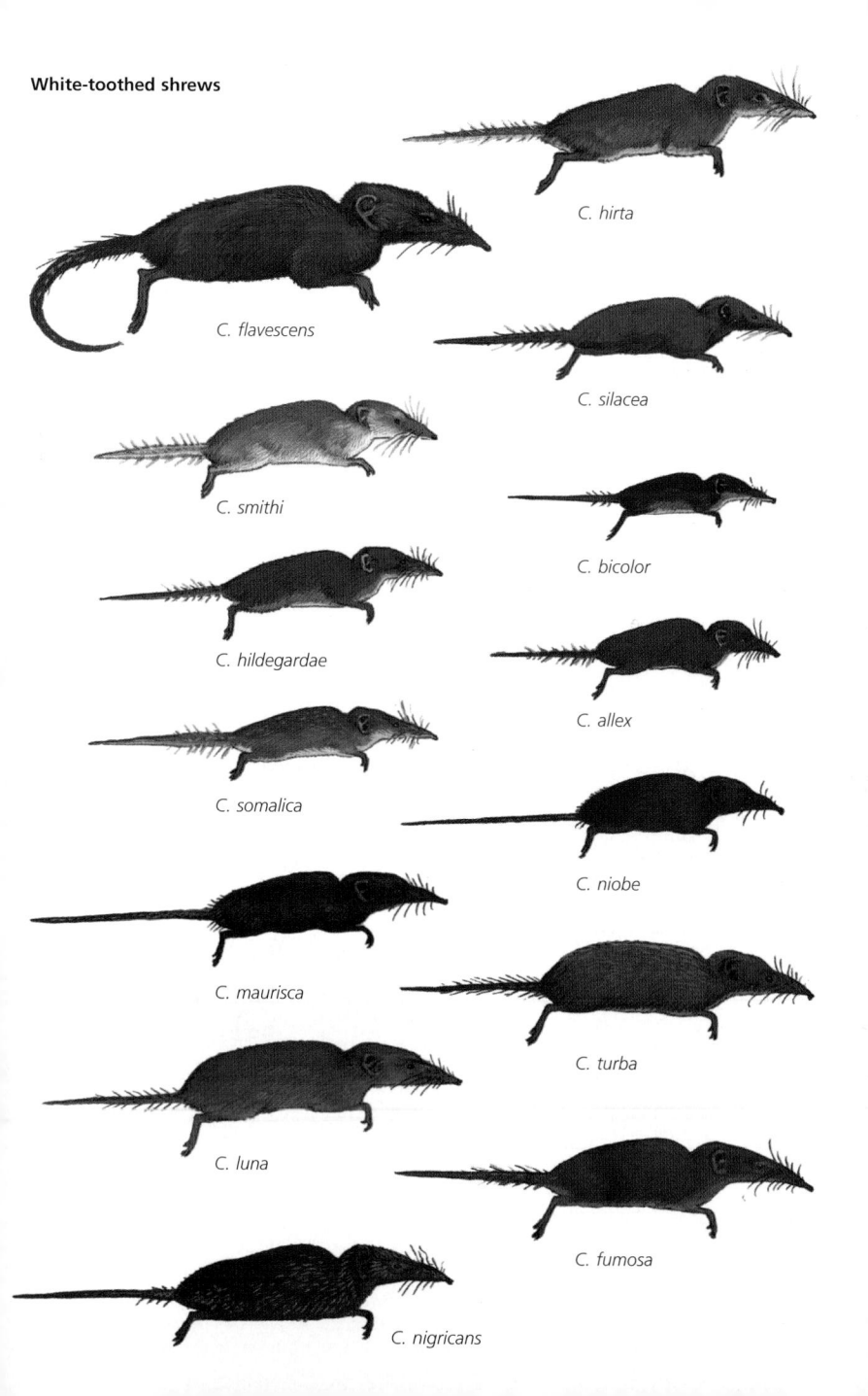

HARES Lagomorpha

Hares specialise in feeding on coarse vegetation in unstable and often cold environments.

HARES Leporidae

This family consists of medium-sized, soft-furred animals with very short, furry tails, relatively large ears, small mouths and muscular hindlegs.

CAPE HARE *Lepus capensis*

SIZE HB 40–68cm. T 7–15cm. W 1–3.5kg.
DESCRIPTION Back is variable light shades of brown, buff or grey while the chest is normally sandy coloured. There are muted contrasts on face and nape of neck. Incisors are without deep grooves and a forehead spot is rare. Great regional variation. Over 30 subspecies named including the small, desert-dwelling *L. c. habessinicus* (Horn of Africa).
HABITAT Prefers completely open grasslands, steppes and subdesert. Will move into cleared or regularly fired grasslands (only to be displaced by scrub hares if there is extensive woody regrowth) but is seldom found in montane areas.
FOOD High proportion of herbs and fire-dependent grasses, cropped close to the ground.

SCRUB HARE *Lepus saxatilis* (syn. *L. crawshayi*)

SIZE HB 41–58cm. T 7–17cm. W 1.5–4.5kg.
DESCRIPTION Back is variable darker shades of brown to grey, with all-white underparts and well-defined pattern contrasts on the face. The nape of the neck is warm russet and a forehead spot is common. Incisors have deep grooves and the muzzle is more projecting than in the Cape Hare. There is enormous regional variation, especially in the length of the ears. Over 30 races have been named, including *saxatilis*, *whytei*, *crawshayi*, *victoriae*, *ansorgei*, *fagani* and *canopus*.
HABITAT Prefers scrubby grasslands, grassy areas within woodlands, secondary growth, cultivation mosaics and stony, wooded steppes; common in upland and montane grasslands.
FOOD Rank grass species, which are cropped less close to the ground. In E Africa takes fewer herbs than Cape Hare.

STARCK'S HARE *Lepus starcki*   see map above

SIZE HB est. 42–60cm. T 7–12cm. W 2–3.5kg.
DESCRIPTION Back is mottled tawny, becoming grey on the rump. Nape, sides, chest and legs are tawny and the underparts are white. Tail is all white or with black stripe. Ears have a prominent black tip.
HABITAT High-altitude moorlands (2,500–4,000m) in Ethiopia.
FOOD Common moorland grasses (*Agrostis*, *Eleusine*, *Festuca*, *Pennisetum* and *Poa*) are likely food plants.

RIVERINE RABBIT *Bunolagus monticularis*   see map on p.96

SIZE HB 42–58cm. T 8–15cm. W 2–3kg.
DESCRIPTION A long-eared, medium-sized hare with relatively short hindfeet, a brown tail and a very conspicuous dark line separating the white chin and bib from the darker muzzle and cheeks. There are conspicuous pale eye rings and white fringes along the upper edges of the ears.
HABITAT Dense vegetation bordering seasonal rivers in the Karoo where salt-loving plants, such as *Salsola* and *Lycium*, predominate. Digs short burrows which it plugs with debris when not in use.
FOOD Browses on common shrubs, i.e. *Salsola*, *Kochia* and the ubiquitous *Mesembryanthemum*.
BEHAVIOUR Solitary, with male home ranges of about 20ha and female 13ha. Activity is nocturnal. Single young, weighing only 40g at birth, are reared in a fur- and grass-lined burrow.

Cape Hare

Scrub Hare

Starck's Hare

Riverine Rabbit

COMMON RABBIT *Oryctolagus cuniculus*

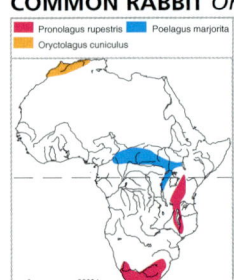

SIZE HB 30–50cm. T 3–8cm. W 0.8–3kg.
DESCRIPTION Small, short-limbed, brown-coated rabbit or 'digging hare', with shorter ears and a rounder head than true hares. The tips of the ears are never black.
HABITAT Bushy and broken country in N Morocco and NW Algeria, avoiding densely wooded land and desert.
FOOD Grass and herbs; bark in winter.
BEHAVIOUR Live on the surface when predators and the climate allow. The digging of dens, burrows or warrens is likely to represent a response to a combination of environmental pressures. As with all hares, rabbits produce a variety of scents which help to regulate their social behaviour.

UGANDA GRASS-HARE *Poelagus marjorita*   see map above

SIZE HB 44–50cm. T 4–5cm. W 2–3kg.
DESCRIPTION Resembles Common Rabbit but fur is coarser, the nose more protuberant and the hindfeet proportionately shorter.
HABITAT Moist, wooded grasslands associated with rocky or broken ground. It shelters in dense vegetation, rock clefts and self-made 'scrapes'.
FOOD Grasses (preferably short), grass seeds, herbs and, occasionally, cultivated crops.
BEHAVIOUR Continuous breeders. The helpless young are born in a nest (blocked by the mother with a vegetation barrier). Mainly nocturnal and solitary or in very small groups.

ROCK HARES *Pronolagus*

Chunky, grizzled hares with a red or dark tail, a grey head and reddish limbs.

SMITH'S RED ROCK HARE *Pronolagus rupestris*   see map above

SIZE HB 38–53cm. T 5–12cm. W 1.3–2.5kg.
DESCRIPTION Grey-headed with a bright russet rump and legs. The red tail normally has a black tip. The black colour is variable and the fur is soft and dense.
HABITAT Stony country where dense bush, grass and rocks are intermingled.
FOOD Mainly grazers.

NATAL RED ROCK HARE *Pronolagus crassicaudatus*

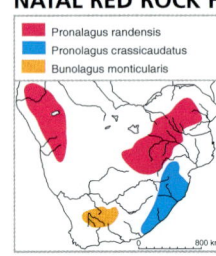

SIZE HB 46–56cm. T 3.5–11cm. W 2.4–3kg.
DESCRIPTION Pale grey band across the cheek, russet fore- and hindlegs and rump, and an all-russet tail. Fur is dense, harsher than in other rock hares.
HABITAT Steep, grassy hillsides with scattered rocks and boulders along the eastern seaboard of South Africa and S Mozambique from East London to the R. Maputo, and from sea-level up to 1,550m. Shelters among the rocks in tussocks or dense, low vegetation.
FOOD Grasses are grazed at night. Often move to higher elevations to graze and may do so in close proximity to each other.

JAMESON'S RED ROCK HARE *Pronolagus randensis*   see map above

SIZE HB 42–50cm. T 6–13.5cm. W 1.8–3kg.
DESCRIPTION Light grey head with brownish flecks and a light, warm-coloured rump and back legs. The red-brown tail has a black tip. Fur is very soft and silky.
HABITAT Rocky hills, valleys and gorges in 2 widely separate areas of S Africa (Zimbabwe–Transvaal and Namibia). Shelter among rocks and tussocks during the day. Very agile among boulders and able to run over very steep surfaces.
FOOD Fresh green flushes of grasses are favoured and are usually grazed in proximity to rocks and koppies at night.

Common Rabbit

Uganda Grass-hare

Smith's Red Rock Hare

Jameson's Red Rock Hare

Natal Red Rock Hare

ROPE SQUIRRELS *Funisciurus*

Small, thin, soft-furred squirrels with a fluffy, rather flimsy tail. In spite of loud calls, rope squirrels are difficult to see and their main defence is to freeze or move behind the nearest tree. Rope squirrels subdivide into three sub-groups. The most terrestrial and insectivorous are the Ribboned and Lunda Rope Squirrels. The Fire-footed, Red-cheeked and Thomas's Rope Squirrels are less insectivorous but also spend time on the forest floor. The third group, Lady Burton's, Kintampo and Congo Rope Squirrels are more arboreal and feed mainly on fruit and leaves. All rope squirrels make large nests of well-shredded plant material hidden in natural crevices.

RIBBONED ROPE SQUIRREL *Funisciurus lemniscatus*

SIZE HB 15–18cm. T 13–19cm. W 100–150g.
DESCRIPTION Olive-coloured with two dark and two pale stripes.
HABITAT Ranges from R. Sanaga to R. Zaïre and R. Aruwimi.
FOOD About 40% animal matter and 60% fruits and seeds.
BEHAVIOUR Almost all food is collected on the ground.

LUNDA ROPE SQUIRREL *Funisciurus bayoni*

SIZE HB 16–19.5cm. T 13–17cm. W 110–160g.
DESCRIPTION Back is greyish olive-green, with a fine black grizzle.
HABITAT Mosaic of rainforest and moist woodlands in NE Angola and SW Zaïre.
FOOD Not known.

THOMAS'S ROPE SQUIRREL *Funisciurus anerythrus*

SIZE HB 16–23cm. T 13–20cm. W 200–220g.
DESCRIPTION Back is brownish olive, with variable pale flank stripes.
HABITAT Margins of the R. Zaïre, R. Ogooué and other rivers.
FOOD In Gabon, about 80% fruits and 20% animal matter.
BEHAVIOUR Lives in the lower strata of dense secondary growth along the margins of rivers and swamps, spending much of its time on the ground.

FIRE-FOOTED ROPE SQUIRREL *Funisciurus pyrropus*

SIZE HB 13.5–26.6cm. T 10–20cm. W 160–300g.
DESCRIPTION Velvety-furred with rich rufous limbs and face.
HABITAT Undergrowth and especially palm groves under a closed canopy.
FOOD In Gabon, about 75% fruits and about 18% animal matter.
BEHAVIOUR Forages mostly on the ground. Often heard before it is seen, utters a series of strident, bird-like chirps or a loud 3-syllable call.

RED-CHEEKED ROPE SQUIRREL *Funisciurus leucogenys*   see map above

SIZE HB 17–21.5cm. T 13–20cm. W 200–300g.
DESCRIPTION Olive-brown back is punctuated by a line of pale or orange spots. The face is usually orange-red.
HABITAT Lowland and montane forests. Restricted to forest floor and low levels in old mature rainforest.
FOOD Not known in detail. Mainly fallen fruits.

Ribboned Rope Squirrel

Lunda Rope Squirrel

Thomas's Rope Squirrel

Red-cheeked Rope Squirrel

Fire-footed Rope Squirrel

NOTE: not to scale

LADY BURTON'S ROPE SQUIRREL *Funisciurus isabella*

- Funisciurus congicus
- Funisciurus isabella
- Funisciurus substriatus
- Paraxerus alexandri

SIZE HB 15–18cm. T 13–18cm. W 100–115g.
DESCRIPTION Dark with pale stripes delimiting four bold black stripes running from head to tail.
HABITAT Occurs patchily between R. Zaïre and R. Cross in Gabon, lower Cameroon and in montane forest in the Highlands.
FOOD In Gabon, fruits (80%) and leaves (about 10%). Also small quantities of animal matter and mushrooms.
BEHAVIOUR Woven nests are sealed when occupied by the young.

KINTAMPO ROPE SQUIRREL *Funisciurus substriatus* — see map above

SIZE HB 15–18cm. T 14–20cm. W est. 100–150g.
DESCRIPTION Olive-coloured with short, poorly defined light and dark stripes on the flanks. May be a rare or vulnerable species.
HABITAT Woodlands and forest edges in the 'Dahomey Gap' area between Nigeria and Ghana.
FOOD Not recorded.

CONGO ROPE SQUIRREL *Funisciurus congicus* — see map above

SIZE HB 14.5–15.6cm. T 16–17cm. W 108–113g.
DESCRIPTION Back grizzled brown, with a long white side-stripe and a narrower dark line below it.
HABITAT Ranges over a large part of Zaïre basin and W Angola.
FOOD Spends about half of its time on the ground, foraging for fallen seeds and fruit.
BEHAVIOUR Very vocal, often seen in groups numbering up to 4.

AFRICAN PYGMY SQUIRREL *Myosciurus*

AFRICAN PYGMY SQUIRREL *Myosciurus pumilio*

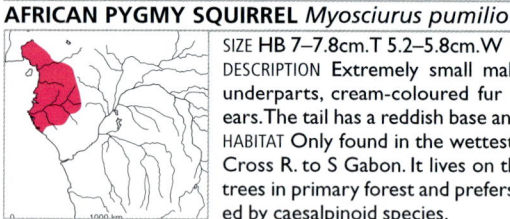

SIZE HB 7–7.8cm. T 5.2–5.8cm. W 15–18g.
DESCRIPTION Extremely small mahogany-coloured squirrel with pale underparts, cream-coloured fur around eyes and mouth, and white ears. The tail has a reddish base and a darker terminal bush.
HABITAT Only found in the wettest area of the Bight of Biafra from the Cross R. to S Gabon. It lives on the trunks and larger branches of tall trees in primary forest and prefers tree communities that are dominated by caesalpinoid species.
FOOD Mainly invertebrates (often collected from resin sites). Buds and young leaves and fruits are also taken.
BEHAVIOUR Shy, tending to hide at any disturbance. It can move very fast.

Lady Burton's Rope Squirrel

Kintampo Rope Squirrel

Congo Rope Squirrel

African Pygmy Squirrel

NOTE: not to scale

ROPE SQUIRRELS *Funisciurus* (continued)

CARRUTHERS'S MOUNTAIN SQUIRREL *Funisciurus carruthersi*

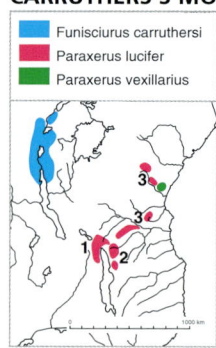

- Funisciurus carruthersi
- Paraxerus lucifer
- Paraxerus vexillarius

SIZE HB 20–26cm. T 18–20cm. W 200–336g.
DESCRIPTION Olive-green with cloud-grey underside and a black and yellow barred tail with a black tip.
HABITAT Between 1,500 and 2,800m in the mountain chains of E Zaïre and W Uganda, especially in stands of African wild plums (*Prunus africanum*).
FOOD Various fruits and seeds (e.g. *Bridelia* and *Strombosia*); occasionally insects.
BEHAVIOUR Large, globular nests, lined with finely shredded bark, are constructed in dense tangles.

BUSH SQUIRRELS *Paraxerus*

Short, thick fur, very variable (and sometimes bright) colour patterns and a tendency to slightly longer ear pinnae are typical features of bush squirrels.

COOPER'S MOUNTAIN SQUIRREL *Paraxerus cooperi* see map on p.102
SIZE HB 19–20cm. T 19cm. W est. 200–300g.
DESCRIPTION Grizzled olive-green back and pale grey underparts mixed with a yellowish sheen. Hands, feet and thighs are of variable colour, sometimes deep russet.
HABITAT Montane and intermediate forests in the Cameroon highland area.
FOOD Fruits and flowers of the tallow tree (*Pentadesma*) have been noted.

TANGANYIKA MOUNTAIN SQUIRREL *Paraxerus lucifer* see map above
SIZE HB 20–33cm. T 16–27cm. W est. 650–750g.
DESCRIPTION Three separate populations (see map). All have soft fur with warm tints on the face, feet and base of the tail and silvery-tipped dove-grey undersides. In *P. l. byatti* tints are muted, back is grizzled olive and tail is barred with dark brown and fine cream cross-bars. In the larger *P. l. laetus* face, limbs and rump are more strongly russet and tail is more thickly haired with bold black and white bars. *P. l. lucifer*, the largest race, is richly red all over, with a black back and half-hidden black bars in the thick red tail.
HABITAT Montane forests of E Tanganyika (*P. l. byatti*), the eastern side of L. Malawi (*P. l. laetus*) and north and west of L. Malawi (*P. l. lucifer*).
FOOD Fruits, nuts and invertebrates.

LUSHOTO MOUNTAIN SQUIRREL *Paraxerus vexillarius* see map above
SIZE HB 24cm. T 21cm. W est. 650–700g.
DESCRIPTION Bright orange hands, feet and tail tip, with a dark olive-green back, dove-grey belly and black and white barred tail.
HABITAT Confined to montane forests of W Usambaras and sandwiched between two isolated mountain forests occupied by *P. l. byatti*.
FOOD Fruits and seeds.

RED-BELLIED COAST SQUIRREL *Paraxerus palliatus* see map on p.106
SIZE HB 17–25cm. T 10–27cm. W est. 200–550g.
DESCRIPTION Pepper-and-salt grizzled with orange limbs, underparts and face. Subspecies: *P. p. palliatus* (centre of range): black and orange tail. *P. p. tanae* (north of range): orange tail. *P. p. ornatus* (south of range): dark red and black tail. *P. p. vincenti* (Mt Namuli): melanic back and tail.
HABITAT Coastal forests and evergreen thickets, lowland riverine forests; isolate (*P. p. vincenti*) in montane forest on Mt Namuli.
FOOD Fruits, berries, seeds and various plant parts.

Cooper's Mountain Squirrel *P. cooperi*
Green Squirrel *P. poensis* (page 106)
Carruthers's Mountain Squirrel *F. carruthersi*
Tanganyika Mountain Squirrel *P. l. byatti*
Tanganyika Mountain Squirrel *P. l. laetus*
Tanganyika Mountain Squirrel *P. l. lucifer*
Lushoto Mountain Squirrel *P. vexillarius*
Red-bellied Coast Squirrel *P. p. vincenti (Namuli Mt variant)*
Red-bellied Coast Squirrel *P. p. ornatus (southern variant)*
Red-bellied Coast Squirrel *P. p. palliatus*

GIANT AND SUN SQUIRRELS *Protoxerini*

An exclusively African group, these squirrels have particularly robust jaws and teeth which enable them to feed on the hardest of nuts. Mainly arboreal and very agile, crossing from tree to tree in the canopy.

RUWENZORI SUN SQUIRREL *Heliosciurus ruwenzori*

SIZE HB 20–26cm. T 22–28cm. W 205–377g.
DESCRIPTION Thickly and densely furred squirrel with a grizzled grey upperside contrasting strongly with white underside. Tail is boldly barred in grey and white. Tends to carry the tail in line with the body.
HABITAT Montane forests between 1,600 and 2,700m in E Zaïre and W Uganda, Rwanda and Burundi. Has adapted to secondary growth and cultivation mosaics.
FOOD Fruits of dominant trees. Insects and lichen have also been recorded.

GAMBIAN SUN SQUIRREL *Heliosciurus gambianus*
(Includes Small Sun Squirrel *H. g. punctatus*) see map above
SIZE HB 17–27cm. T 18–26cm. W 250–350g.
DESCRIPTION Variably coloured squirrel with a grizzled back and head and lighter underparts. Tail is boldly barred (about 14 rings) and there is a pale surround to the eyes.
HABITAT Woodlands and savannahs and montane habitats from Senegal to Ethiopia and Kenya; south of the forest block from Angola to Tanganyika. Enclaves in forest areas are considered to be the product of 'engulfment' after changes in climate. Descends to ground to visit isolated trees but prefers branch travel.
FOOD Fruits, seeds and the pods of *Acacia*; animal foods are also taken.

ZANJ SUN SQUIRREL *Heliosciurus undulatus*

SIZE HB 20–25cm. T 21–28cm. W est. 250–380g.
DESCRIPTION Back is tawny grizzled and underparts are cream. Tail is barred in brown and cream.
HABITAT Lowland and montane forests and thickets, and secondary growth, east of the Gregory Rift from Mt Kenya to R. Rufiji, and on Zanzibar and Mafia Is.
FOOD Fruits and seeds, palm dates, leaves and buds. Insects are of seasonal importance.

MUTABLE SUN SQUIRREL *Heliosciurus mutabilis*

SIZE HB 20–28cm. T 17–20cm. W 200–380g.
DESCRIPTION Upperparts are grizzled brown or orange, with tones from pale to nearly black. Underparts also vary from white to fawn or grey. Tail has a narrow, indistinct barring in similar tints to the body.
HABITAT Lowland to montane forests and thickets, including riverine strips and cultivation mosaics, from the R. Rufiji southwards to Zimbabwe and Mozambique.
FOOD Various plant foods; occasionally insects and small vertebrates.

RED-LEGGED SUN SQUIRREL *Heliosciurus rufobrachium* see map above
SIZE HB 20–27cm. T 18–30cm. W 250–400g.
DESCRIPTION Upperparts are grizzled, graduating to warm reddish tints on the outer surfaces of the limbs. Underside is paler cream-coloured (often with sparse fur). Tail is barred with black and white (about 18 bands of each). Loud calls and a flicking tail are particularly noticeable.
HABITAT Very common at low and medium altitudes from Senegal eastwards across the R. Zaïre basin to Uganda to the Gregory Rift.
FOOD Fruits, palm dates, leaves, buds; occasionally animal material.

Ruwenzori Sun Squirrel

Gambian Sun Squirrel

Red-legged Sun Squirrel

Zanj Sun Squirrel

Mutable Sun Squirrel

WESTERN PALM SQUIRREL *Epixerus ebii*

- Epixerus wilsoni
- Epixerus ebii

SIZE HB 26–29cm. T 27–31cm. W est. 450–700g.
DESCRIPTION Large squirrel with a grizzled grey back and a warm orange to red underside. The very conspicuous black-fringed tail has black and white bars across the upperside and fine longitudinal stripes, fading into an orange brush, on the underside. The muzzle is more protuberant than in giant squirrels.
HABITAT Palm forests and mature rainforest in mainly coastal areas from Sierra Leone to Ghana.
FOOD Fruits and nuts are collected on the tree or from the ground.

BIAFRAN BIGHT PALM SQUIRREL *Epixerus wilsoni* see map above

SIZE HB est. 26–29cm. T 27–31cm. W 500–620g.
DESCRIPTION Large squirrel with a grizzled grey back. The face and underparts are cream, with warmer tints on the wrists and rump. The tail has a predominantly white upperside, with bold black bars or chevrons and a warm-coloured stem on the underside. The head is broad and flat, with a long robust muzzle. (It is distinguishable from the western species mainly by cranial differences.)
HABITAT Lowland rainforests near the coast from S Cameroon to R. Zaïre. Areas with abundant palms are preferred.
FOOD Fruits and nuts (98% in Gabon); occasionally animal foods.

AFRICAN GIANT SQUIRREL *Protoxerus stangeri*

- Protoxerus stangeri
- Protoxerus aubinnii

SIZE HB 22–40cm. T 24–36cm. W 540–1,000g.
DESCRIPTION Large grizzled squirrel with a disproportionately large, rounded head which is predominantly grey. The back and limbs are of warm tints, very variable in colour and intensity. The yellowish underside is often semi-naked. Nose, ears and eyelids also tend to be naked. The long, black and white tail has about 18 bars. Nineteen subspecies have been described.
HABITAT Exclusively limited to well-developed equatorial rainforests, in tall swamp forest and at altitudes up to 2,000m.
FOOD Mainly fruits, seeds and nut kernels of numerous rainforest trees (87.6% in Gabon, with 8.5% leaves, 3.5% mushrooms and traces of animal matter).

SLENDER-TAILED SQUIRREL *Protoxerus aubinnii* see map above

SIZE HB 23–27cm. T 27–33cm. W est. 300–400g.
DESCRIPTION A largish, very dark squirrel with a long, slender, tapered tail with very fine black and olive annulations. The short, dense coat is very fine and silky and covers upper- and underparts equally.
HABITAT Moist high forests from Liberia to Ghana, with a marked preference for palms.
FOOD Fruits, particularly palm dates. Unlike the Giant Squirrel, which prefers to eat only the kernels, this species has been recorded feeding on the husks.

Western Palm Squirrel

African Giant Squirrel

Biafran Bight Palm Squirrel

Slender-tailed Squirrel

ANOMALURES Anomaluridae

Also known as 'scaly tails' because their tails are strengthened by pairs of pointed scales on the underside, these are mainly gliding rodents with slender bodies concealed by long, fine fur and (in the gliders) by the gathered membrane or 'patagium'.

LORD DERBY'S ANOMALURE *Anomalurus derbianus*

SIZE HB 27–38cm. T 22–30cm. W 450–1,100g.
DESCRIPTION Predominantly grey or brown with a rippling silvery grizzle to the tips of the very long, fine textured fur. The membranes are similarly coloured above but black bristle hairs reinforce the hem of the membrane behind the elbow strut. 16 subspecies have been named.
HABITAT Moist rainforests to relatively dry woodlands at various altitudes.
FOOD A specialist in certain barks and bark wound exudates (notably those of *Julbernardia*, *Newtonia*, *Cynometra*, *Pentaclethra* and *Dialium*). In addition, fruits, flowers, leaves, nuts and occasional insects.
BEHAVIOUR Nocturnal and lives in vertical hollow tree trunks. It is possible that unique 'pruning' behaviour in this species results in a form of 'farming' of its preferred food trees. Pruning away of all growing shoots is especially severe around the bases of these trees. Thus, in keeping their flight paths clear, the anomalures eventually kill off potential competitors for their food trees.

PEL'S ANOMALURE *Anomalurus peli*

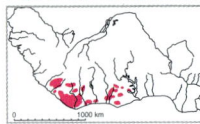

SIZE HB 40–46cm. T 32–45cm. W 1,300–1,800g.
DESCRIPTION Black back and face vividly outlined with pure white borders around the ears and on the muzzle. Underside and tail are also white, as are the borders to the flight membranes.
HABITAT Moist high forests with numerous tall emergents and palm trees.
FOOD Bark supplemented by fruits (especially oil and other palm dates), leaves and flowers.
BEHAVIOUR Wholly nocturnal and emerges well after sunset. Contact calls described as deep hoots.

LESSER ANOMALURE *Anomalurus pusillus*

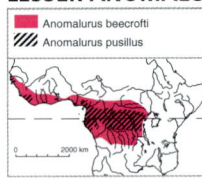

■ Anomalurus beecrofti
▨ Anomalurus pusillus

SIZE HB 18.5–24.6cm. T 13.8–20cm. W est. 200–300g.
DESCRIPTION Back coloration varies from near black to mottled tan. The membrane adjoining the tail is usually yellower while the lateral membranes are dark grey. The head is grey without borders around the ears.
HABITAT Has a strictly equatorial distribution.
FOOD Probably bark and fruits including drupes of parasol trees (*Musanga*).
BEHAVIOUR Has been found sheltering in hollow trees in lowland rainforest.

BEECROFT'S ANOMALURE *Anomalurus beecrofti* — see map above

SIZE HB 25–31cm. T 16–24cm. W est. 640–660g.
DESCRIPTION Very variably coloured with a prominent, narrow snout. The underside is always yellow-orange to some degree and similar warm tints occur on the back in some populations. Often has a white spot on the forehead but does not have a dark 'mask' around the eyes.
HABITAT Tropical rainforests from Sierra Leone to E Zaïre, from sea-level up to 2,500m. Marked preference for palm groves.
FOOD Fruits, especially palm dates, bark, leaves and occasional insects.
BEHAVIOUR Rests in holes and will also hide in the junctions between palm fronds or cling to the sheltered underside of major tree branches close to the trunk.

Pel's Anomalure

Lord Derby's Anomalure

Lesser Anomalure

Beecroft's Anomalure

ZENKER'S FLYING MOUSE *Idiurus zenkeri*

SIZE HB 6.5–9cm. T 7–13cm. W 14–17.5g.

DESCRIPTION A miniature scaly-tail resembling a very silky-furred, tawny-coloured, snub-nosed mouse, with a membrane like those of the larger anomalures. The very long tail is fringed on the underside by two rows of short stiff hairs. Zenker's Flying Mouse also has sparse, very long hairs on the upperside of the tail. It utters a shrill mouse-like squeak and is a very efficient, fast and agile glider.

HABITAT Very moist equatorial rainforests, from Cameroon to the R. Zaïre, and between the R. Aruwimi and R. Zaïre to the foothills of Ruwenzori and Kivu.

FOOD Oil-palm pulp, occasional insects and possibly exudates or nectar.

BEHAVIOUR Roosts in hollow trees (more rarely under bark), sometimes in ones or twos but more usually in groups that may number up to 100. It has been suggested that Zenker's Flying Mouse may travel many km in a night to feed. However, nothing is known of its feeding behaviour. The notched upper incisors project from the mouth, which may mean that the food requires sharp chiselling.

LONG-EARED FLYING MOUSE *Idiurus macrotis*

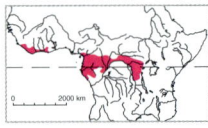

SIZE HB 8–11cm. T 13–19cm. W 25–35g.

DESCRIPTION A small scaly-tail of slightly more robust build than Zenker's Flying Mouse and with darker fur. This species is pale grey in colour with a brownish sheen. The ears and the face are somewhat longer than Zenker's and the tail is proportionately shorter, with similar short, stiff hairs on the underside. Dense, short fur covers the rest of the tail.

HABITAT Equatorial lowlands (like Zenker's Flying Mouse). The overall range is similar but the Long-eared Flying Mouse appears to be rarer than Zenker's in the eastern part of their ranges.

FOOD Not known.

BEHAVIOUR This species sometimes shares hollow trees with Zenker's Flying Mouse (and with bats).

CAMEROON SCALY-TAIL *Zenkerella insignis*   see map above

SIZE HB 18–23cm. T 15–17cm. W est. 180–220g.

DESCRIPTION Superficially resembling a large dormouse, this scaly-tail has no trace of a membrane (although its loose, woolly coat might cushion short, spread-eagled leaps). Head and body are a soft slate grey with ochre tints on the forearm, lower shin and cheeks. Underparts are very pale grey and the tail is black and bushy. The strip of paired scales on the underside of the tail resembles that of other scaly-tails and implies a similar degree of support while at rest. The ankles have a brush of highly specialised 'spoon-hairs' over a glandular area. Its function and operation are not known.

HABITAT Only known from Cameroon to Gabon. Animals thought to be scaly-tails have been seen moving among low-level vines by means of very fast springy leaps. May also inhabit understorey and canopy.

FOOD Not known.

Zenker's Flying Mouse

Cameroon Scaly-tail

Long-eared Flying Mouse

SPRING HARE Pedetidae

SPRING HARE *Pedetes capensis*

SIZE HB 35–43cm. T 34–49cm. W 3–4kg.
DESCRIPTION Long-tailed, hopping, burrowing rodent with long, soft fur. Hindlegs have 4 toes.
HABITAT Sandy plains, with seasonal cover of grasses.
FOOD Fresh grasses, stems, roots, bases of grasses and fruits.

GUNDIS Ctenodactylidae

Rock-dwelling herbivores that resemble guinea pigs. Diurnal, social animals, with whistling calls.

GUNDIS *Ctenodactylus* (2 species)

SIZE HB 15–21cm. T 3–5cm. W 175–180g.
DESCRIPTION Reddish with a minuscule tail and oval, white-fringed ear. A horny comb is present on the claw of the inner hindtoe.
HABITAT Rock outcrops with abundant crevices in which they shelter.
FOOD Grass, leaves, stalks and flowers.

SENEGAL GUNDI *Felovia vae*

SIZE HB 15–21cm. T 3–5cm. W 200–210g.
DESCRIPTION Dark walnut-brown with a paler reddish underside and a short bushy tail.
HABITAT Rock outcrops in dry or semi-arid regions of Mauritania, Mali and Senegal.
FOOD Various grasses, trees and herbs.

FRINGE-EARED GUNDI *Massouteria mzabi* see map above

SIZE HB 17–24cm. T 3–4cm. W est. 200–220g.
DESCRIPTION Pale tawny with massively enlarged inner ear bullae. Tail is frisked conspicuously.
HABITAT Rocks in very arid areas.
FOOD Grasses, *Acacia* and other desert plants.

PECTINATOR *Pectinator spekei* see map above

SIZE HB 16–18cm. T 4–5cm. W est. 160–160g.
DESCRIPTION Tawny with prominent, frequently flicked tail.
HABITAT Rocky outcrops. Home ranges may be extensive (3km^2).
FOOD Variety of grasses, *Acacia* and other desert plants.

DORMICE Myoxidae (syn. Gliridae)

Small, agile, climbing, nocturnal rodents. Their tails detach easily.

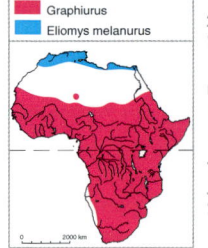

AFRICAN DORMICE *Graphiurus* (14 species)

SIZE HB 7.5–15cm. T 5–11cm. W 18–85g.
DESCRIPTION Usually grey with white undersides. Dark eye mask and prominent ears. Tail bushy. Agile climbers, on sharp-clawed, dextrous fingers.
HABITAT Almost all habitats.
FOOD Invertebrates and small vertebrates, inc. small birds, lizards, eggs.

EASTERN ORCHARD DORMOUSE *Eliomys melanurus*

SIZE HB 10–17cm. T 9–15cm. W est. 45–200g.
DESCRIPTION Tawny forehead and a dorsal midline flanked by grey. Mask and jaw-line black.
HABITAT Mediterranean N African littoral in woodlands, oases, sand dunes and rocky country.
FOOD Fruits, nuts, buds, invertebrates and occasional vertebrates.

Spring Hare
Pedetes capensis

Common Gundi
Ctenodactylus gundi

Senegal Gundi
Felovia vae

Fringe-eared Gundi
Massouteria mzabi

Pectinator
Pectinator spekei

Eastern Orchard Dormouse
Eliomys melanurus

Woodland Dormouse
Graphiurus murinus

BLESMOLS Bathyergidae

Compact, subterranean rodents. The mouth closes behind the sharp white incisors.

DUNE BLESMOLS *Bathyergus* (2 species)

SIZE HB 17–33cm. T 3–7cm. W 500–750g.
DESCRIPTION Large blesmols with very long, pointed claws and grooved incisors. Species: Cape Dune Blesmol *B. suillus*, large, cinnamon; Namaqua Dune Blesmol *B. janetta*, slate grey.
HABITAT Restricted to sandy habitats in extreme south-west of Africa.
FOOD Roots, bulbs and grass stolons.

COMMON BLESMOLS *Cryptomys* (7 species)

SIZE HB 13–21.5cm. T 1–2.5cm. W 100–300g.
DESCRIPTION Velvety-furred with broad palms and relatively small nails.
HABITAT Drier soils outside main forest blocks.
FOOD Roots, bulbs, grass, leaves and occasional invertebrates.
BEHAVIOUR Food-gathering is seasonal; burrows are extended in the rains and collected roots brought back to stores. Colonies vary in size and some species are solitary.

CAPE BLESMOL *Georychus capensis* *see* map below

SIZE HB 14–20.5cm. T 2–4cm. W 124–360g.
DESCRIPTION Cinnamon and orange back, black head and pale to white underparts.
HABITAT Cape littoral and scattered upland areas, coastal sand dunes, and valleys with sandy soils.
FOOD Stores roots and bulbs harvested from very shallow burrows.

SILKY BLESMOL *Heliophobius argenteocinereus*

SIZE HB 10–20cm. T 1.5–4cm. W 142–168g.
DESCRIPTION Coat is long, grey, sandy or reddish and paler below.
HABITAT Well-drained, sandy soils on rocky hillsides, open plains or in woodlands.
FOOD Roots and tubers, including lablab (*Dolichos*) and pulses (*Vigna*).

SAND-PUPPY (NAKED MOLE-RAT) *Heterocephalus glaber*

SIZE HB 8–10cm. T 2–5cm. W 30–80g.
DESCRIPTION Resembles a newborn, even foetal, animal. Its transparent skin goes pale or bright red depending on body heat and circulation.
HABITAT Plains, thickets, dry savannahs and open woodlands.
FOOD The roots of dominant trees and the bulbs and tubers of other common plants.
BEHAVIOUR Celebrated as the prime example of a highly social mammal which exhibits division of labour (as in bees and termites).

ROOT-RATS Rhizomyidae

Chunky, tunnelling rats with diminutive ears, small eyes and prominent orange incisors.

ROOT-RATS *Tachyoryctes* (provisionally 11 species)

SIZE HB 16–28cm. T 5–10cm. W 160–600g.
DESCRIPTION Robust, with variable colouring, size and skull structure. The Giant Root-rat *T. macrocephalus* is a very large, highly distinctive species living at 3,000–4,100m in Ethiopia.
HABITAT Uplands (including very high-altitude Afro-alpine grasslands).
FOOD Roots, tubers, stems and bulbs are indiscriminately taken underground within a short radius of the hole.

Cape Dune Blesmol
Bathyergus suillus

Common Blesmol
Cryptomys hottentotus

Silky Blesmol
Heliophobius argenteocinereus

Cape Blesmol
Georychus capensis

Sand-puppy
Heterocephalus glaber

Palestine Mole-rat
Nannospalax ehrenbergi
(A marginal species from Egypt)

Giant Root-rat
Tachyoryctes macrocephalus

Ankole Root-rat
Tachyoryctes ankdiae

PORCUPINES Hystricidae

Large nocturnal rodents that rely on their spines to deter predators.

CRESTED PORCUPINE *Hystrix cristata*

- Hystrix cristata
- Hystrix africaeaustralis
- Known overlap area

SIZE HB 60–100cm. T 8–17cm. W 12–27kg.
DESCRIPTION Very large, black-bodied rodent with long, black and white spines and prominent crest. Black rump. Short rattle quills.
HABITAT Savannahs, woodlands, steppes and uplands. Sometimes found along forest margins or galleries. Prefers hilly or rocky country.
FOOD Roots, bulbs, bark and fallen fruits. Root crops, maize and cucumbers.
BEHAVIOUR Family groups often share a burrow or cave but foraging is a solitary activity during which animals can travel more than 15km in a night.

SOUTH AFRICAN PORCUPINE *Hystrix africaeaustralis*

SIZE HB 75–100cm. T 10–17cm. W 10–24kg.
DESCRIPTION Very large rodent with a sweeping, erectile neck crest. White rump. Long rattle quills.
HABITAT Found mainly south of the equator in most habitats from sea-level up to about 3,000m.
FOOD Mainly roots, bulbs, tubers and bark, with occasional scavenging from carcasses or old skeletons.
BEHAVIOUR Usually grunts while foraging.

BRUSH-TAILED PORCUPINE *Atherurus africanus*

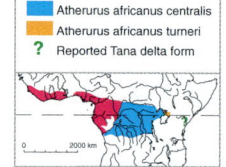

- Atherurus africanus africanus
- Atherurus africanus centralis
- Atherurus africanus turneri
- ? Reported Tana delta form

SIZE HB 36–60cm. T 15–23cm. W 1.5–4kg.
DESCRIPTION Long-bodied, low-slung brown rodent with very bristly fur on the limbs and face, progressing to very sharp, thick quills on the back and shorter ones on the rump and tail.
HABITAT Rainforests, where a preference for valley bottoms may reflect their need for natural shelters (eroded rock or root systems).
FOOD Fallen fruits, roots, tubers and stems. Oil-palm, crabwood and ginger fruit are especially favoured but animal foods are rarely taken.
BEHAVIOUR Groups of up to 20 animals (usually 6 to 8) inhabit an area of 2–5ha. They sleep in their burrows during the day and are active much of the night.

CANE-RATS Thryonomyidae

Medium-sized to large, robust rodents with grizzled brown coats, prominent chisel-like orange incisors, short tails and short, strong legs with sharp digging claws. Exclusively African.

SAVANNAH CANE-RAT *Thryonomys gregorianus*

SIZE HB 35–51cm. T 6.5–14cm. W 2.6–7.5kg.
DESCRIPTION Has a bulbous nose, short tail and deeply grooved incisors.
HABITAT Mainly areas of reliable rainfall and rank grass growth in tropical Africa east of Nigeria. It is especially common in elephant grass (*Pennisetum purpureum*).
FOOD Stems of elephant grass; also *Setaria*, *Hyparrhenia*, *Exotheca* and *Melinus*. The ginger (*Aframomum*) is eaten in wet, well-wooded areas. Fruits, bark and roots are also eaten.
BEHAVIOUR Mainly nocturnal. Uses habitual paths between feeding areas and shelter.

MARSH CANE-RAT *Thryonomys swinderianus*

SIZE HB 43–58cm. T 17–26cm. W 4.5–8.8kg.
DESCRIPTION Distinguished by its slightly larger size, longer tail, less protuberant nose and restricted fine grooving of the incisors.
HABITAT Beds of *Setaria*, *Echinochloa*, *Sorghastrum* and *Hyparrhenia* in seasonally waterlogged valley bottoms throughout moister parts of Africa.
FOOD Dominant grasses within its habitat.
BEHAVIOUR Has a highly characteristic whistle. Mainly nocturnal.

Rattle quill and rear view of Crested Porcupine

Crested Porcupine

Rattle quill and rear view of South African Porcupine

Brush-tailed Porcupine

Savannah Cane-rat

Marsh Cane-rat

DASSIE RAT Petromuridae
The only living representative of this family.

DASSIE RAT *Petromus typicus*

SIZE HB 13.5–21cm. T 11.5–17cm. W 170–262g.
DESCRIPTION Squat, coarse-furred rodent with long, hairy tail and flattened head. Colour varies from pale grey or ochre, through shades of brown, to nearly black.
HABITAT Rocky outcrops.
FOOD Leaves, stems and heads of grasses.
BEHAVIOUR Likes to sun-bathe in pairs or small groups but is very shy and flees for shelter at any disturbance. Urine is used to mark particular rocks and forms characteristic yellow-white streaks near the dens.

JERBOAS Dipodidae
Nocturnal, jumping rodents with long hindlegs. Efficient deep diggers in sandy soil.

DESERT JERBOAS *Jaculus* (2 species)

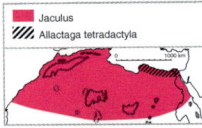

SIZE HB 17–32cm. T 14–22cm. W 50–71g.
DESCRIPTION Hindfeet elongated and hair-tufted. Three toes. Nose flat, used to tamp soil. Tail long and tufted, held in a curl and acts as tripod with hindlegs.
HABITAT Arid environments. Species: *J. jaculus* (mainly sand dunes in Sahara), *J. orientalis* (mainly steppe on Mediterranean littoral).
FOOD Seeds, stems and roots of desert grasses.
BEHAVIOUR Deep burrows. Mainly solitary but form temporary groups of 4 or 5.

FOUR-TOED JERBOA *Allactaga tetradactyla*   see map above

SIZE HB 24–30cm. T 15–20cm. W est. 20–40g.
DESCRIPTION Sandy-coloured, with 4 toes, long ears and snub-nosed. Long tail has a white tip.
HABITAT Restricted to gravel plains that lie between Alexandria in Egypt and the Gulf of Sirte in Libya.
FOOD Grass seeds and roots.

PSEUDO-HAMSTERS Mystromyinae
Resembles the smallest Eurasian hamsters. Lone survivor of an archaic group.

WHITE-TAILED MOUSE *Mystromys albicaudatus*   see map above

SIZE HB 10.5–18.4cm. T 50–97cm. W 75–111g.
DESCRIPTION Plump, short-tailed, large-eyed, with soft grey upperparts and a white underside.
HABITAT Savannah grasslands and scrub in the South African uplands and Cape region.
FOOD Seeds, green vegetable matter and insects.
BEHAVIOUR Lives in crevices and burrows where it makes a nest of shredded material.

CRESTED RAT Lophiomyinae
In a subfamily of its own, it is generally regarded as being distantly related to the Eurasian hamsters.

CRESTED (MANED) RAT *Lophiomys imhausi*

SIZE HB 25.5–36cm. T 14–21.5cm. W 590–920g.
DESCRIPTION Slow-moving, woolly grey fur, black and white on face.
HABITAT Dry woodlands and montane forests, especially juniper in NE Africa.
FOOD Fruits, shoots, leaves, roots and insects.
BEHAVIOUR Mainly nocturnal. Skilful, but slow climber; hands manipulate foods while squatting.

Dassie Rat
Petromus typicus

Four-toed Jerboa
Allactaga tetradactyla

Lesser Egyptian Jerboa
Jaculus jaculus

White-tailed Mouse
Mystromys albicaudatus

Crested Rat
Lophiomys imhausi

TATERA (NAKED-SOLED) GERBILS *Tatera* (11 species)

SIZE HB 12–16cm. T 14–17cm. W est. 60–125g.
DESCRIPTION Variously coloured with long hindlegs, naked-soled feet, large eyes and ears, and a prominent, hairy muzzle.
HABITAT Most of sub-Saharan Africa (except rainforest areas) and margins of Sahara. *Tatera* gerbils inhabit well-drained, sandy areas.
FOOD Seeds, stems and roots of grasses; also roots, bulbs and insects.

TATERILLUS GERBILS *Taterillus* (8 species)

SIZE HB 10–14cm. T 14–17cm. W est. 50–80g.
DESCRIPTION Eyes are particularly large. Skull has a very large cavity in the palate.
HABITAT Mainly Sudanic and Sahelian savannahs and steppes along the southern borders of the Sahara.
FOOD Various plant foods and (probably) insects.

DWARF GERBIL *Desmodilliscus braueri*

SIZE HB 5–7cm. T 3.5–5cm. W est. 8–15g.
DESCRIPTION Fawn with white spots behind the ears, small hindfeet, tail shorter than body. Large cheek pouches.
HABITAT Sahelian steppes from Mauritania to Sudan.
FOOD Presumed to be grass seeds.

HAIRY-FOOTED GERBIL *Gerbillurus* (4 species)

SIZE HB 8–12cm. T 10–13cm. W 22–40g.
DESCRIPTION Small, pale-coloured Gerbils with long tails and large, hairy hindfeet.
HABITAT Arid areas of SW Africa, with a preference for sandy soils. Hairy-footed gerbils excavate warrens where they live in small groups.
FOOD Seeds and probably insects.

NAMAQUA GERBIL *Desmodillus auricularis*

SIZE HB 10–14cm. T 8–10cm. W 39–70g.
DESCRIPTION Variably coloured with short hindlegs. The tail is shorter than the body and there is white fur behind the flesh-coloured ears.
HABITAT Open pans and compacted calcareous soils in SW African deserts.
FOOD Seeds of grasses (mainly) and of shrubs and trees.

WALO *Amodillus imbellis*

SIZE HB 10.5–11cm. T est. 13–15cm. W est. 40–60g.
DESCRIPTION Reddish fawn with a long, hairy tail. The base of the ears and brows to the large eyes are white.
HABITAT Recorded from sandy desert in Somalia.
FOOD The very feeble jaw structure suggests that only soft foods are taken, possibly fruits and soft-bodied insects.

Bushveld Gerbil
Tatera leucogaster

Emin's Gerbil
Taterillus emini

Dwarf Gerbil
Desmodilliscus braueri

Bushy-tailed Hairy-footed Gerbil
Gerbillurus vallinus

Walo
Amodillus imbellis

Namaqua Gerbil
Desmodillus auricularis

DENDROMURINES Dendromurinae

Now exclusive to Africa. The living genera probably represent relicts of radiation.

CLIMBING MICE Dendromus (11 species)

Dendromus
Megadendromus nicolausi
Dendroprionomys rousseloti
Prionomys batesi

SIZE HB 5–10cm. T 6.5–11.5cm. W 7–23g.
DESCRIPTION Large-headed with long, semi-prehensile tails, long, extremely dextrous toes and a specialised, 'padded hook' hand structure.
HABITAT Tall grass and shrubby secondary growth.
FOOD Specialist grass-seed-eaters.

GIANT CLIMBING MOUSE Megadendromus nicolausi

SIZE HB 11–13cm. T 9–10.5cm. W 49–66g.
DESCRIPTION Dark brown with pale underside. Tail long, fine.
HABITAT High altitudes in the Bale massif in central Ethiopia.
FOOD Probably grass seed.

VELVET CLIMBING MOUSE Dendroprionomys rousseloti   see map above

SIZE Unavailable.
DESCRIPTION Velvety-furred, dark brown with tawny flanks and a white underside.
HABITAT Only known from the zoological gardens on the banks of the R. Zaïre at Brazzaville.
FOOD Thought to include insects.

DOLLMAN'S CLIMBING MOUSE Prionomys batesi   see map above

SIZE HB est. 5.5–6.5cm. T est. 9.5–10cm. W est. 10–15g.
DESCRIPTION Shrew-like. Velvet fur, tawny-brown. Eye mask. Forefeet lack a thumb.
HABITAT Moist rainforest zone between the R. Dja and R. Zaïre.
FOOD Not known.

LARGE-EARED MOUSE Malacothrix typica

Malocothrix typica
Deomys ferugineus

SIZE HB 7–8cm. T 3.2–4cm. W 10–20g.
DESCRIPTION Small, prettily marked with ash-grey streaks on the back and flanks and a tawny face and shoulders. Nocturnal.
HABITAT Areas of short grass and karoo bush growing on or close to calcareous pans in dry SW Africa.
FOOD Seeds and green plant parts.

LINK RAT Deomys ferugineus

SIZE HB 12–14.5cm. T 15–21.5cm. W 40–70g.
DESCRIPTION Long legs, pointed, narrow head, enormous ears. Nocturnal and crepuscular.
HABITAT Seasonally flooded forest floors between Cameroon and the Victoria Nile.
FOOD Mainly insects, crustaceans, slugs and some fallen fruits (notably palm-nut husks).

FAT MICE Steatomys (6 species)

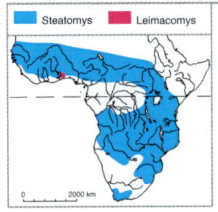

Steatomys   Leimacomys

SIZE HB 5–14cm. T 3–75cm. W est. 15–30g.
DESCRIPTION Small mice with large ears and short limbs and tail. Upperparts sandy brown, underparts white. Often very fat and lethargic.
HABITAT Savannahs, woodlands and (marginally) semi-arid environments.
FOOD Seeds, bulbs, roots, insects, grass.

TOGO MOUSE Leimacomys buettneri

SIZE HB 11.8cm. T 3.7cm. W est. 50–60g.
DESCRIPTION Brown with short tapered tail, paler fawn flanks.
HABITAT Not known but collected within the 'Dahomey Gap', a savannah–forest-mosaic region.
FOOD Delicate muzzle suggests small, soft-bodied insects or unripe seeds.

Chestnut Climbing Mouse
Dendromus mystacalis

Giant Climbing Mouse
Megadendromus nicolausi

Velvet Climbing Mouse
Dendroprionomys rousseloti

Dollman's Climbing Mouse
Prionomys batesi

Large-eared Mouse
Malacothrix typica

Link Rat
Deomys ferugineus

Togo Mouse
Leimacomys buettneri

Common Fat Mouse
Steatomys pratensis

POUCHED RATS Cricetomyinae
Sluggish, greyish brown animals, with large cheek pouches. All dig burrows. Strictly nocturnal.

LESSER POUCHED RAT *Beamys hindei*

- B. hindei / C. gambianus also
- C. emini / occurs in these ranges
- C. gambianus
- C. (gambianus) cosensi

SIZE HB 13–18.7cm. T 10–15.5cm. W 55–150g.
DESCRIPTION Grey or brown upperparts, white underparts and mottled tail. A climber, strictly nocturnal.
HABITAT Sandy riverbanks in forest, thicket or dense woodland, from Kenya to Malawi. Subspecies: *hindei* (coastal), *major* (montane).
FOOD Fruits and seeds; occasionally animal foods.

GIANT POUCHED RATS *Cricetomys* (2 species)
SIZE HB 28–45cm. T 36–46cm. W 1–1.4kg.
DESCRIPTION Brown or grey, with large, naked ears. The terminal half of the long tail is white. Good climbers. Strictly nocturnal.
HABITAT Very varied (*C. gambianus*); only lowland rainforest (*C. emini*).
FOOD Fruits, seeds, nuts, roots and leaves.

POUCHED MICE *Saccostomus* (2 species)
- Saccostomus
- Delanymys brooksi

SIZE HB 11.5–19cm. T 3–8cm. W 40–85g.
DESCRIPTION Grey or greyish brown with short, limp fur, enormous cheek pouches, and short legs and tail. Strictly nocturnal.
HABITAT Savannahs, woodlands and semi-arid habitats in S and E Africa.
FOOD Seeds, fruits and occasionally insects.

PYGMY ROCK MICE Petromyscinae
2 rare, relict genera. Small brown mice with distinctive teeth.

PYGMY ROCK MICE *Petromyscus* (4 species)
SIZE HB 7.5–11.5cm. T 7.5–10.5cm. W 17–25g.
DESCRIPTION Brown with broad, flattened heads and prominent ears and whiskers.
HABITAT Arid regions of SW Africa from S Angola to the Cape.
FOOD Mainly seeds.

DELANEY'S MOUSE *Delanymys brooksi*   see map above
SIZE HB 5–6cm. T 8.5–10.5cm. W 5g.
DESCRIPTION Long hindlegs, 5 mobile fingers and a vestigial thumb. Long tail.
HABITAT High-altitude (1,700–2,625m) marshes in E Zaïre and W Uganda, among sedges.
FOOD Grass and sedge seeds (possibly unripe); perhaps also fruits.

GROOVE-TOOTHED RATS Otomyinae
Stocky, shaggy, blunt-faced rats with short legs and tail. Vegetarian; feed on rank grasses.

GROOVE-TOOTHED RATS *Otomys* (12 species)
- Otomys
- Parotomys

SIZE HB 12–22cm. T 6–12cm. W 100–260g.
DESCRIPTION Varied colouring, blunt muzzle large ears. Placid.
HABITAT Grasslands, marshes, dense secondary growth and savannah.
FOOD Green grass and herb stems; bark; occasionally roots and seeds.

WHISTLING RATS *Parotomys* (2 species)
SIZE HB 12–17cm. T 8–12cm. W 90–155g.
DESCRIPTION Shaggy, large-eyed, short-legged, diurnal rats. Whistle loudly.
HABITAT Burrows in dry, sandy environments in SW Africa.
FOOD Grass stems and seeds. Stems and leaves of xerophytic shrubs.

Lesser Pouched Rat
Beamys hindei

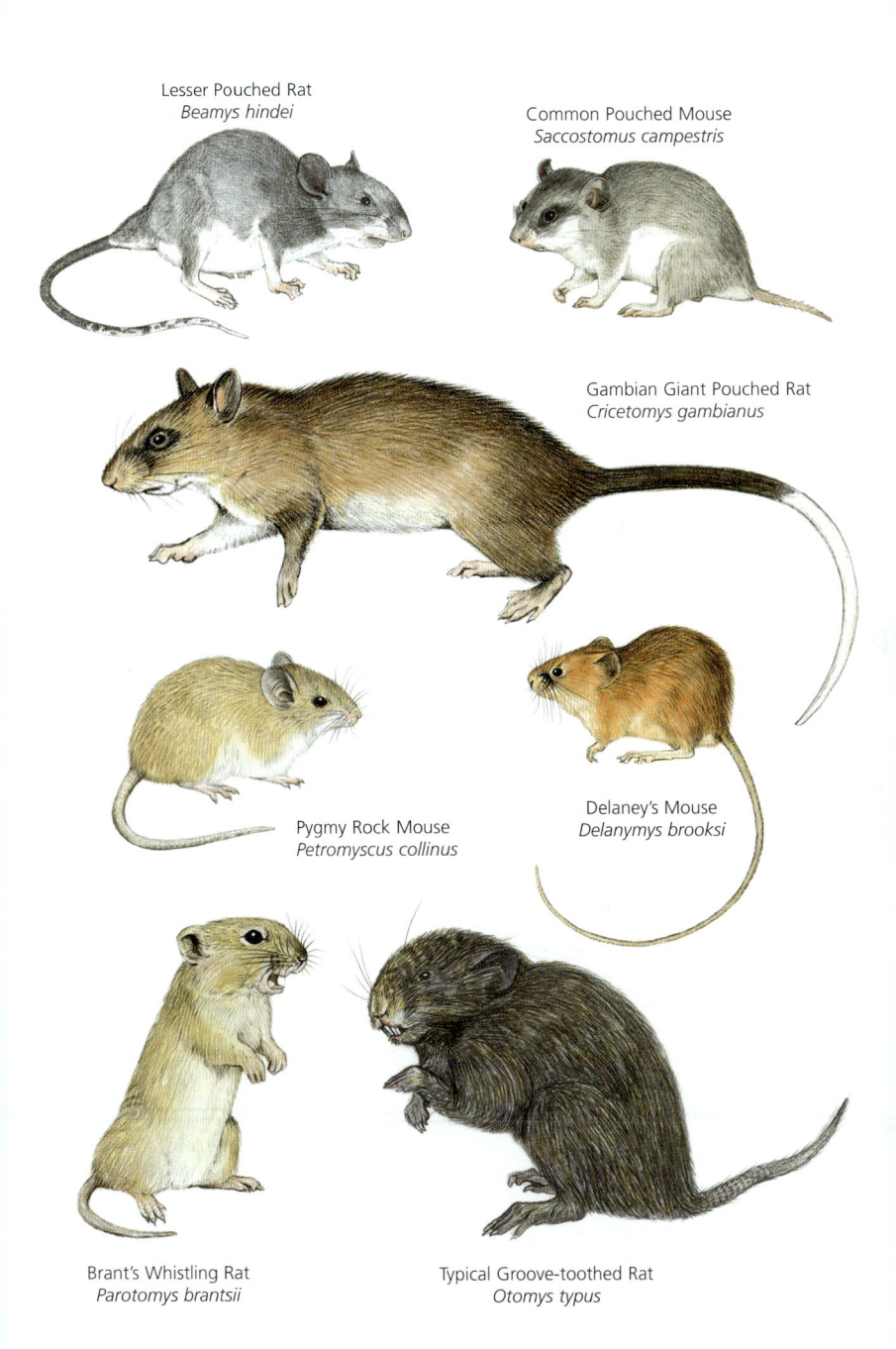

Common Pouched Mouse
Saccostomus campestris

Gambian Giant Pouched Rat
Cricetomys gambianus

Pygmy Rock Mouse
Petromyscus collinus

Delaney's Mouse
Delanymys brooksi

Brant's Whistling Rat
Parotomys brantsii

Typical Groove-toothed Rat
Otomys typus

MURID RATS AND MICE Muridae

A diverse group numbering over 30 genera and 150 species. Murid rats and mice range from 2 to 170g in weight and may have a long or short tail, limbs, nose and ears.

SPINY MICE *Acomys* (11 species)

SIZE HB 7–12cm. T 4–10cm. W 10–40g.
DESCRIPTION Mice with short limbs and very spiny, coarse fur. Upperparts rufous to grey or brown, underparts white or tinted.
HABITAT Deserts and dry areas from the Mediterranean to the Cape.
FOOD Opportunistic; seeds, leaves, dry plant matter, invertebrates.

URANOMYS MOUSE *Uranomys ruddi*   see map below
SIZE HB 8.5–13.5cm. T 5–8cm. W est. 30–60g.
DESCRIPTION Chunky, short legs, brush-textured coat. Colour ranges from black to grey, fawn or russet.
HABITAT Tropical species showing a preference for *Hyparrhenia* grassland with borassus palms (*Palmyra borassus*). Very disconnected records from Senegal to Uganda to Malawi.
FOOD Omnivorous. Little known.

BRUSH-FURRED MICE *Lophuromys* (9 species)

SIZE HB 8.5–16cm. T 5.5–15cm. W 20–100g.
DESCRIPTION Compact mice with short legs and tails. Dark or speckled coats have a brush-like texture. Diurnal and nocturnal.
HABITAT Moist tropical Africa from sea-level to about 3,000m.
FOOD Invertebrates, especially ants, carrion and plant material.

BROAD-HEADED STINK MICE *Zelotomys* (2 species)

SIZE HB 11.5–14cm. T 8.5–11.5cm. W 50–65g.
DESCRIPTION Broad-headed mice with grey-brown or flecked grey upperparts and pale underparts and cheeks. Tail and limbs off-white. Upper incisors protuberant. Have a very strong smell.
HABITAT S and E Africa, in arid and semi-arid (*Z. woosnami*) or grassy savannahs and scrub dominated by sword grass, *Imperata*.
FOOD Invertebrates, notably myriapods (*Z. hildegardeae*). *Z. woosnami* takes more seeds.

LONG-FOOTED RATS *Malacomys* (5 species)   see map above

SIZE HB 12–18cm. T 14–21cm. W 50–150g.
DESCRIPTION Long-legged, short-furred, large ears, conical muzzle. Black eye-mask.
HABITAT Very moist forest floor close to streams and swamps from Guinea to Uganda and L. Tanganyika.
FOOD Invertebrates and vegetable matter (fruits, seeds and roots); occasional small vertebrates.

VELVET RAT *Colomys goslingi*

SIZE HB 11.5–14cm. T 14.5–18cm. W 50–75g.
DESCRIPTION Long-limbed, long-tailed, swollen rhinarium, profuse whiskers. Dense, velvet fur brown above, pure white below.
HABITAT Margins of forest streams and swamp forests among palms, gingers and arrowroots. Ranges from Cameroon and Angola to L. Tanganyika. Also by streams in Kenya and Ethiopia.
FOOD Aquatic insects, worms, slugs and crustaceans; occasionally vegetable matter.

Cairo Spiny Mouse
Acomys cahirinus

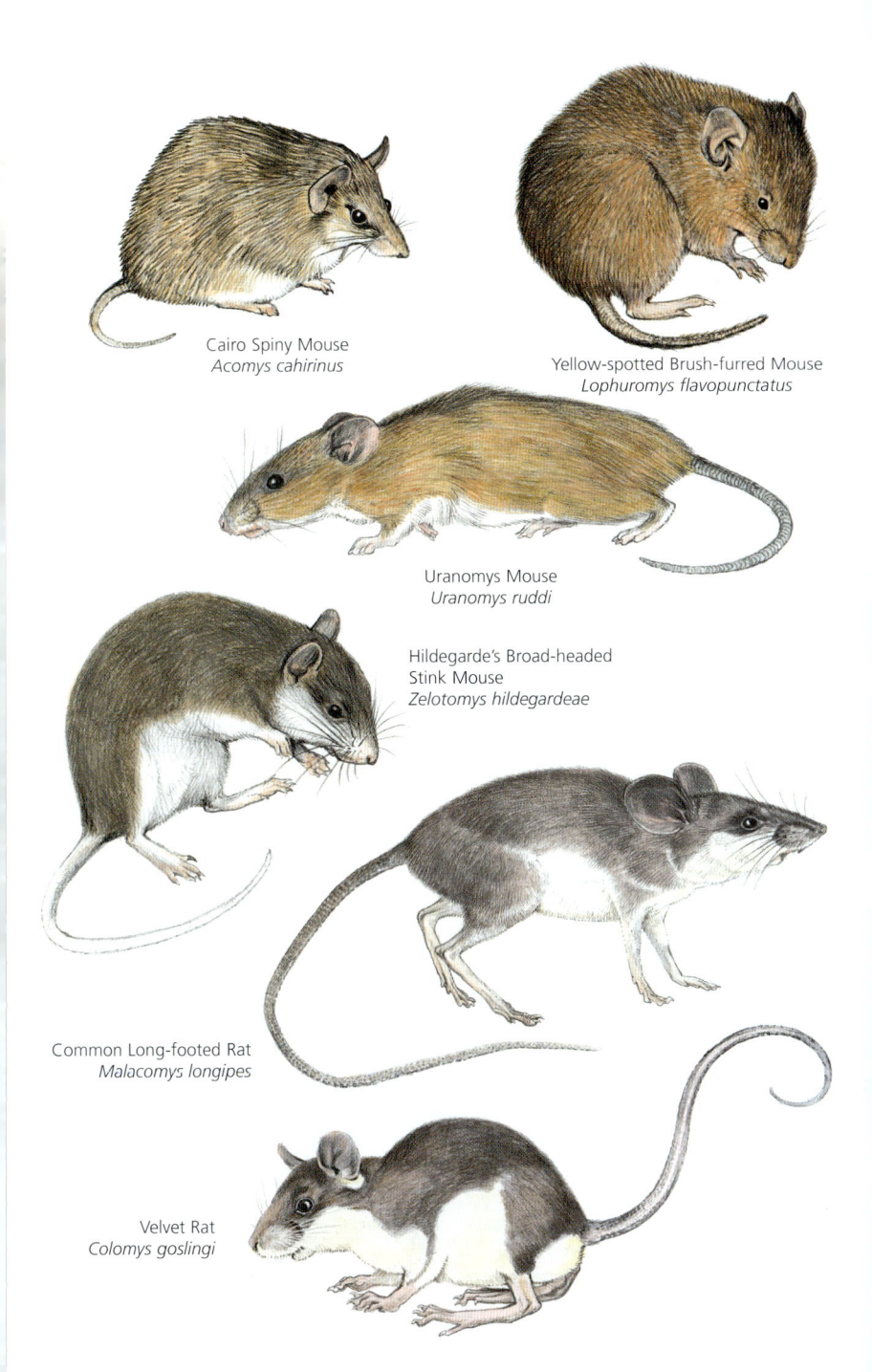

Yellow-spotted Brush-furred Mouse
Lophuromys flavopunctatus

Uranomys Mouse
Uranomys ruddi

Hildegarde's Broad-headed
Stink Mouse
Zelotomys hildegardeae

Common Long-footed Rat
Malacomys longipes

Velvet Rat
Colomys goslingi

PLATE 58 WOODLAND MICE AND BUSH-RATS

NARROW-FOOTED WOODLAND MICE *Grammomys* (11 species) no map
SIZE HB 8–14cm. T 12–22cm. W est. 28–65g.
DESCRIPTION Arboreal. Slender; prominent, oval ears and long, finely haired tail. Guard hairs on rump.
HABITAT Mainly moister vegetation types from Guinea to the Indian Ocean coast.
FOOD Fruits, seeds, stems and other vegetable matter; occasionally insects.

ACACIA RATS *Thallomys* (4 species) no map
SIZE HB 12–17cm. T 13–21cm. W est. 63–100g.
DESCRIPTION Arboreal. Long, slightly hairy tail, large, round ears and sharp, curved claws on short feet. Bold black eye-mask.
HABITAT Dry *Acacia*-dominated woodlands and savannahs of E and S Africa.
FOOD Buds, leaves, seeds, gum; occasionally roots and insects.

SHAGGY SWAMP RATS *Dasymys* (5 species) no map
SIZE HB 12–19cm. T 10–18cm. W 80–165g.
DESCRIPTION Robust, shaggy; somewhat flattened, disc-like face, and rounded pink ears.
HABITAT Wetter grassy areas of sub-Saharan Africa in marshes, especially at higher altitudes.
FOOD Stems, roots, shoots and flowers of plants in waterlogged habitats.

BUSH-RATS *Aethomys* (10 species) no map
SIZE HB 12–19cm. T 12–21cm. W est. 50–150g.
DESCRIPTION Streaky, soft fur of very variable colour (by species and region).
HABITAT Strong preference for rocky habitats in S and E Africa, population in Nigeria (*A. stannarius*).
FOOD Grass, stems, leaves and seeds.

TARGET RAT *Stochomys longicaudatus* no map
SIZE HB 12–17.5cm. T 18.5–25cm. W 50–104g.
DESCRIPTION Dark reddish. The long black bristles on its rump have been likened to arrows.
HABITAT Equatorial lowland forests from the R. Cross (Nigeria) to W Uganda.
FOOD Fruits, seeds and possibly some insects.

RUSTY-NOSED RATS *Oenomys* (2 species) no map
SIZE HB 13–18cm. T 14–21cm. W 50–121g.
DESCRIPTION Shaggy brown with red or orange nose and rump. Semi-arboreal and nocturnal.
HABITAT Forest belt from Guinea to central Kenya. Favour secondary growth in clearings.
FOOD Green leaves, stems, shoots, buds and green seeds; also insects.

MOUNT OKU MOUSE *Lamottemys okuensis* no map
SIZE Unavailable.
DESCRIPTION Shaggy brown, semi-arboreal.
HABITAT Secondary growth in montane habitats surrounding Mt Oku, Cameroon uplands.
FOOD Not known.

BROAD-FOOTED THICKET RATS *Thamnomys* (2 species) no map
SIZE HB 12–16cm. T 18–22cm. W est. 50–100g.
DESCRIPTION Arboreal; broad feet, long tail. Back is brown, dense grey underfur.
HABITAT Montane forests in E Zaïre, Uganda, Rwanda and Burundi.
FOOD Plant material, including leaves and seeds.

DEPHUA MICE *Dephomys* (2 species) no map
SIZE HB 11.5–13.5cm. T 18–20.5cm. W est. 40–65g.
DESCRIPTION Arboreal; broad hindfeet, long tail, conical head. Fur has fine guard hairs on rump.
HABITAT Secondary and swampy palm forests and scrub from Sierra Leone to Ghana. Nocturnal.
FOOD Not recorded.

Common Narrow-footed Woodland Mouse
Grammomys dolichurus

Acacia Rat
Thallomys paedulcus

African Shaggy Swamp Rat
Dasymys incomptus

Kaiser's Bush-rat
Aethomys kaiseri

Target Rat
Stochomys longicaudatus

Rusty-nosed Rat
Oenomys hypoxanthus

Mount Oku Mouse
Lamottemys okuensis

Broad-footed
Thicket Rat
Thamnomys venustus

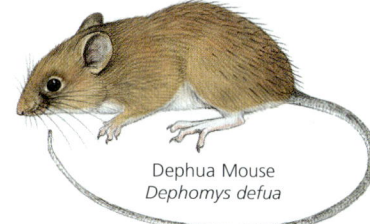

Dephua Mouse
Dephomys defua

ZEBRA MICE *Lemniscomys* (10 species)

- Lemniscomys
- *Mylomys dybowski*
- *Desmomys harringtoni*

SIZE HB 9–14cm. T 9.5–15cm. W est. 18–70g.
DESCRIPTION Grass mice with variable numbers of dorsal stripes, some with light unbroken lines, others fragmented into dashes. All have a near-black dorsal midline. Species: *L. barbarus, L. bellieri, L. griselda, L. hoogstraali, L. linulus, L. macculus, L. mittendorfi, L. rosalia, L. roseveari, L. striatus*.
HABITAT African grasslands south of the Sahara (and one species, *L. barbarus*, in Morocco). The ranges of several species overlap and they partition the habitat in such areas but broaden their niches when free of competition.
FOOD Grass stems, leaves and seeds. Insects are periodically taken.
BEHAVIOUR Very fecund, a single pair can produce 4 litters of up to 12 (usually 4 or 5) young in less than 4 months.

FOUR-STRIPED GRASS MOUSE *Rhabdomys pumilio* see map on p.138

SIZE HB 9–13.5cm. T 8–13.5cm. W 30–40g.
DESCRIPTION Grass mouse with four black stripes along its back, with two pale interstripes and a dorsal buff line in the centre. A compact mouse with relatively small ears, sometimes orange or red.
HABITAT Limited to cooler grasslands in S Africa and in the E African mountains; very discontinuous distribution.
FOOD Vegetarian: stems, leaves and seeds of grass.

Four-striped Grass Mouse
Rhabdomys pumilio

Buffoon Zebra Mouse
Lemniscomys macculus

Note: the rats illustrated opposite are currently being reviewed and their nomenclature revised. A lot remains to be learned about these rodents, which are variable both individually and regionally.

Zebra and Grass Mice

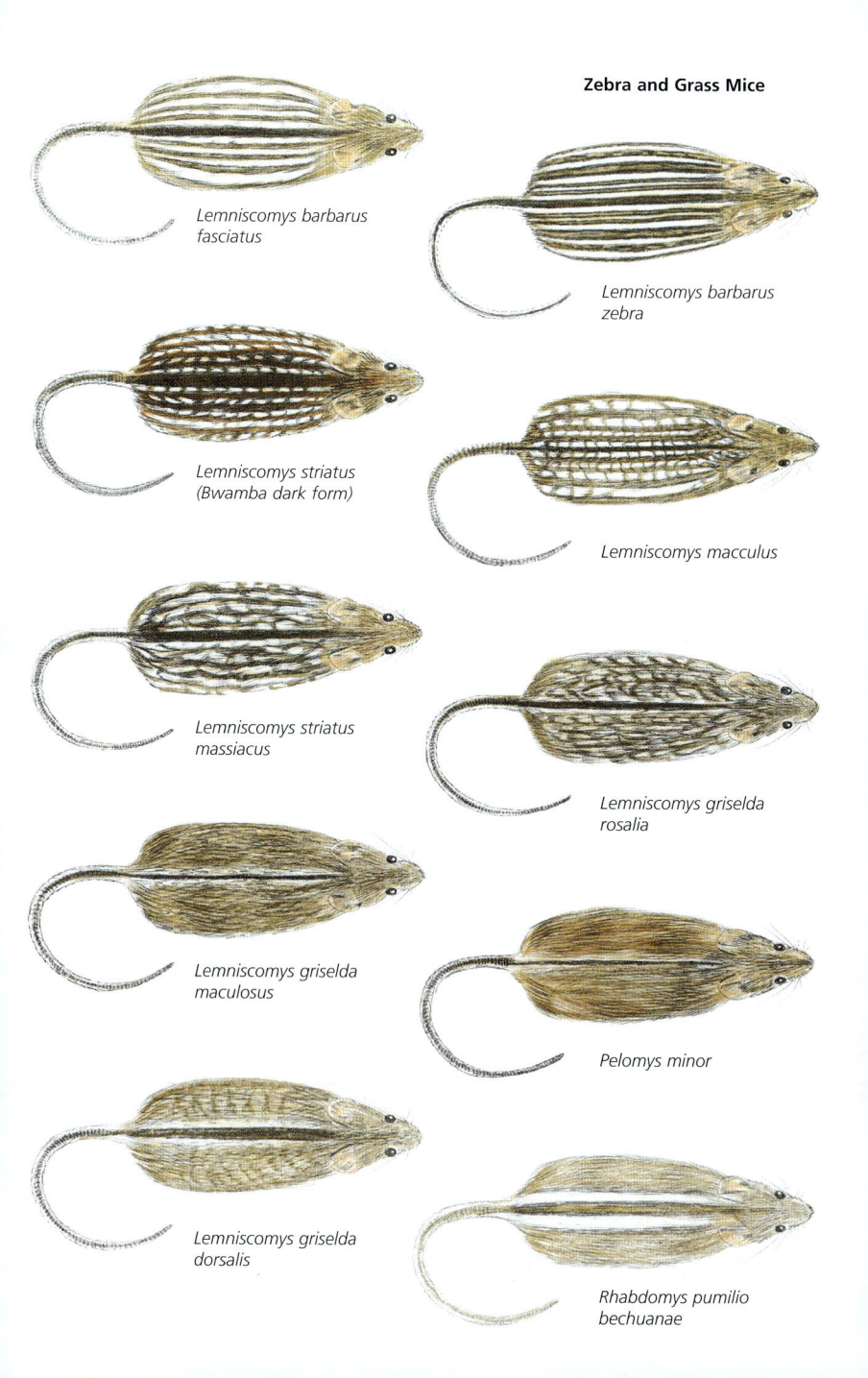

Lemniscomys barbarus fasciatus

Lemniscomys barbarus zebra

Lemniscomys striatus (Bwamba dark form)

Lemniscomys macculus

Lemniscomys striatus massiacus

Lemniscomys griselda rosalia

Lemniscomys griselda maculosus

Pelomys minor

Lemniscomys griselda dorsalis

Rhabdomys pumilio bechuanae

CARNIVORES Carnivora
A group of 'animal-eaters' comprising 7 families: Dogs, Mustelids, Mongooses, Hyaenids, Viverrids Nandinids and Cats.

DOGS AND ALLIES Canidae
These relatively long-legged, long-muzzled carnivores are adapted to running down prey in relatively open and dry environments.

COMMON (GOLDEN) JACKAL *Canis aureus*
SIZE HB 65–105cm. T 18–27cm. W 6–15kg.
DESCRIPTION Sand-coloured with black-tipped tail. Back streaky fawn. Active at night, in the early morning and evening.
HABITAT Dry, open country from sea-level to over 3,000m. Depends on secure burrows or dens, especially on plains.
FOOD Omnivorous. Invertebrates and small vertebrates. Bulbs, berries and fallen fruits.
BEHAVIOUR Several families may form group territories where there is access to super-abundant resources (i.e. rubbish tips). The barks and yelps resemble those of dogs.

SIDE-STRIPED JACKAL *Canis adustus*
SIZE HB 70–80cm. T 35–45cm. W 7.3–12kg.
DESCRIPTION Drabber, shorter legged and shorter eared than other jackals, can generally be distinguished by the white tip to its tail. Mainly nocturnal.
HABITAT Various savannah and thicket types to the edges of forest. Common in various montane habitats up to 2,700m.
FOOD Omnivorous. Invertebrates and small vertebrates, fallen fruits, unripe maize, carrion and organic rubbish.
BEHAVIOUR May travel as family group, more frequently solitary. Wide repertoire of growls, yaps, whines and screams.

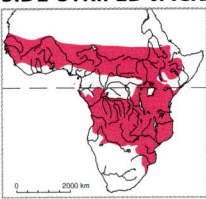

BLACK-BACKED JACKAL *Canis mesomelas*
SIZE HB 70–100cm. T 30–35cm. W 6.5–13.5kg.
DESCRIPTION Slender, long-legged with large ears and a black back (streaked with white). Limbs and flanks are variously fawn to rufous. Tail black tipped.
HABITAT Close association with dry *Acacia* savannahs. In the southern part of its range it occupies most habitat types.
FOOD Omnivorous but small and medium-sized mammals and carrion are taken. Food is bolted and regurgitated in response to the pups' begging.
BEHAVIOUR Form hierarchical family groups. Vocal communication in South Africa (where they are the only jackal) includes howling. In areas of overlap, only the Golden Jackal howls.

ETHIOPIAN WOLF (formerly 'Simien Fox') *Canis simensis*
SIZE HB 90–100cm. T 25–34cm. W 11.5kg (female), 14–18.5kg (male).
DESCRIPTION Tall, large-eared, dog-like. Rich russet-red above, with white underparts and a black tip to the tail.
HABITAT Mainly Afro-alpine meadows and *Helichrysum* moorlands in areas of high rodent density.
FOOD Giant Mole-rats (*Tachyoryctes macrocephalus*) comprise nearly 40% of the prey captures (and the main mass of the diet) on Bale massif. Smaller rodents, hares and carrion make up the rest.
BEHAVIOUR Cohesive, highly hierarchical packs live in regularly demarcated territories of 5–15km^2.

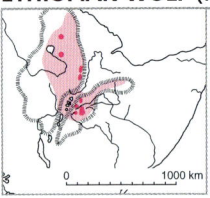

Common (Golden) Jackal

Side-striped Jackal

Black-backed Jackal

Ethiopian Wolf

RED FOX *Vulpes vulpes*

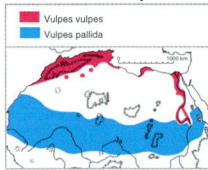

SIZE HB 50–55cm. T 33–40cm. W 4–8kg.
DESCRIPTION Back may be sandy red or greyish, surrounded by red or yellowish flanks, limbs, neck, face and tail. Tail tip, throat and chin are white. Ears, nose, whisker patch, forepaws, and sometimes the belly, are black. The most frequently heard call is a loud, multiple wow-bark.
HABITAT Cultivated and urban land, settlements, desertic steppe, scrub, woodlands and hillsides up to 4,500m. Red foxes dig or modify burrows.
FOOD Omnivorous: vertebrates and carrion, invertebrates, fruits and household debris.
BEHAVIOUR Social grouping varies but pairs occupy large territories in impoverished habitats.

RÜPPELL'S FOX *Vulpes rueppelli*

SIZE: HB 40–48cm. T 25–38cm. W 2–4.5kg.
DESCRIPTION Very large-eared, slender fox with a soft, thick coat and rich, bushy tail. The grizzled fur tends to be greyish on the sides, with a sandy-yellow or brown flush on the midline (from forehead to tail), elbows and heel. Apart from black whisker patches, the ears and face are very pale, as are the underside and limbs. The tip of the tawny tail is white and above its 'violet gland' (near the root) is dark brown. The loud call is a harsh, yelping bark. This is a strictly nocturnal, cool-adapted fox.
HABITAT Sand and stone deserts where burrows are commonly excavated under slabs of stone or the roots of bushes.
FOOD Rodents, reptiles, insects and occasional fruits (dates). Ruppell's Foxes can tolerate a total absence of water.
BEHAVIOUR Commonly solitary or in pairs, this very vocal species has brittle hacking calls, a high-pitched whistle, trilling (when tense) and hissing (in warning). There is also a barking loud call. Breeding is thought to be seasonal, with 3 or 4 blind helpless young born in late winter after a gestation of just under 2 months.

SAND (PALE) FOX *Vulpes pallida* see map above

SIZE HB 38–45cm. T 23–28cm. W 2–3.6kg.
DESCRIPTION Small, very pale fox with large ears, long legs and a relatively thin coat. It has sandy-fawn upperparts and a pale to white underside.
HABITAT S Sahara and Sahel from Mauritania to the Red Sea, in steppe country, sandy and stony deserts. Dig extensive burrows and tolerate heat well.
FOOD Small vertebrates (mainly rodents and lizards) and invertebrates.
BEHAVIOUR Active from dusk till dawn. Unable to survive under totally waterless conditions.

CAPE FOX *Vulpes chama* see map above

SIZE HB 54–62cm. T 29–39.5cm. W 2.5–3.5kg.
DESCRIPTION Lightly built, slender fox, with bushy tail, medium to large ears and a fine-tapered muzzle. The face, underside and base of tail are tawny cream. The loud call is a high-pitched 'wow', ending in 2 or 3 yaps. Nocturnal.
HABITAT Open *Acacia* grasslands, steppe, subdesert scrub and open grassy areas within bushland. Digs burrows or lies up in dense vegetation during the day.
FOOD Predominantly invertebrates and mice; also other small vertebrates, carrion, fallen fruits and grass.
BEHAVIOUR Forages alone but females have been observed out with subadult young.

Red Fox

Sand Fox

Rüppell's Fox

Cape Fox

ROYAL (HOARY) FOX *Vulpes cana*

SIZE HB 40–60cm. T 29–41.5cm. W 2–3kg.
DESCRIPTION Densely furred, sandy-coloured fox with 'frosted' grey sides, white underparts and a furry, sandy tail that has densely packed, very long, dark guard hairs. Large, funnel-like ears are scantily haired. The general demeanour is very cat-like and animals are invariably very evasive and timid.
HABITAT Marked preference for rocky mountainous regions up to 2,000m. Possibly the relic of an Ice Age fauna. Thought to prefer natural crevices and rock shelters.
FOOD Insects, supplemented by fruits and small vertebrates.
BEHAVIOUR Extremely sensitive to sound and very shy, escaping notice with a fast ground-hugging run.

FENNEC FOX *Vulpes zerda*

Otocyon megalotis
Vulpes zerda

SIZE HB 37–41cm. T 18–21cm. W 0.8–1.5kg.
DESCRIPTION Very small, rather short-legged fox with huge ears and a very small, pointed muzzle. The loud call is a brief shuddering howl, descending in pitch and repeated serially. Strictly nocturnal.
HABITAT Sand-dune deserts and steppes with light, sandy soils. Self-dug burrows are extensive and dry grass is brought in to line the resting chamber.
FOOD Desert grasshoppers and other desert invertebrates. Lizards, rodents and birds, and occasionally fruits and roots, are also taken. An extremely fast and efficient digger in sand, both to catch prey and to escape detection. It can survive without surface water.
BEHAVIOUR Most frequently seen in pairs but up to 10 animals have been recorded in a group.

BAT-EARED FOX *Otocyon megalotis* see map above

SIZE HB 47–66cm. T 23–34cm. W 3–5.3kg.
DESCRIPTION Long-limbed, large-eared 'foxes' with a thickly furred, black-tipped tail and black-tipped ears, feet and muzzle. The eyes are contained within a dark 'mask'. Relatively quiet, they occasionally utter a series of thin, wailing howls. Contact calls among bat-eared foxes are bird-like mewings.
HABITAT Dry, open country, especially *Acacia* savannahs and associated plains, grasslands and steppes.
FOOD Termites, especially harvester termites (*Hodotermes*), beetles and other invertebrates; also, marginally, small vertebrates and fruits.
BEHAVIOUR A permanent pair is the basic social unit, often accompanied by up to 6 recent offspring.

WILD DOG *Lycaon pictus*

Lycaon pictus
Former range

SIZE HB 76–112cm. T 30–41cm. W 18–36kg.
DESCRIPTION Large, blotchy dog with prominent, round ears and a tufted tail. The tail tip is almost always white and the broad, powerful muzzle always black. Each individual's pattern of blotches is unique but there are family and regional resemblances.
HABITAT Woodlands, savannahs, grasslands and steppes at all altitudes.
FOOD Exclusively mammals. Wild dogs prefer to feed on the commonest medium-sized antelopes not more than twice their own weight. Specialised pack-hunters, rely on an unconcealed fast chase of up to 5km at a steady 48kmh. Their strategy is to snap and tear at the rear and sides of running prey until it tires.
BEHAVIOUR The social behaviour of a pack centres on a breeding pair, with non-breeding adults assisting in the feeding (by regurgitation) of litters that can number up to 16 puppies. All pack members are subordinate to the breeding pair.

Royal Fox

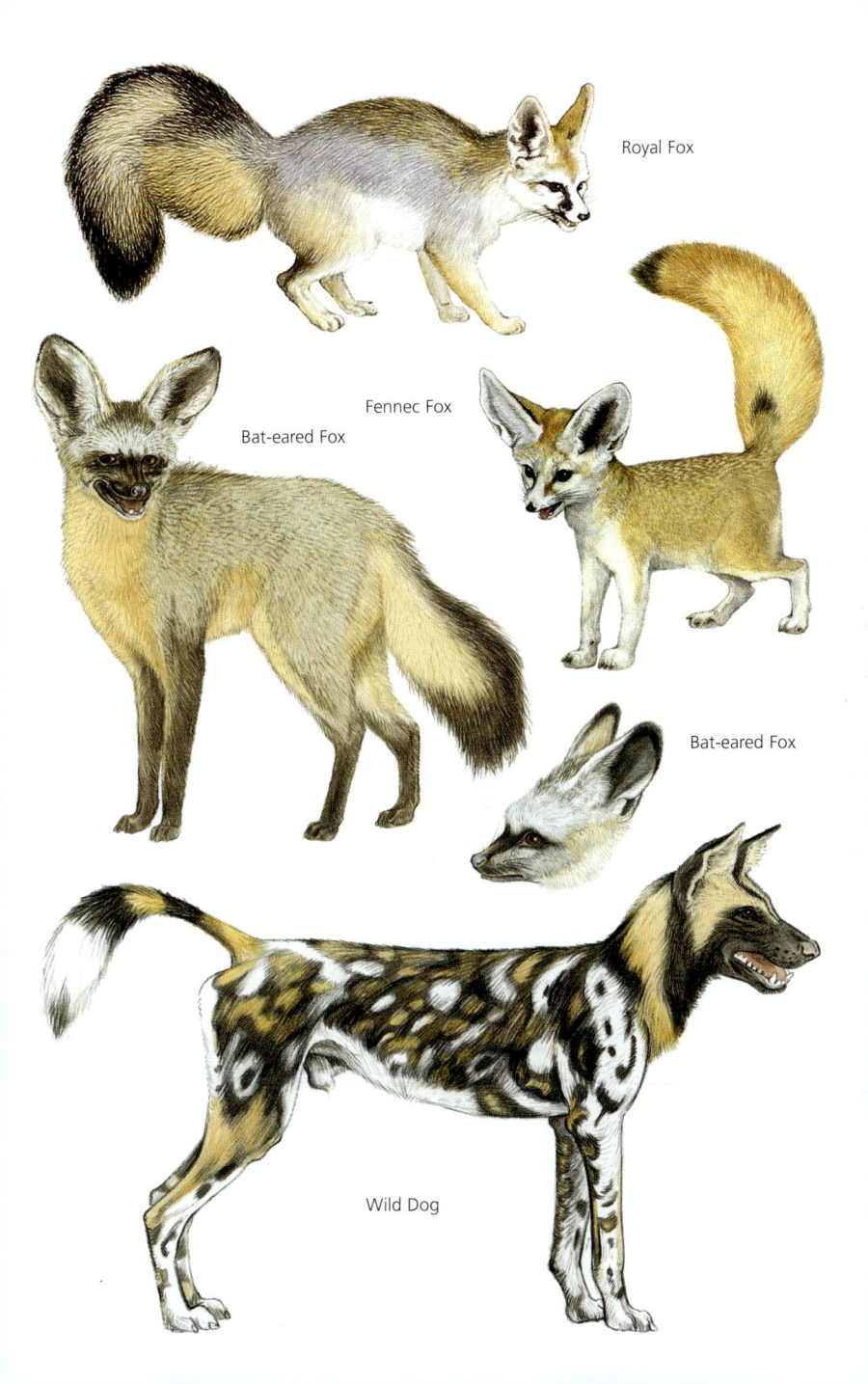

Fennec Fox

Bat-eared Fox

Bat-eared Fox

Wild Dog

MUSTELIDS Mustelidae

Mainly bird, mammal and fish predators of northern temperate origin.

'WEASELS' Mustelinae: A grouping of all the non-amphibian African mustelids.

WEASEL (LEAST) *Mustela nivalis*

SIZE HB 20–29cm. T 7–13cm. W 124–250g.
DESCRIPTION Brown upperparts and a white underside.
HABITAT Mediterranean littoral and Atlas Mts, mainly in farmland.
FOOD Rats, mice, frogs, lizards, small birds, rabbits and insects.

POLECAT *Mustela putorius*

SIZE HB 35–45cm. T 12–16cm. W 700–1,500g.
DESCRIPTION White ears, and face marked with a black eye mask and hood.
HABITAT From sea-level up to 2,000m in the Atlas Mts west of the Riff.
FOOD Small mammals, reptiles, frogs, birds and insects; very occasionally fish and fruits.

LIBYAN STRIPED WEASEL *Ictonyx libyca*   *see* map above

SIZE HB 22–30cm. T 12–19cm. W 500–750g.
DESCRIPTION Conspicuous, with long, erectile hair, mainly white upperparts and narrow black stripes down the back. Nocturnal. Side-swinging movements give a remarkably snake-like impression.
HABITAT Sahara desert, mainly on its margins and mountains.
FOOD Rodents and other small mammals, reptiles, invertebrates, birds and their eggs.

ZORILLA *Ictonyx striatus*

SIZE HB 30–38cm. T 22–30cm. W 700–1,400g.
DESCRIPTION Small carnivore with strong claws on the forelegs, black underparts and a well-furred white tail.
HABITAT Very patchily distributed, scarce or absent in most heavily wooded areas. Prefers upland grasslands or steppe.
FOOD Invertebrates are the main staple but rodents form the bulk of the diet in some localities during certain seasons. Snakes and other reptiles are also commonly taken in some localities. Hares are a recorded prey animal.

STRIPED (WHITE-NAPED) WEASEL *Poecilogale albinucha*

SIZE HB 25–36cm. T 13–24cm. W 230–350g.
DESCRIPTION Small, very elongated with very short legs but powerfully clawed paws and a conspicuous black and white striped back, underside black.
HABITAT Occurs in numerous widely separate localities. Main centres of distribution are extensive grasslands or high veld with perennial, dense rodent populations.
FOOD Almost exclusively rodents, with occasional birds and eggs.
BEHAVIOUR Normally solitary or in pairs. Larger groups include single females with young.

RATEL (HONEY BADGER) *Mellivora capensis*

SIZE HB 60–77cm. T 16–30cm. W 7–16kg.
DESCRIPTION Chunky, lumbering carnivore with a white forehead and variably coloured mantle. The neck and shoulders are very muscular and the broad forepaws are armed with massive claws.
HABITAT Commonest in open woodland but occurs in forest, waterless desert, in Afro-alpine moorland and coastal scrub.
FOOD Opportunistic omnivore, specialising in the excavation of social insects, mice, trap-door spiders, dung beetles, larvae, scorpions, etc.
BEHAVIOUR Ratels have very large, overlapping ranges, and normally forage singly, but 2 animals are very often seen together.

Weasel

Libyan Striped Weasel

Polecat

Striped Weasel

Zorilla

Ratel (Honey Badger)

OTTERS Lutrinae

These long-bodied, long-tailed, amphibious carnivores have dense waterproof fur, a blunt, short face and a prominent moustache of whiskers.

SWAMP OTTER *Aonyx congica*

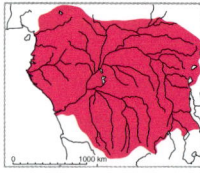

SIZE HB 78–97cm. T 40–59cm. W 15–25kg.
DESCRIPTION White bib, nose and ears and a prominent black patch between the eyes and nostrils. Body rich sepia with some frosting on head and neck.
HABITAT Rivers, swamps and ponds close to or surrounded by rainforest.
FOOD Fish, frogs, earthworms, crabs, molluscs and other vertebrates and invertebrates.
BEHAVIOUR Excellent swimmer. Forages singly but family parties have been observed in Cameroon rivers.

AFRICAN CLAWLESS OTTER *Aonyx capensis*

SIZE HB 72–92cm. T 40–71cm. W 12–34kg.
DESCRIPTION Blunt, unwebbed fingers and toes, and almost vestigial fingernails. Head broad. Massive neck and crown are visibly modelled by well-developed neck and jaw muscles. Colour on face variable but dark area between eye and nostril is never sharply isolated (as it is in the Swamp Otter).
HABITAT Rivers, streams, marshes, lakes and dams with adequate cover.
FOOD Freshwater crabs consistently form the major part of the diet. Frogs comprise a lesser, more seasonal, part of the otter's diet, as do fish, small mammals, birds and molluscs.
BEHAVIOUR Normally forage singly or as a mother with young. However, adults may be quite tolerant and spend time together. It is possible that related animals along a stretch of 3–20km of river or coast may share a group or clan territory. Very vocal.

COMMON OTTER *Lutra lutra*

SIZE HB 60–90cm. T 35–47cm. W 6–18kg.
DESCRIPTION The short face has prominent eyes and a brush of stiff whiskers on the muzzle. Coat can vary from light tan or grey tints to deep dark brown. Strong, well-clawed, webbed toes. The Common Otter makes chirping contact calls and a soft whistle of alarm. Largely nocturnal.
HABITAT Now found only in a very few localities. Need dense vegetation for cover and safe retreats in holes, hollow trees etc. for breeding.
FOOD Mainly fish but also frogs, crabs and many small animals.
BEHAVIOUR Solitary individuals, pairs or families range over 12–24km of shoreline (and some up to 60km) on which they use up to 40 habitual resting spots (each well spaced from the next).

SPOT-NECKED OTTER *Lutra maculicollis* see map above

SIZE HB 60–65cm. T 35–40cm. W 4–6.5kg.
DESCRIPTION Sleek, slender with long tail and well-webbed, clawed toes. Apart from the brown and white blotching of the throat and underparts, which is very variable, the colour is a uniform, deep chocolate brown. A thin, high whistle is the most characteristic call.
HABITAT Clear water seems to be an important determinant in distribution (it is mainly a diurnal fisher).
FOOD Fish and frogs; also crabs, molluscs, aquatic insects and larvae, and various other vertebrates and invertebrates.
BEHAVIOUR Usually solitary, may form small family parties. It forms groups of up to 20 animals in L. Victoria.

Swamp Otter

African Clawless Otter

Common Otter

Spot-necked Otter

MONGOOSES Herpestidae

Small to medium-sized carnivores with long bodies and tails and shortish legs. All have inconspicuous ears, small eyes and a more or less pointed muzzle. Primarily terrestrial.

SURICATE (MEERKAT) *Suricata suricata*

SIZE HB 24.5–31cm. T 19–24cm. W 620–970g.
DESCRIPTION Ochre-grey with rotund body, muscular, well-clawed forearms, a round head and tubular muzzle. Eye-masks of black skin and fur. Pale underside prominently displayed when the animal stands upright. Banded rump.
HABITAT Kalahari *Acacia* bush, Karoo scrub and Highveld rangelands. Favour dry, open, often stony, country with short or sparse woody growth, mainly short grasses and extensive open pans.
FOOD Mainly insects associated with grassland and herbivore herds: termites, larvae and pupae.
BEHAVIOUR Packs of about 10 (up to 30) animals may include several breeding pairs. Aggression is seldom obvious (although adults may squabble over food).

BANDED MONGOOSE *Mungos mungo*

SIZE HB 30–45cm. T 15–30cm. W 1.5–2.25kg.
DESCRIPTION Chunky, coarse-haired with short, muscular, well-clawed legs. Prominently banded rump. Larger and darker in moist habitats, and smaller and paler in drier habitats. Strictly diurnal.
HABITAT Forest/cultivation mosaics to arid Acacia scrub and open, short grasslands. Closely associated with termitaries.
FOOD Termites and beetle larvae (especially in rangelands); cryptic litter fauna in more forested areas, supplemented by small vertebrates.
BEHAVIOUR Live in packs that can reach about 40 members before dividing into smaller groups with an average of between 15 and 20 members.

GAMBIAN MONGOOSE *Mungos gambianus*

SIZE HB est. 33–36cm. T est. 18–22cm. W est. 1–2kg.
DESCRIPTION Compact, coarse-haired with plain grey upperparts, ochraceous underparts and dark outer surfaces to the limbs. Diurnal.
HABITAT Moist savannahs, forest/cultivation mosaics, grasslands and woodlands.
FOOD Invertebrates with some vertebrates.
BEHAVIOUR Highly social and twitters continuously while foraging in long grass.

LIBERIAN MONGOOSE *Liberiictis kuhni*

SIZE HB 40–45cm. T est. 18–22cm. W 2–2.3kg.
DESCRIPTION Long-clawed, long-nosed with thick dark coat and bushy tail. The very undershot mouthparts, chin and chest are off-white.
HABITAT Known from stream banks in secondary and deciduous forest.
FOOD Earthworms and insect larvae are found in streambeds and sump areas by energetic digging with the claws, followed by sniffing and grubbing with the snout.

SAVANNAH MONGOOSE *Dologale dybowski*

SIZE HB 22–33cm. T 16–23cm. W est. 250–400g.
DESCRIPTION Grizzled with powerful claws on the forefeet and a thick, bushy tail. Throat displays prominent reverse 'cow-lick' of fur.
HABITAT Only known from moist savannahs and margins of rainforest in NE Zaïre, S Sudan and NW Uganda.
FOOD Unknown, but is associated with termitaries. Possibly fossorial invertebrates and small burrowing vertebrates.

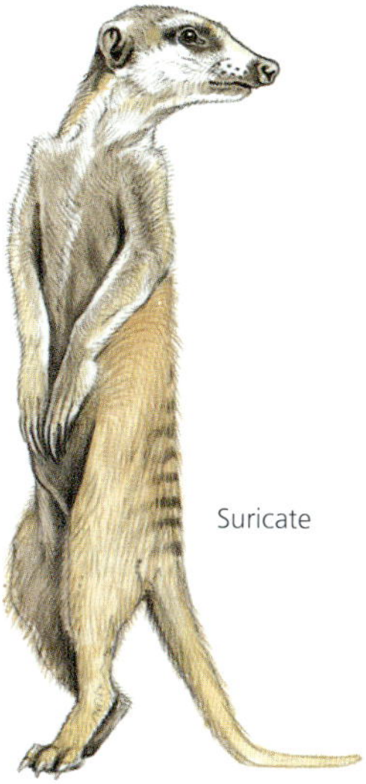

Suricate

Banded Mongoose

Gambian Mongoose

Liberian Mongoose

Savannah Mongoose

DWARF MONGOOSE *Helogale parvula*

SIZE HB 18–28cm. T 14–19cm. W 210–350g.
DESCRIPTION Easily distinguished by its small size, rather infantile features, smooth, finely grizzled coat and its diurnal and social habits.
HABITAT Savannahs, thickets and woodlands, typically with numerous termitaries for shelter. Avoid very arid, open country.
FOOD Invertebrates, notably crickets, grasshoppers, termites and spiders. Also rodents, lizards, snakes and birds.
BEHAVIOUR Social species, forms packs averaging over 8 individuals (range 2–20), with more females than males and fluctuating numbers of young.

SOMALI DWARF MONGOOSE *Helogale hirtula* see map above

SIZE HB est. 20–27cm. T est. 15–18cm. W est. 220–330 g.
DESCRIPTION Very small with shaggier fur than the Dwarf Mongoose. Social and diurnal.
HABITAT Horn of Africa, limited to thicket and deciduous woodlands. Can live without water.
FOOD Invertebrates and vertebrates.

CUSIMANSES *Crossarchus*

Dark, shaggy mongooses with a snout-like nose and a tubular muzzle. Diurnal, social mongooses that form family parties numbering up to 20 animals.

COMMON CUSIMANSE *Crossarchus obscurus*

SIZE HB 30–37cm. T 15–25cm. W 1–1.5kg.
DESCRIPTION Tubby, long-nosed, strongly clawed. Paler underfur. Shaggy dark outer fur that gives unkempt appearance.
HABITAT Rainforest zone between Sierra Leone and Nigeria. Inhabits the floor of the rainforest, notably in areas of dense undergrowth.
FOOD Insects, earthworms, snails, myriapods, crabs and invertebrates; also vertebrates, including their eggs.
BEHAVIOUR Quick and energetic forager. Keeps in touch with frequent chirps, churrs and twitters.

FLAT-HEADED CUSIMANSE *Crossarchus platycephalus* not illustrated
(Sometimes treated as a subspecies of *C. obscurus*) see map above

SIZE HB est. 30–36cm. T est. 15–25cm. W est. 1–1.5kg.
DESCRIPTION Externally resembles Common Cusimanse. Shaggy, with black guard hairs over a thick brown undercoat.
HABITAT Tropical rainforest between the R. Cross (Nigeria) and R. Zaïre. Very patchily distributed.
FOOD Forest floor invertebrates and small vertebrates.

ALEXANDER'S CUSIMANSE *Crossarchus alexandri* see map above

SIZE HB 35–44cm. T 22–32cm. W 1–2kg.
DESCRIPTION Continuous crest from crown to tail. Shaggy, with long-muzzled, short-furred face.
HABITAT Rainforest in Zaïre basin and W Uganda. Favours seasonally flooded swamp forest.
FOOD Earthworms, snails, slugs, beetles and other invertebrates; also small vertebrates and fallen fruits.
BEHAVIOUR Social. Mainly diurnal. Commonly grunts and twitters while foraging.

ANSORGE'S CUSIMANSE *Crossarchus ansorgei* see map above

SIZE HB est. 32–36cm. T est. 20–22cm. W est. 0.6–1.5kg.
DESCRIPTION Thick brown fur on the body, black limbs and tail. Thick muzzle flat-fronted and blunt.
HABITAT Known only from high deciduous rainforest and said to avoid disturbed and cultivated land.
FOOD Insect larvae, eggs and small vertebrates.

Somali Dwarf Mongoose

Dwarf Mongoose

Common Cusimanse

Alexander's Cusimanse

Ansorge's Cusimanse

PLATE 68 SOLITARY MONGOOSES

SMALL GREY MONGOOSE *Herpestes pulverulenta*
SIZE HB 28–37cm. T 23–36cm. W 370–800g.
DESCRIPTION Uniformly grizzled grey with thickly furred tail.
HABITAT Bushy country in all habitat types south of the Orange R. Prefers rocky ground, hillsides and the coastal plain.
FOOD Mainly invertebrates, insects, crabs, larvae, earthworms, snails; also rodents, reptiles, birds.
BEHAVIOUR Seen singly, in twos, or in small family groups.

ICHNEUMON (EGYPTIAN) MONGOOSE *Herpestes ichneumon*
Herpestes ichneumon
Herpestes naso

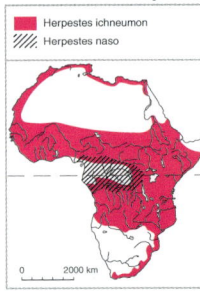

SIZE HB 45–60cm. T 33–54cm. W 2.2–4.1kg.
DESCRIPTION Long-bodied, low-slung with a slender, almost snake-like head. Long, tapered tail ends in a black tassel. In most postures legs are concealed by long fur, increasing its reptile-like form.
HABITAT Commonest on floodplains, littorals, and broad river valleys; also rolling moist savannahs and clearings where grass is dominant.
FOOD Rodents, reptiles, frogs, birds and various invertebrates.
BEHAVIOUR Normally seen singly or in small family parties. Larger associations form around 2 or more females, their immediate young and some previous young.

LONG-SNOUTED MONGOOSE *Herpestes naso*   see map above
SIZE HB 52–59cm. T 36–43cm. W 3–4.2kg.
DESCRIPTION Dark, shaggy with relatively long legs, a thick tail and pointed muzzle. Head is greyer than the deep sepia-black grizzled body and tail.
HABITAT Main forest block north of the R. Zaïre where they live close to clear forest streams.
FOOD Known to eat snails (a rare prey for carnivores), reputed to take carrion and likely to feed on rodents.

SLENDER MONGOOSE *Herpestes sanguinea*
SIZE HB 26–34cm. T 23–31cm. W 350–800g.
DESCRIPTION Long-bodied, short-legged, partly arboreal, extremely variable in colour. Numerous subspecies.
HABITAT All wooded, savannah, thicket and forest habitats; also occurs in extensive papyrus and forest swamps.
FOOD Rodents, insects, reptiles, frogs, birds (including nestlings and eggs). Insect larvae (notably blowfly larvae at carcasses).
BEHAVIOUR Mainly diurnal foragers. Both sexes hold exclusive territories of variable size. Adult males may tolerate smaller males but confrontations within and between sexes are common.

YELLOW MONGOOSE *Cynictis penicillata*
SIZE HB 25–40cm. T 18–30cm. W 440–800g.
DESCRIPTION Dainty, rather weak-looking limbs and sharply tapered face. Commonly sun-bathe in the early morning.
HABITAT Favours sandy areas, often valley bottoms or clearings within wooded country.
FOOD Invertebrates, especially beetles, their larvae and harvester termites.
BEHAVIOUR Hierarchical packs numbering up to 50 animals are dominated by a breeding pair.

Small Grey Mongoose

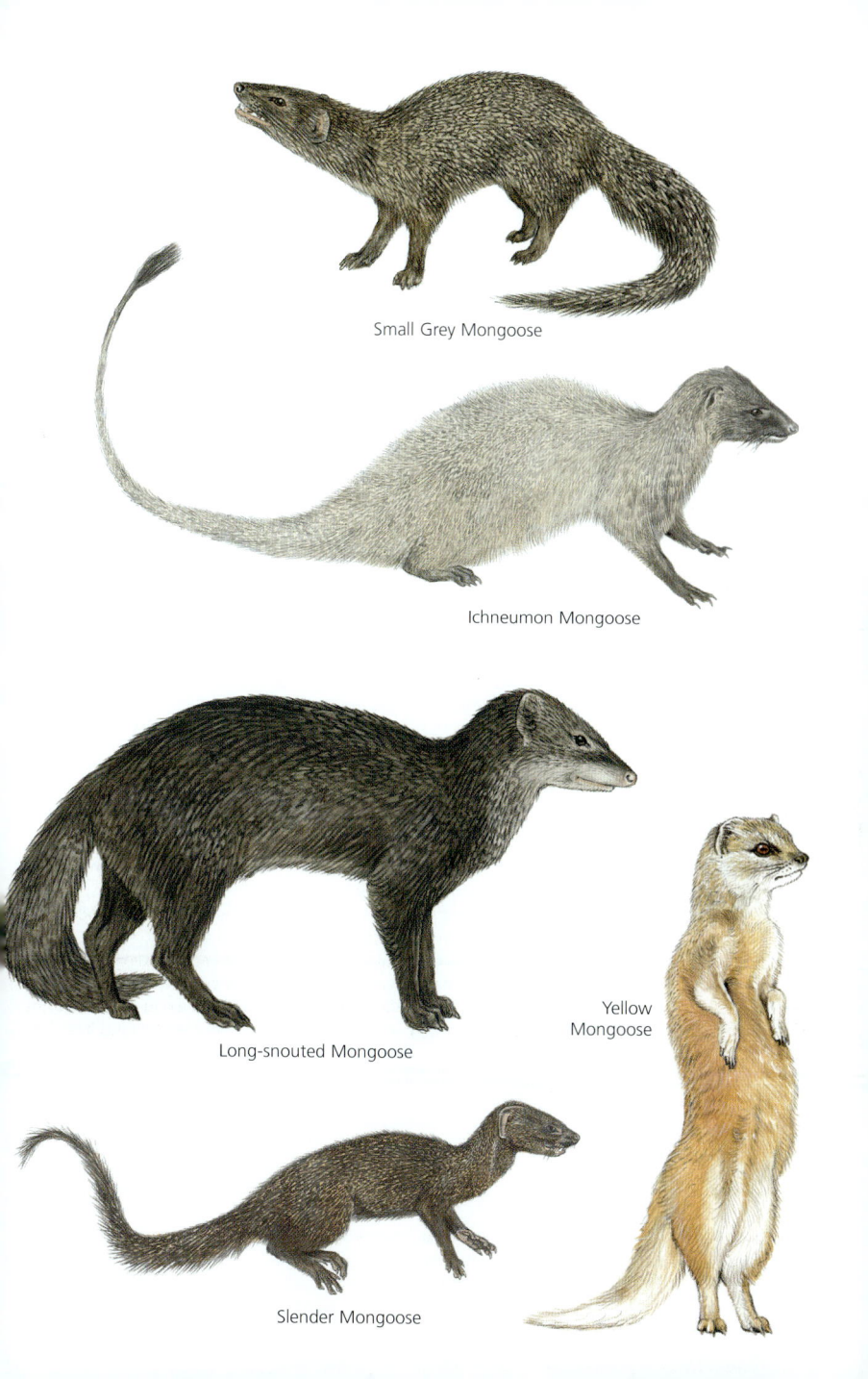

Ichneumon Mongoose

Long-snouted Mongoose

Yellow Mongoose

Slender Mongoose

MARSH MONGOOSE Atilax paludinosus

SIZE HB 46–64cm. T 32–53cm. W 2.2–5.0kg.
DESCRIPTION Dark brown with thick, shaggy fur on the neck, body and tail but short, sleek fur on the fingered hands and feet. The hands have soft, naked palms and sensitive, flexible fingers. The blunt, slightly upturned muzzle is distinctive. 16 subspecies have been described
HABITAT River courses and lake-shore areas in otherwise inhospitable regions. More generally distributed in forested or humid areas and are one of a small community of animals living in *Papyrus* swamps.
FOOD Freshwater crabs, snails, mussels, frogs, lungfish (*Protopterus*) and catfish (*Clarias*); insect larvae, reptiles, small mammals, birds and their eggs, fruits.
BEHAVIOUR Territorial and forage individually or in pairs with young. During droughts territories appear to be used more intensively and activity (which is predominantly nocturnal) may continue well into the day. Loud bark-growls are uttered as a threat against intruding mongooses or dogs. Moans and purrs (contact?) and bleats (excitement) are also uttered on occasion.

MELLER'S MONGOOSE Rhynchogale melleri

SIZE HB 44–50cm. T 28–40cm. W 1.7–3.1kg.
DESCRIPTION Dark, muddy-coloured with long legs and tail, shaggy, coarsely grizzled fur and a blunt, broad and rather retroussé nose. Somewhat domed forehead and a wide, swollen upper lip. A distinctive feature is the prominent 'reverse cow-licks' of long fur on each side of the throat. Where these meet the cheek fur there is something of a ruff.
HABITAT Moist areas with thick grass and abundant termitaries, particularly in wide, shallow and well-watered valleys.
FOOD Termites, particularly harvester termites (*Hodotermes*) and the larger *Macrotermes*. Also takes termite-eating snakes and centipedes, and grasshoppers, beetles and frogs have also been recorded. Fallen fruits may be locally or seasonally important. Termites can only be taken in small numbers at a time because this mongoose is not a digger.
BEHAVIOUR Solitary and little-known, extremely shy and reclusive.

WHITE-TAILED MONGOOSE Ichneumia albicauda

SIZE HB 47–71cm. T 35–50cm. W 2.0–5.2kg.
DESCRIPTION Somewhat fox-like, with thick, silver-tinted coat. Unlike the Dog Mongoose (4 toes), this species has 5 toes. Nocturnal.
HABITAT Flourishes in grassy savannahs, tropical woodlands, grassy clearings in former forest areas, cultivation, suburbia and ranchlands.
FOOD Mainly invertebrates: termites, beetles and their larvae preferred. Mice, frogs and reptiles also frequent, fruits very infrequent.
BEHAVIOUR Although normally solitary, adult females are known to share home ranges amicably with adult offspring. As many as 9 individuals have been seen foraging together

SELOUS'S MONGOOSE Paracynictis selousi

SIZE HB 35–48cm. T 28–43cm. W 1.3–2.2kg.
DESCRIPTION Delicate-looking with bushy, white-tipped tail. Almost wholly nocturnal.
HABITAT Open, short grass; well-drained, sandy country with open Mopane (*Colophospermum*) scrub, *Baikiaea* teak woodland and fire-climax Miombo (*Brachystegia*) woodland with open floors.
FOOD Invertebrates, with a strong preference for beetles and their larvae, termites and grasshoppers. Mice, reptiles and frogs are commonly eaten; birds only rarely.
BEHAVIOUR Finds most food by smell. Often visits cattle pens to dig for dung-beetle larvae. Burrows are dug slowly and laboriously but are important as key landmarks and refuges. Normally seen singly out in the open..

Marsh Mongoose

Meller's Mongoose

White-tailed Mongoose

Selous's Mongoose

BUSHY-TAILED MONGOOSE *Bdeogale crassicauda*

- Bdeogale crassicauda
- Bdeogale omnivora
- Bdeogale jacksoni
- Probable range
- Bdeogale nigripes

SIZE HB 40–50cm. T 20–30cm. W 1.3–2.1kg.

DESCRIPTION Brown or black with bushy, tapered tail, relatively prominent ears and blunt dog-like muzzle. Colouring varies locally but is relatively uniform, with long black guard hairs over paler, dense underfur. Limbs black or deep brown.

HABITAT Coastal thickets, dry forests and well-vegetated valleys in the moister eastern Miombo (*Brachystegia*) woodlands; also dense vegetation around rocky outcrops and escarpments.

FOOD Ants and termites; also caterpillars, crickets, grasshoppers, beetles, their larvae and other invertebrates, mostly picked off the ground or vegetation. Snakes and lizards, burrowing toads and rodents are more rarely eaten. Very active prey appears to confuse bushy-tailed mongooses but more acquiescent prey is dealt with deliberately by means of deep, forceful bites.

SOKOKE DOG MONGOOSE *Bdeogale omnivora*

SIZE HB 34–45cm. T 18–24cm. W est. 0.7–1.6kg.

DESCRIPTION Small with pale cream-coloured body and dark brown limbs and tail. There are longer, black-tipped guard hairs in the tail, on the rump and more sparsely on the back. Head and shoulders are palest, almost white. Predominantly nocturnal.

HABITAT Only known with certainty from coastal forests between the R. Galana and Mombasa. The Sokoke forest consists of very old Miombo (*Brachystegia*) woodland growing on white marine sands. The animals shelter in small riverine patches of evergreen thicket but forage more widely. They range through a mosaic of forest, savannah and cultivation.

FOOD The first specimens collected contained insects, birds and fruits.

JACKSON'S MONGOOSE *Bdeogale jacksoni*   *see* map above

SIZE HB 52–57cm. T 27–36cm. W 2–3kg.

DESCRIPTION Often regarded as a montane isolate of the Black-legged Mongoose, distinguished by much longer fur, especially on the tail, and very yellowish tints on the neck and throat. Mainly nocturnal and crepuscular.

HABITAT Montane forests and bamboo zones on the Kenya mountains; also recorded from lowland forest immediately south of Mt. Elgon.

FOOD Adult diet consists of insects, mostly army ants of the genus *Anona*; also caterpillars, beetles, millipedes, snails, lizards and snake eggs. About 80% of the juvenile's diet is rodents (compared with over 5% in adults), with the rest mostly lizards, beetles and birds. Coping with well-defended columns of army ants may therefore depend on maturity and learning.

BLACK-LEGGED MONGOOSE *Bdeogale nigripes*

SIZE HB 55–65cm. T 35–40cm. W est. 2–3.5kg.

DESCRIPTION Large pale mongoose with black limbs and a white tail (face and rump are also white in some individuals). The tail is long but only moderately bushy. Fur on the body is dense and thick but relatively short. Shoulders may be grey or show an upward extension of the black or sepia forelimb colour.

HABITAT Lowland rainforests between the R. Cross in Nigeria to the Western Rift Valley. Within this extensive range it is localised but nowhere very common.

FOOD Mainly ants, notably army ants (*Dorylus* and *Myrmecaria*), and other insects; also a variety of invertebrates, including snails and crabs. Vertebrates, including rodents and frogs. Fallen fruits are taken occasionally.

Bushy-tailed Mongoose

Sokoke Dog Mongoose

Jackson's Mongoose

Black-legged Mongoose

HYAENAS Hyaenidae

Long-legged, long-necked carnivores with large eyes and ears and a blunt muzzle. They have complex social relationships regulated by scent signals, loud calls and elaborate behaviour.

STRIPED HYAENA *Hyaena hyaena*

SIZE HB 100–120cm. T 25–35cm. W 25–55kg.

DESCRIPTION Tall, slender with long, thick neck, pointed ears, large eyes and a blunt black muzzle with a pointed, dog-like nose. A crest runs from crown to tail.

HABITAT Arid steppes and subdesert, *Acacia* scrub and dry savannahs, open montane habitats and rocky escarpments.

FOOD Omnivorous and opportunistic but primarily adapted to coping with bones and carrion.

BEHAVIOUR Depends on whether or not Spotted Hyaena is present. Where the 2 species co-exist Striped is quieter, more retiring and perhaps more solitary and cryptic

BROWN HYAENA *Hyaena brunnea* *see* map above

SIZE HB 110–125cm. T 25–30cm. W 40–55kg.

DESCRIPTION Resembles dark, heavily caped Striped Hyaena but with a vivid cream-coloured throat, dark brown or slate body and shorter black tail.

HABITAT Currently limited to the Kalahari Desert, the Namibian coastal littoral and less inhabited borderlands in South Africa and Zimbabwe.

FOOD Primarily carrion, especially during the dry season or when nomadic herds pass through. Almost entirely nocturnal.

BEHAVIOUR Home ranges are occupied by a small number of closely related adults (up to 3 males and 5 females), their immediate young and some subadults, numbering up to 14 in total.

SPOTTED HYAENA *Crocuta crocuta*

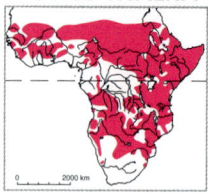

SIZE HB 100–180cm. T 25–36cm. W 40–90kg.

DESCRIPTION Powerfully built, dog-like, with a black muzzle and black tip to the short, brushy tail. Females average 12% heavier than males. Its loud, long-distance call, a repetitive and reverberating 'whoo-up', carries for up to 5km. Less frequent is its famous 'laugh', a shrill, social-appeasement call.

HABITAT Open savannahs, all *Acacia* communities, montane moors and grasslands, various dry steppes with abundant herbivores preferred.

FOOD Opportunistic carnivore and scavenger wherever animal waste, from the feeding of other carnivores or humans, or the vicissitudes of nature, is available.

BEHAVIOUR Where food is plentiful a single clan can number over 100 (with a range of 35–80 adults).

AARDWOLF *Proteles cristata*

SIZE HB 55–80cm. T 20–30cm. H 40–50cm. W 8–12kg.

DESCRIPTION Slender, cream or tawny with narrow, well-spaced stripes and dark brown feet, tail tip and muzzle. Long crest on neck and back.

HABITAT Presence depends on 2 genera of harvester termites (*Trinervitermes* and *Hodotermes*). These termites flourish best in heavily grazed and trampled grasslands and savannahs, especially on sandy plains and plateaus.

FOOD Harvester termites. The availability of the nocturnal *Trinervitermes* and the more diurnal *Hodotermes* may partly determine the times at which Aardwolves are active. Small numbers of scarab and tok-tockie beetles, grasshoppers, moths and a few small vertebrates are also eaten.

BEHAVIOUR Defended territories vary in extent (1–2km^2 in habitats with a high density of termite mounds).

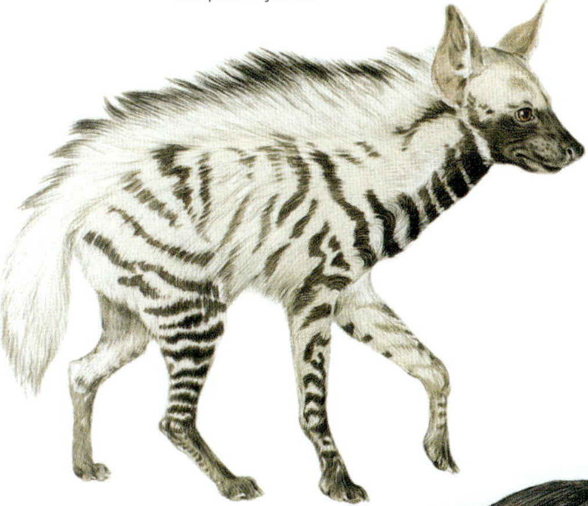

Striped Hyaena

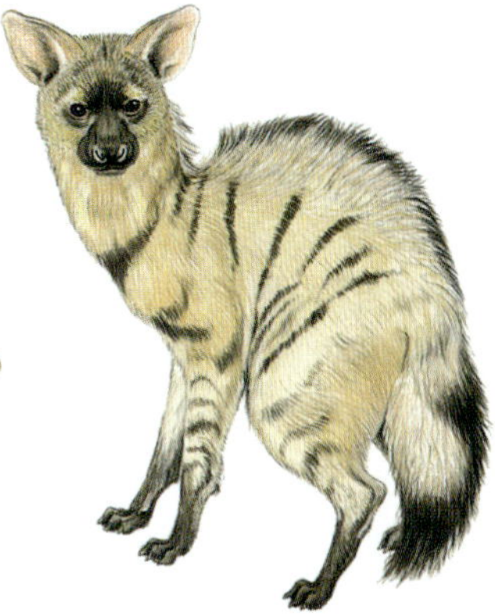

Aardwolf

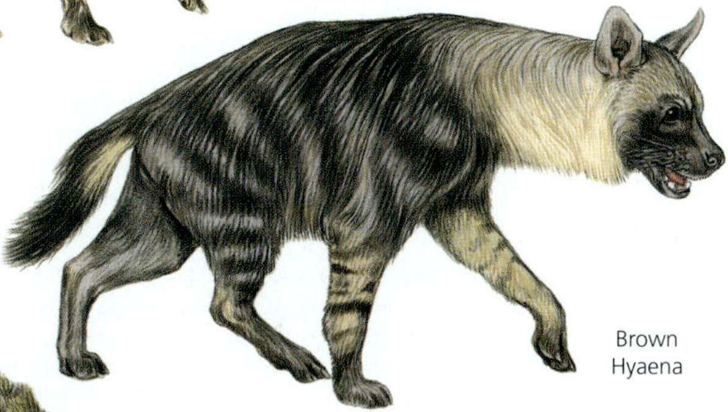

Brown Hyaena

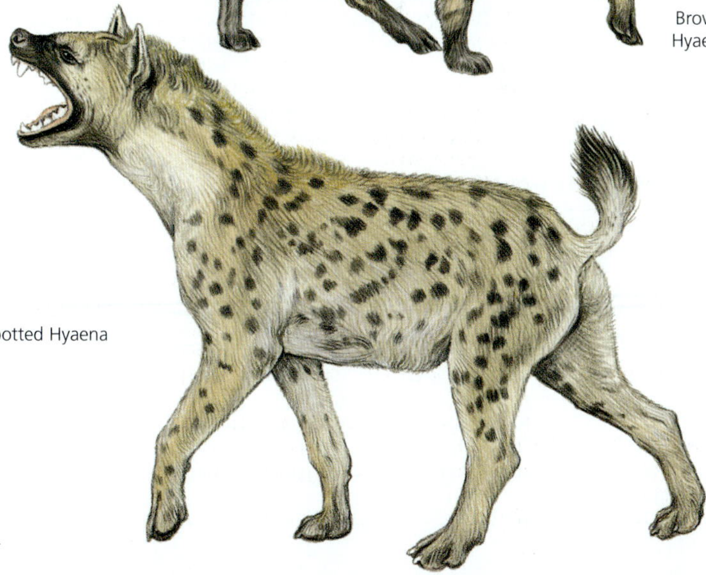

Spotted Hyaena

GENETS AND CIVETS Viverridae

Cat-like carnivores. Solitary foragers but some form short-lived family associations. Civets are almost wholly terrestrial; they are larger, coarse-furred, with blunt claws fixed in dog-like pads.

GENETS *Genetta*

Slender, long-bodied, cat-like carnivores. Predominantly arboreal, they have soft fur, retractile claws, a spotted or blotched coat pattern.

COMMON GENET *Genetta genetta* (and allies)

SIZE HB 40–55cm. T 40–51cm. W 1.3–2.25kg.
DESCRIPTION Rather coarse fur and a short crest along the spine. Ringed tail is nearly as long as the body and strongly tapered. The dark brown spots are small, numerous and linear on a sandy background. Differently coloured morphs (red or grey-black) co-exist in the same area.
HABITAT A wide range of drier habitats, from seasonally arid woodlands to sparsely bushed near-desert, especially rocky country. Can live without water.
FOOD Local vertebrates (rodents, birds or reptiles), invertebrates and fruits.

BLOTCHED GENET *Genetta tigrina* (incl. *maculata* and allies)

SIZE HB 40–55cm. T 40–54cm. W 1.2–3.1kg.
DESCRIPTION Soft-furred, short-legged without a well-defined dorsal crest.
HABITAT Most of sub-Saharan Africa except the Horn of Africa and SW Africa. Rainforest, riverine vegetation, secondary growth, moist woodlands and all moist forest and woodland mosaics.
FOOD Mainly rodents, but more invertebrates and fruits than Common Genet.

MIOMBO GENET *Genetta angolensis*

SIZE HB 44–48cm. T 38–43cm. W 1.3–2kg.
DESCRIPTION Dark grey or brownish with a dorsal crest and irregularly spotted coat. The underside of the paws and the feet are blackish. Face dark with contrasting white flashes below eyes and muzzle.
HABITAT Miombo (*Brachystegia*) woodlands from Angola to Tanzania, preference for the moister woodlands, riverine vegetation and forest galleries.
FOOD Rodents are likely to be the main staple; also invertebrates.

SERVALINE GENET *Genetta servalina*

SIZE HB 41–50cm. T 35–44cm. W 1–2kg.
DESCRIPTION Narrow face, rather long legs, very soft, dense, short fur and no dorsal crest (a short crest on the back of the neck may sometimes extend to the shoulders). Exclusively nocturnal.
HABITAT Rainforest, apparently absent from Upper Guinea. Both lowland and montane forests.
FOOD Ground-dwelling rodents, tree hyraxes, birds, insects and fruits have been recorded.

GIANT GENET *Genetta victoriae*

SIZE HB 55–60cm. T 45–50cm. W 2.5–3.5kg.
DESCRIPTION Dense soft fur, long legs and a fine, narrow muzzle. Black spots are very numerous (but subject to individual variation).
HABITAT NE Zaïre and W Uganda. Patchily distributed in forests, low and medium altitudes.
FOOD Birds, termites, oil palm seeds, carrion and fruits reported.

Common Genet

Blotched Genet

Miombo Genet
(Mozambique form)

Servaline Genet

Giant Genet

ETHIOPIAN GENET *Genetta abyssinica*

SIZE HB 40–50cm. T 40–45cm. W 1.3–2kg.
DESCRIPTION Pale, sandy with five black stripes running down the back. Fur short, fairly coarse and of uniform length. Forefeet distinguished by absence of fur between digit pads and 'palm'.
HABITAT Recorded from Red Sea coast to Ethiopian highlands in woodlands. Precise range and preferred habitats not yet known.
FOOD Presumed to resemble other genets.

HAUSA GENET *Genetta thierryi* *see* map above

SIZE HB 38–45cm. T 37–45cm. W 1.3–1.5kg.
DESCRIPTION Tan with blotchy spots following linear patterns down the back, often rich reddish orange. There is no crest and spotting is generally sparse on the face and forequarters.
HABITAT Sparsely distributed in drier savannahs from Guinea to Cameroon. Eastern limits uncertain.
FOOD Not known.

JOHNSTON'S GENET *Genetta johnstoni*

SIZE HB 40–52cm. T 40–54cm. W est. 1–3kg.
DESCRIPTION Thick soft coat. Large eyes and fine muzzle. Upperparts tawny with rows of spots down flanks and back (become larger and more regular as they approach midline). Short dorsal crest.
HABITAT Known from rainforest in Liberia and Guinea (also W Ivory Coast?).
FOOD Not recorded but likely to include soft-bodied insects.

AQUATIC GENET *Osbornictis piscivora*

SIZE HB 45–50cm. T 35–42cm. W est. 1.2–2.5kg.
DESCRIPTION Lightly built, densely furred unspotted genet with large, protuberant eyes, relatively small ears and a 'moustache' of conspicuous, downwardly deflected white whiskers.
HABITAT Shallow headwaters of streams (preferably clear and flowing over red clays and sands) within a forest type dominated by Limbali trees (*Gilbertiodendron*).
FOOD Fish, which are caught in the mouth with a very rapid strike. The long tail is black tipped, tapered and marked by incomplete dark rings which have a rich orange suffusion near the body but become darker towards the tip.

CENTRAL AFRICAN 'LINSANG' *Poiana richardsoni*

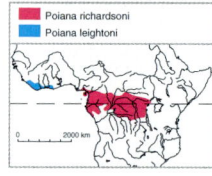

SIZE HB 33–38cm. T 35–40cm. W 500–700g.
DESCRIPTION Very slender, small-muzzled, small-eared, long-tailed genet but differs in dentition and skull.
HABITAT Rainforests. These nocturnal, highly arboreal linsangs are thought to move every few days, presumably on regular circuits, sleeping in nests during the day and rarely coming to the ground.
FOOD Arboreal vertebrates, invertebrates and fruits.

WEST AFRICAN 'LINSANG' *Poiana leightoni* *see* map above

SIZE HB 30–38cm. T 35–40cm. W est. 500–700g.
DESCRIPTION Very long, soft-furred tail, marked with dark asymmetrical chevrons (not parallel rings). Has small, sometimes irregular spots that are well spaced but a continuous black-brown line runs down the spine. The underside is unspotted and pure white.
HABITAT Only known from rainforest in E Liberia and W Ivory Coast, where it is reputed to live in tree crowns above 30m.
FOOD Young birds, insects and plant material, including kola fruits.

Ethiopian Genet

Hausa Genet

Johnston's Genet

Aquatic Genet

West African 'Linsang'

Central African 'Linsang'

AFRICAN CIVET *Civettictis civetta*

SIZE HB 68–95cm. T 40–53cm. W 7–20kg.
DESCRIPTION Shaggy, low-slung, dog-like animal with ornate pattern of bands and blotches on body and tail, black limbs and boldly marked face mask with pale forehead, white muzzle and black eye patches. Hair is coarse and loose, crest extends from forehead to tail tip. Mainly nocturnal. Normal gaits are a slow, tentative, low-headed walk or a steady trot. Very conspicuous dung middens called 'civettries', strongly scented with anal gland secretions. Independently scents landmarks in territories with large perineal glands. Normally silent but growls deeply and coughs explosively if harrassed. Eight named subspecies.
HABITAT Most abundant in forested or partly forested mosaics, in cultivated and marshy areas. It occurs only in dry, open country where dense cover grows along watercourses, around stone outcrops and in broken gullied land. Most often seen on well-established pathways.
FOOD Omnivorous: vertebrates and plants (mainly roots, shoots and fruits). Able to eat poisonous fruits, such as *Strychnos*, distasteful insects, such as stink locust (*Zonoceras*), millepedes and dangerous snakes. Also able to feed irregularly and can fast for up to 2 weeks. Prey either approached cautiously or disabled in sudden, rushing lunge. Vertebrates bitten deeply, shaken violently, then dropped. Kills prey up to the size of a hare or mongoose. Large prey torn into pieces and bolted.
BEHAVIOUR Solitary except while breeding. Probably territorial. Up to 4 young born after 60–72 days' gestation in burrow, crevice, termitary or in dense vegetation. Young develop quickly, begin to take solid food at 1 month and adopt adult behaviour at 5 months. Young 'freeze' until detected but hiss and spit when threatened. They make a soft, clucking contact note which persists into adulthood as a 3-note 'duff, duff, duff' contact call or courtship signal.

AFRICAN PALM CIVET Nandinidae

The African Palm Civet is the single survivor of a very ancient carnivore family distantly related to all the 'cat-like' Feliforms: viverrids, mongooses, hyaenids and cats.

AFRICAN PALM CIVET *Nandinia binotata*

SIZE HB 45–58cm. T 50–62cm. W 2–3.2kg.
DESCRIPTION Very inconspicuous. Mottled brown with long body and tail, well-clawed feet and distinctively textured soles to the hindlegs. The inner toes on all feet separated from other digits and function like thumbs during manipulation of foods or twigs. Strong, flexible limbs allow it to descend head down. Also drop spread-eagled from considerable heights. Two pale spots on the shoulders prominent. Olive-green eyes have a conspicuously vertical pupil. Arboreal. Two subspecies: *N. b. binotata* (main forest blocks), and *N. b. arborea* (E African isolates).
HABITAT Mainly rainforest but also flourishes in cultivation mosaics. This may be due to partiality for the fruits of colonising trees, such as the umbrella tree (*Musanga*), sugar plums (*Uapaca*), corkwood (*Myrianthus*) and wild figs.
FOOD The above-mentioned fruits, fleshy pulp of oil palms and numerous other fruits form seasonal staples. However, Palm Civets are omnivorous and highly opportunistic, catching roosting birds, nestlings, rodents, lizards, fruit bats and insects. They also take carrion. Prey stalked and pounced on, bitten repeatedly and bolted whole or in very large pieces. Become active shortly after nightfall, forage for about 4 hours, rest up and then forage again for 3–4 hours before dawn. Hide in a crevice or hole, where available, but more usually in a vine tangle, or even curled up in an exposed tree fork.
BEHAVIOUR Mainly solitary but home ranges overlap extensively, with 12 or more animals using a common resource, such as a grove of fruiting trees. Up to 4 young are born in a hollow tree after a 2-month gestation.

African Civet

African Palm Civet

sketches of African Palm Civets

SERVAL *Felis serval*

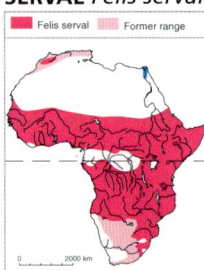

SIZE HB 67–100cm. T 24–35cm. W 11kg (6–12.5kg) (female), 13kg (10–18kg) (male).

DESCRIPTION Tall, spotted cat with very large ears, a small muzzle and shortish tail. In SW Uganda and E Zaïre finely freckled Servals can be nearly as common as the more widespread, bold-spotted morph (both occur in the same litter). Various forms of melanic Serval through to all-black animals also occur.

HABITAT Grass savannahs, subalpine and montane mosaics of moorland, forest and glades. Abundant along the margins of forest galleries, reedbeds and marshes.

FOOD Wide range of small mammals, birds, reptiles and insects; occasionally fruits. Grass-dwelling rodents are the main prey and times when local rodents are active strongly influence hunting patterns. High leaps or springs, with a powerful downward strike by the claws, are employed against larger prey, such as young antelopes and snakes as well as rodents. The Serval plucks birds and hares, and typical 'play' or tossing often changes imperceptibly into deliberate plucking. It will cache parts of a larger prey, returning later to uncover and consume it. Prey is sometimes disembowelled and the viscera left uneaten.

BEHAVIOUR Has small, defended core territories but shares much larger areas (from 2 to 30km^2) with other Servals.

CARACAL *Felis caracal*

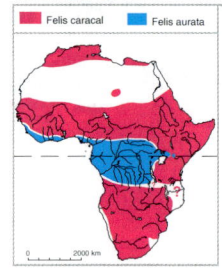

SIZE HB 62–91cm. T 18–34cm. W 8–13kg (female), 12–19kg (male).

DESCRIPTION Colour varies by region, age, stage of moult and wear and tear, but generally with a reddish fawn coat variably frosted with a fine grey freckle. Sometimes melanistic. Muzzle is exceptionally short and small for such a tall cat but powerful jaw muscles underlie the broad cheeks and rounded face.

HABITAT Plains and rocky hills in country with a short wet season and limited grass cover. *Acacia* and *Commiphora* woodlands, thickets and Karoo scrub are preferred.

FOOD Depending on the locality, hyraxes, hares, small monkeys, antelopes and rodents make up the bulk of the diet. Birds such as partridges and doves are locally and seasonally important. Reptiles and fruits may also be occasional foods. The Caracal stalks its prey to within range of its prodigiously long and fast bounds or spring, which is powered by disproportionately long and muscular hindlegs.

BEHAVIOUR Mostly solitary, forms pairs or small mother–young groups for the period of mating and rearing. Repertoire of growls, spits, hisses and miaows but also a highly distinctive coughing call during breeding season.

GOLDEN CAT *Felis aurata* see map above

SIZE HB 61–101.5cm. T 16–46cm. W 5.5–18kg (males heaviest).

DESCRIPTION Powerful, with even limb proportions, a heavy muzzle and small, black-backed ears. Adult sizes are very variable, as is the proportion of the tail. Colour and pattern are also varied, the background colour from red or yellow to smoky grey. All have boldly spotted bellies and inner limb fur, but spots range from fine freckles to large rosettes, from faint to bold, and from partial to overall. Before all this variation was understood, many races and species were described.

HABITAT Mostly in lowland forest zone; also in secondary vegetation along rivers in outlying areas. Also at high altitudes in several mountainous areas in moorland, bamboo and montane forest.

FOOD Duikers, monkeys, rodents and birds. In the Ruwenzori Mts, feeds mainly on rats, hyraxes and Red Duikers. Francolins and guinea fowl are also commonly taken.

BEHAVIOUR Has been observed repeatedly dashing up trees and down again which suggests that it may rely less upon leopard-like ambushes and more upon exceptional alertness and quick dashes.

Serval

Caracal

Golden Cat

SCALY ANT-EATERS Pholidota

Highly specialised scaly ant-eaters, pangolins are typified by long, very muscular tails and horny scales, which are cornified extrusions of the outer skin (or enlargements of the miniature scales that cover many rodent and insectivore tails).

PANGOLINS Manidae

LONG-TAILED PANGOLIN *Uromanis tetradactyla*

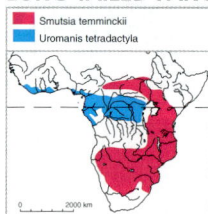

SIZE HB 30–40cm. T 55–80cm. W 2.2–3.25kg.
DESCRIPTION Small, arboreal, with a very long tail and black face and underparts. The muzzle is naked and pointed. Active by day but very wary and difficult to spot.
HABITAT Very localised; never far from permanent water and watercourses. Sleeps in tree hollows or in hollowed-out insect nests.
FOOD Tree ant species that occur in swampy areas.
BEHAVIOUR Uses habitual routes and sleeping-holes in a well-known home range.

TREE PANGOLIN *Phataginus tricuspis*

SIZE HB 25–43cm. T 35–62cm. W 1.6–3kg.
DESCRIPTION Has very numerous, thin scales, resembling fir-cone scales in texture but with serrated ('3-cusped') points. Tail is tipped with a sensitive, thumb-like pad.
HABITAT All through lowland rainforest block (and outliers) but especially favours secondary growth.
FOOD Mainly termite species that are mostly found on the ground; also ants. Most foraging is on the surface and in leaf litter. The tail sometimes helps sweep insects within range of the flickering tongue. Predominantly nocturnal.
BEHAVIOUR Adult females highly sedentary and sleep in self-dug holes used for long periods. Forage within overlapping home ranges of some 3 or 4ha. Adult males more nomadic.

GIANT PANGOLIN *Smutsia gigantea*

SIZE HB 75–100cm. T 50–70cm. W 30–35kg.
DESCRIPTION Largest pangolin. Powerfully built with precise geometric pattern of brunette scales which darken and change both texture and shape with age. The hindlegs leave prints that resemble those of a small elephant. At the front, weight is taken on the wrist, with long sharp claws folded inwards and facing to the rear. The tail, unlike that of the Ground Pangolin, often leaves a heavy drag mark.
HABITAT Forest and forest mosaics but survives in secondary grasslands. Totally water dependent.
FOOD Termites and ants. Other insects and larvae are also taken. Even water-beetles (*Dytiscidae*) are licked off the surface of pools (it is an able swimmer).
BEHAVIOUR Solitary. Individuals have been known to inhabit a very limited locality for up to 2 years but their seasonal and overall ranges are poorly known.

GROUND PANGOLIN *Smutsia temminckii* see map above

SIZE HB 34–61cm. T 31–50cm. W 7–18kg (males up to 50% heavier than females).
DESCRIPTION Rotund with broad, rounded scales and heavy, graviportal hindlegs. Very broad, relatively short tail.
HABITAT High- and low-rainfall areas with both sandy and rocky soils, in woodlands, savannahs and grasslands. The main determinant is an abundance of ants and termites of a few specific types.
FOOD Mainly ants.
BEHAVIOUR Although capable of digging a burrow, prefers to use natural shelters or disused holes of other species.

Long-tailed Pangolin

Tree Pangolin

Giant Pangolin

Ground Pangolin

AFROTHERIA (superorder)
Ancient radiation of uniquely African mammals that evolved during Africa's continental isolation (100–50MYA). The Aardvark, elephants, sea-cows, hyraxes, elephant shrews, otter shrews and golden moles all share the genetic markers for Afrotheria.

AARDVARK Tubulidentata
The modern aardvark is distinguished by many peculiarities, notably in the teeth, which lack enamel and are composed of densely packed tubules surrounded by columns of dentine, the whole tooth being contained in a sleeve of dental cement. These peg-like molar teeth are at the back of a slender, toothless snout.

AARDVARK Orycteropodidae

AARDVARK *Orycteropus afer*

SIZE HB 100–158cm. T 44–63cm. H 58–66cm. W 40–82kg.

DESCRIPTION The Aardvark's long nose, squared-off head and tapered tail are rather delicately built extensions in comparison with the massive body and the muscular limbs, which are armed with great, nailed digits. The fur on many old individuals can become heavily abraded but young animals are well furred. The Aardvark is a shy nocturnal animal and rarely seen. Its burrows, spade-like scratchings and tracks are more commonly seen than the animal itself. The snout is not at all pig-like, being soft, mobile, rounded and furry, with dense hair around the nostrils (see detail opposite).

HABITAT Patchily distributed in a large part of sub-Saharan Africa with past extensions down the Nile valley and Hoggar/Tassili Mts. The Aardvark is normally rare or absent in rainforest. It is found in areas with a year-round abundance of ants, termites and beetle larvae. The earth that is preferred for digging warrens may be some distance from foraging areas so nightly walks between the two are normal in some localities. Very hard or stony soils and regularly flooded areas are avoided. In highly stratified hills the Aardvark may select a particular stratum for its more regularly used warrens. Temporary 'camping' holes of only a few metres in length are more frequent than the much longer warren complexes, which can have 8 or more entrances and descend as deep as 6m.

FOOD Termites, ants and larvae are foraged for at night, beginning an hour or two after dusk. Most food is found on or very close to the surface but subterranean termitaries, ants' nests and beetle caches may be extensively excavated. However, the colonies of social insects are seldom entirely destroyed (the deterrent is probably a critical concentration of defending soldiers). Insects are swept into the small mouth by the long, sticky tongue.

BEHAVIOUR Solitary, but females sometimes accompanied by one or two young. Large warrens may be used by more than two or three animals. The only recorded sounds are a grunt and, in extreme fear, a bleat. The Aardvark lives up to 18 years.

GOLDEN MOLES Chrysochloridae
A very ancient and little-known group of subterranean mammals with shiny coats of very dense fur and streamlined, formless appearance. All have a blunt, bare nose, digging forelegs, with one or more greatly enlarged claws, and less developed hindlegs. They have no visible eyes, ears or tails. They live in various habitats. Some have been seen to catch food on the surface but most species obtain the greater part of their invertebrate diet underground. They make various types of molehills and subsurface tunnels that betray their presence. They should not be confused with root-rats, or blesmols, which are rodents.

Aardvark

Detail of Aardvark nose

Stuhlmann's Golden Mole
Chrysochloris stuhlmanni

GOLDEN MOLES Chrysochloridae

Subterranean mammals with shiny coats of dense fur. Streamlined, formless appearance. Blunt, bare noses, digging forelegs, with enlarged claws, less developed hindlegs. All feed on invertebrates.

NARROW-HEADED GOLDEN MOLES *Amblysomus* (4 species)

SIZE HB 10–13cm. W 21–75g.
DESCRIPTION Long body and a small, narrow head. Hair bases are grey.
HABITAT *A. gunningi* only known from one montane locality. *A. julianae* localised in drier uplands.

YELLOW GOLDEN MOLE *Calcochloris obtusirostris*

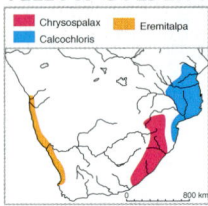

SIZE HB 97–108mm. W 20–30g.
DESCRIPTION Long-bodied with variably coloured upper surfaces but yellow underfur.
HABITAT Light sandy soils and dunes in S Mozambique and vicinity.

FORTY-TOOTHED GOLDEN MOLES *Chlorotalpa* (5 species)

SIZE HB 95–138mm. W 40–75g.
DESCRIPTION Compact, rounded skull and metallic sheen.
HABITAT Dry sandy soils from Somalia and Angola to South Africa.

CAPE GOLDEN MOLES *Chrysochloris* (3 species)

SIZE HB 98–110mm. W est. 25–35g.
DESCRIPTION Expanded, rounded back to skull. A long second claw.
HABITAT Cape Province and central and E African montane highlands.

GIANT GOLDEN MOLES *Chrysospalax* (2 species)   see map above

SIZE HB 148–230mm. W 125–538g.
DESCRIPTION 'Double-hull' structure over brain-case caused by expanded cheekbones.
HABITAT Deep soils in E Cape (*C. trevelyani*). Borders of marshes in SE Africa (*C. villosus*).

CRYPTIC GOLDEN MOLES *Cryptochloris* (2 species)   see map above

SIZE HB 79–90mm. W est. 20–30g.
DESCRIPTION Rounded forehead and skull. Silvery sheen with grey, white and fawn hairs.
HABITAT Sand dunes at Port Nolloth and Companies Drift, W Cape.

DESERT GOLDEN MOLE *Eremitalpa granti*   see map above

SIZE HB 76–86mm. W 16–30g.
DESCRIPTION Pale silvery fur and disproportionately large head. Three thin claws of equal length.
HABITAT Sand dunes along the Namib coastline, preferring areas of dune-grass.

Giant Golden mole
Chrysospalax villosus

Golden mole skull shapes and proportions

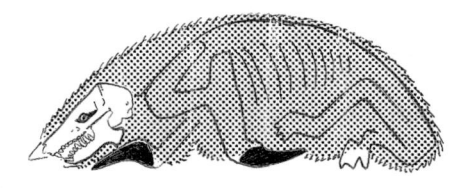

Narrow-headed Golden mole
Amblysomus hottentottus

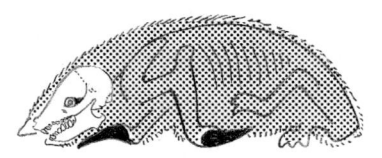

Cape Golden mole
Chrysochloris asiatica

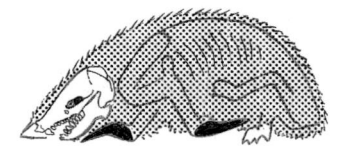

Yellow Golden mole
Calcochloris obtusirostris

Cryptic Golden mole
Cryptochloris wintoni

Forty-toothed Golden mole
Chlorotalpa duthiae

Desert Golden mole
Eremitalpa granti

ELEPHANT SHREWS or SENGIS Macroscelidea

Mouse- or rat-sized animals with large eyes and ears, slender limbs and a long, bare tail. They have a long, tubular snout protruding from a strongly tapered skull bearing 50–60 teeth. Most species are brownish and some have bold markings on the face or back.

SOFT-FURRED ELEPHANT SHREWS or SENGIS Macroscelidinae

Fine-boned and soft-furred, these are superficial surface-gleaners of small invertebrates (also fruits and seeds) in shaded but dry environments.

LESSER ELEPHANT SHREWS *Elephantulus* (10 species)

SIZE Total length 210–280mm. W 25–70g.
DESCRIPTION Mouse-sized, naked-tailed with large eyes and ears, a fine-pointed proboscis and long hindlegs. There are rings of white or paler fur around the eyes. Coat colour often closely matches local soil colour.
HABITAT Relatively dry but seasonal, bushy or scrubby habitats are preferred. Minimise exposing themselves to predation by remaining under vegetation and rocks and only crossing open ground at high speed. Some species dig burrows; others maintain conspicuous paths which are daily cleared of litter by scuffling with the legs; yet others use vacant rodent holes.
FOOD A wide range of invertebrates, pounced upon in leaf litter (and near the dung piles of herbivores). Some species occasionally eat fruits and seeds. Rapid daily traverses along pathways in small, well-known territories serve to exclude trespassers and rehearse rapid escape from predators. However, the main function of such runs is to gather food.
BEHAVIOUR Both males and females exclude their own sex from territories but may tolerate adult-sized offspring in home ranges of 0.25–0.6ha. Territorial displays involve fluffing out the fur and strutting on tip-toe (which displays the white or contrasting colour of the legs and underside). Very intense, rapid activity is followed by long periods of quiescence in well-concealed, shady observation posts. All species are predominantly or wholly diurnal and several sun-bathe before becoming fully active. Communicate with squeaky calls and by drumming the hindlegs.

FOUR-TOED ELEPHANT SHREW *Petrodromus tetradactylus*

Petrodromus tetradactylus
Macroscelides proboscideus

SIZE HB 165–220mm. T 130–180mm. W 150–280g.
DESCRIPTION Brown, rat-sized with a large head and ears and conspicuous facial markings. Legs are light coloured and very slender, with only four toes.
HABITAT Mainly in dense evergreen undergrowth in caesalpinoid forests, woodlands and thickets.
FOOD Mainly ants and termites; also crickets, grasshoppers and other litter invertebrates.
BEHAVIOUR Most active in the early morning and evening, scuffling litter to find food. Rapping of the hindlegs is presumed to be a territorial advertisement and alarm signal.

ROUND-EARED ELEPHANT SHREW *Macroscelides proboscideus* see map above

SIZE HB 105–115mm. T 114–130mm. W 31–47g.
DESCRIPTION Grizzled, mouse-sized with rounded, hairy ears, small eyes and a short muzzle. Colour varies from grey to buff or brown.
HABITAT Areas of low Karoo scrub in SW African arid zone.
FOOD Ants and termites.

Rufous Elephant Shrew
Elephantulus rufescens

Four-toed Elephant Shrew
Petrodromus tetradactylus

Round-eared Elephant Shrew
Macroscelides proboscideus

Sketches of Rufous Elephant Shrew

GIANT ELEPHANT SHREWS Rhynchocyoninae

Elegant, long-legged animals the size of a large rat with a long, naked, white-tipped tail and a very long, tapering snout. The proboscis protrudes well beyond the mouth (which is inconspicuous, as are the very rapid movements of the long, tapered tongue). Their pungent smell derives from a gland behind the anus. They favour moister habitats where they feed on relatively cryptic invertebrates (larvae, termites, ants, beetles, spiders, myriapods and earthworms), which they find by noisily turning over litter and soil with their paws and well-reinforced but flexible nose.

They require relatively well-drained soils and abundant dry leaf litter in order to construct their 1m-wide leaf-mound shelters, which are piled over shallow, body-sized scoops in the soil. Each animal makes and maintains 10 or more such retreats in its territory. They serve as the night-rests of these exclusively diurnal animals, as nurseries for the young and occasional day-time refuges. Constructed in the early morning, when leaves are damp, limp and compressible (and the sound of raking and tamping them is muffled), they provide concealment from a variety of predators. The presence of the right conditions for the building of dry, comfortable leaf mounds is probably the single most important requisite for giant elephant shrews. Territories average 1.7ha.

A broad, compressed skull and ground-hugging crouch allow these animals to occupy very little space within their leaf mounds, where they sleep in a posture that leaves them ready for instant action. Physiologically they appear well adapted to digest toxic or difficult foods, such as ants and myriapods. However, some millipedes may be taken less frequently or avoided. That these animals show relatively little change over some 30 million years suggests that their micro-habitats, and the niches they occupy within them, must have retained a remarkable degree of stability.

CHEQUERED ELEPHANT SHREW *Rhynchocyon cirnei*

Rhynchocyon cirnei
Rhynchocyon petersi
Rhynchocyon chrysopygus

SIZE HB 235–315mm. T 190–263mm. W 408–440g.
DESCRIPTION The back is marked with a complex pattern of longitudinal dark bands on an agouti-grizzled background with pale (even white) spots or flecks. In the humid Zaïre basin and mountains north of L. Nyasa (formerly L. Malawi) this pattern becomes difficult to see because the overall colour becomes very dark. In SE Tanzania and Mozambique the pattern is very variable, with suffusions of orange-red and black that could suggest long-term hybridisation with the black and red Zanj Elephant Shrew.
HABITAT Forests and gallery forests at low, medium and high altitudes. *R. c. reichardi* (with colouring that closely resembles a grass-mouse) inhabits grassland during the wet season, only retreating into galleries or relict forest patches in the dry season.
FOOD As other species but grasshoppers and caterpillars are important for some races.

ZANJ ELEPHANT SHREW *Rhynchocyon petersi* *see* map above

SIZE HB 235–315mm. T 190–263mm. W 408–440g.
DESCRIPTION Forequarters orange, graduating to deep red with black rump. Tail orange with white tip.
HABITAT Coastal and montane forest and thickets in E Tanzania and the Kenya coast.
FOOD Cryptic invertebrates in leaf litter.

GOLDEN-RUMPED ELEPHANT SHREW *Rhynchocyon chrysopygus* *see* map above

SIZE HB 235–315mm. T 190–263mm. W 408–440g.
DESCRIPTION The dark body graduates to a metallic yellow rump. The neck is russet and the forehead and face are tawny agouti. Vestigial traces of a spotted pattern similar to that of the Chequered Elephant Shrew are obvious in juveniles and just perceptible in some adults. Thickened skin under the golden rump suggests that damaging bites or slashes inflicted during territorial fights and flights may be targeted on this rump shield.
HABITAT Confined to two very small areas of the Kenya coast where it lives in dry evergreen thickets.
FOOD Grasshoppers and crickets, beetles, spiders, millipedes, ants, centipedes, earthworms and termites (in order of preference).

Chequered Elephant Shrew

Zanj Elephant Shrew

Golden-rumped Elephant Shrew

OTTER SHREWS Tenrecidae, Potamogalinae

These are aquatic animals whose distribution is very restricted. They differ from many small mammals in lacking collar bones. They have a flattened muzzle in which very numerous and stiff vibrissae are embedded. Each whisker is served by nerves and most food is thought to be found by touch, while hunting underwater. Two fused toes on the hindfoot act as combs and are used in frequent and thorough grooming of their waterproof fur.

Of the three potamogales the Giant Otter Shrew has adapted furthest towards a wholly aquatic existence. The tail vertebrae and muscles are larger and more powerful than those in the lumbar area. It is also quite clumsy on land. When harassed it hisses and strikes rather like a snake, and this resemblance may well protect it from some enemies. A metallic lustre to the fur also enhances its reptilian appearance. All species make short but frequent dives with very small animals eaten in the water, but larger prey is brought onto land for killing and eating.

Potamogales are the last relics of a very ancient group of mammals. The exploitation of very peculiar or localised niches seems to have saved them from direct competition from more advanced mammals, such as otters or mongooses. Any appreciable modification of their habitats, whether natural or artificial, is likely to result in their extirpation.

GIANT OTTER SHREW *Potamogale velox*

SIZE HB 29–35cm. T 4.5–9cm. W est. 300–950g.
DESCRIPTION Aquatic mammal with a brown back and white underside. The broad, flat snout is covered in bristles. Flat shields cover the nostrils. The fur is generally very dense and soft but is short and silky on the bladed tail. Vertical flattening of the tail allows a fish-like, side-to-side swimming motion.
HABITAT Rivers within the main forest block from Nigeria to W Kenya. The Giant Otter Shrew occurs in large, fast-flowing rivers, as well as streams, sluggish coastal rivers and swamps. It retreats to burrows and crevices on the riverbank to rest and breed.
FOOD Freshwater crabs, fish, frogs, insects and water molluscs caught in the water at night.

MOUNT NIMBA OTTER SHREW *Micropotamogale lamottei*   see map above

SIZE HB 12–15cm. T 10–20cm. W est. 60–90g.
DESCRIPTION A small, soft-furred, aquatic mammal, uniformly grey-brown in colour, with a slender, rat-like tail. The feet lack any trace of webbing.
HABITAT Waters in the vicinity of Mt. Nimba; montane streams, small rivers, swamps and ditches in surrounding forests, forest–savannah–cultivation mosaics.
FOOD Crabs, fish and insects, mostly hunted at night in the water.

RUWENZORI OTTER SHREW *Mesopotamogale ruwenzorii*   see map above

SIZE HB 12.3–20cm. T 10–15cm. W est. 130–150g.
DESCRIPTION Soft-furred, aquatic mammal with a broad, whiskered nose and minuscule eyes and ears. It is dark brown above and white below. Hands and feet are partially webbed. The tail is slightly flattened vertically.
HABITAT Waters flowing off the Ruwenzori and Kivu massifs; also likely to occur in Itombwe and has been recorded from montane and lowland streams flowing through forest, savannah and cultivation. Digs burrows in riverbanks.
FOOD Worms, insect larvae, small crabs, fish, frogs and tadpoles caught at night in water.

Giant Otter Shrew

Mount Nimba Otter Shrew

Ruwenzori Otter Shrew

HYRAXES Hyracoidea

Hyraxes are small, woolly animals with no visible tail and blunt 'hoofed' digits. Although superficially similar to rodents, they are more closely related to elephant shrews and elephants, and are placed in an order of their own.

HYRAXES Procavidae

Three genera show few easily observable external differences: all are rabbit-sized, woolly and brown, with large-mouthed, deep-jawed heads and rubbery, blunt-fingered hands and feet. Skull and teeth remain the most reliable guide to genera, but each occupies a different niche with a distinct diet and each species has loud and highly distinctive vocalisations. Mainly diurnal.

ROCK HYRAXES *Procavia* (5 species)

SIZE HB 38–60cm. W 1.8–5.5kg.

DESCRIPTION These blunt-faced hyraxes vary in colour both regionally and individually but are generally brown with a paler underside. Species: Cape Rock Hyrax, *P. capensis* (S and SW Africa): black dorsal patch. Ethiopian Rock Hyrax, *P. habessinica* (NE Africa and Arabia): variable dorsal patch. Black-necked Rock Hyrax, *P. johnstoni* (central and E Africa): variable dorsal patch. Kaokoveld Rock Hyrax, *P. welwitchii* (Kaokoveld): pale cream dorsal patch. Red-headed Rock Hyrax, *P. ruficeps* (S Sahara): orange dorsal patch.
HABITAT Mainly rock outcroppings, often in areas where the rocks themselves assist the growth of vegetation by trapping moisture or nutrients.
FOOD Mainly grasses and herbs within easy reach of shelter. Shrubs and trees are also browsed.
BEHAVIOUR Territorial, with single male territories containing up to 25 females and offspring.

BUSH HYRAXES *Heterohyrax* (3 species)

SIZE HB 32–57cm. W 2–3.5kg.

DESCRIPTION Relatively small with conspicuous pale 'eyebrows', a white or off-white underside and a greyish, pepper-and-salt agouti body colour. The snout is more pointed than that of the Rock Hyrax and the animal is altogether more lightly built. Species: Yellow-spotted Hyrax, *H. brucei* (S, E and NE Africa and the Sinai): yellow dorsal spot. Hoggar Hyrax, *H. antinae* (Hoggar Massif): small, with mane but no spot. Matadi Hyrax, *H. chapini* (mouth of the R Zaïre): a large muzzle and brows.
HABITAT Wooded localities on riverbanks, escarpments and rock outcrops. Normally shelters in rocks but may resort to trees or old burrows.
FOOD Leaves, fruits, stems, twigs and bark.
BEHAVIOUR Single colonies can number up to 34 individuals. They utter sustained 5-minute bouts of loud calls, less resonant and deep than that of other hyraxes.

TREE HYRAXES *Dendrohyrax* (3, probably 5 species)

Dendrohyrax validus
Dendrohyrax arboreus
Dendrohyrax dorsalis

SIZE HB 32–60cm. W 1.5–4.5kg.

DESCRIPTION Densely furred, arboreal hyraxes with elongated hands and feet, mostly dark (although pale, cream-coloured morphs are known). Species: Eastern Tree Hyrax, *D. validus* (eastern mountains, islands, coast): naked patch 20–40mm long and dorsal fur russet-coloured. Southern Tree Hyrax, *D. arboreus* (S, E and central Africa): naked patch 23–30mm long and dorsal fur cream–coloured. Western Tree Hyrax, *D. dorsalis* (W and central Africa): naked patch 42–72mm long and dorsal fur white.
HABITAT Forests, moist savannahs, evergreen thickets and mosaics. In higher mountains partially diurnal, in lower forests they are nocturnal and more solitary.
FOOD Leaves, fruits and twigs in the canopy, grasses and sedges on screes. Giant groundsel and numerous aromatic leaves and herbs.
BEHAVIOUR Often live at very high densities. Territorial and aggressive during the mating season.

Black-necked Rock Hyrax
(Mt Kenya race)

*Detail of Rock Hyrax
(Procavia johnstoni) skull*

Yellow-spotted Bush Hyrax

*Detail of Bush Hyrax
(Heterohyrax brucei) skull*

Detail of Eastern Tree Hyrax (Dendrohyrax validus) skull

Eastern Tree Hyrax

*Detail of Southern Tree Hyrax
(D. arboreus) skull*

Southern Tree Hyrax

Detail of Western Tree Hyrax (Dendrohyrax dorsalis) skull

Western Tree Hyrax

ELEPHANTS Elephantidae

AFRICAN ELEPHANT *Loxodonta africana* (probably 2 species)

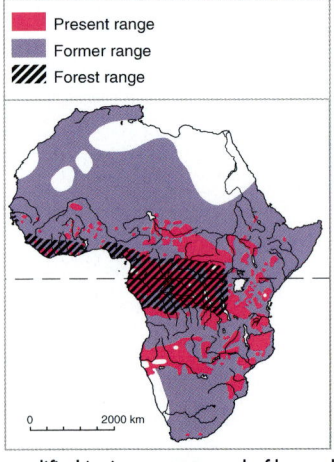

- Present range
- Former range
- Forest range

SIZE Bush Elephant, *L. a. africana*: HB (unstable measure). T 1–1.5m. SH 2.4–3.4m (female), 3–4m (male). W 2,200–3,500kg (female), 4,000–6,300kg (male).
Forest (Pygmy) Elephant, *L. a. cyclotis*: HB (unstable measure). T 0.5–1.2 m. SH 1.6–2.4m (female), 1.7–2.8m (male). W 900–3,000kg (female), 1,200–3,500kg (male).

DESCRIPTION The largest land animals, elephants are easily identifiable in having a trunk, tusks, large ears and pillar-like legs. Their thick skin is only superficially pigmented and the intensity of the melanin layer varies from a dense black to pale grey, brown or, in rare instances, depigmented pink (in patches or overall). Newborn elephants are often very hairy and adults retain coarse, short bristles on the trunk, chin and, as abraded remnants, in the crevices over much of the rest of the body. The large, round ears are not only sound-catching dishes and flagging devices but also a cooling mechanism. The backs of the ears are laced with blood vessels which help to reduce the elephant's overall body temperature when the ears are fanned. The tusks are modified incisors composed of layered dentine and their presence or absence, size, shape, orientation and microstructure are subject to much variation.

The feet are columnar with the original five toes bound into a hoop of tissue, skin and nail above a cushion of elastic tissue. Nails vary from 5 on both fore- and hindfeet to 4 on the forefeet and 3 on the hindfeet, the latter being the norm in Bush Elephants. The smooth but cracked foot pads leave individually recognisable tracks, circular for the forefeet, smaller and more elongated for the hindfeet. Tracks, frequent boluses, occasional urine puddles and extensive harvesting of plants are the most commonly seen signs of elephants.

Trunks are capable of powerful twisting and coiling while gathering food or wrestling with other elephants but can also perform delicate movements, such as picking berries, rubbing eyes or exploring orifices. Trunks can draw up columns of water or dust and their great length can reach up to 7m or burrow down into sand, soil or crevices to reach deeply hidden water.

Subspecies: Bush Elephant, *L. a. africana*; Forest (Pygmy) Elephant, *L. a. cyclotis*.

Because successful adaptation to peculiar ecological conditions depends upon long-maintained family traditions, elephants readily evolve subpopulations. These can show consistent characteristics in size, ear shape, limb proportions, skull and tusk shape, number of nails, skin texture and colour. As a result 25 subspecies have been proposed.

The Forest Elephant *L. a. cyclotis* has recently been shown to be genetically distinct from the Bush Elephant and is probably a different species.

HABITAT Formerly most of Africa except the driest regions of the Sahara. The ability to forage as far as 80km from water greatly augmented their overall range in otherwise marginal areas.

FOOD: Grass and browse are taken in different and changing proportions by season. Elephants consume about 5% of their body weight (i.e. up to 300kg) in 24 hours and vegetation takes about 12 hours to pass through the animal.

BEHAVIOUR: The central social unit in elephant society is the mother and her offspring. Female elephants are not able to conceive until 8 years of age (20 at latest) but once they become mothers they soon become unit leaders, or 'matriarchs'. Gestation lasts 650–660 days and 1, very rarely 2, young are born, with a slight peak of births in the rains. Although they rise to their feet within hours, newborn elephants are visibly unsteady for several weeks (a feebleness that attracts lions and hyaenas). Mothers are alert to all their infant's needs, helping it over all manner of obstacles with trunk and feet. Elephants are thought to live no longer than 65 years.

Bush Elephant

Forest Elephant

ODD-TOED UNGULATES Perissodactyla
HORSES Equidae
AFRICAN HORSES *Equus*

Partially or wholly striped, these large grazing animals have a short, sleek coat. All have a big, long head, with large, flat chewing muscles over deeply rooted tooth rows. The neck is muscular and maned and the body is compact with a deep chest and very muscular haunches. The legs are strong and bony, with hard, single hooves. Horses can be very vocal, with a variety of neighs, barks or brays, squeals and whinnies.

COMMON ZEBRA *Equus quagga* — see plate 87

SIZE HB 217–246cm. T 47–57cm. SH 127–140cm. W 175–250kg (female), 220–322kg (male).

DESCRIPTION A muscular horse with relatively short neck and sturdy legs. The stripes are subject to much regional and individual variation. Patterns are better illustrated than described (see opposite and overleaf).

HABITAT Grasslands, steppes, savannahs and woodlands. These zebras are totally dependent on frequent drinking. They prefer firm ground underfoot so may move off sumplands in the wet season or during flooding.

FOOD Grass of the most available species. Adaptable grazers, they mow short lawns close to the roots but are equally able to take taller flowering grasses. Water shortage may concentrate zebra populations around available waterholes during the dry season. Daily activity is dominated by shifts from open night-time resting areas to pastures, to water and back to sleep or rest.

BEHAVIOUR Up to 6 females and their young live in very stable 'harems' where they are subject to low-key but continuous coercion by the harem stallion. He herds the females in his group whenever they stray and threatens males that come too close. The number of females appears to be limited by the intolerance of established females against incomers.

Common Zebras are extremely vocal, the adult males being particularly noisy during any nocturnal movement. For each social unit the stallion's individual 'song' (a glottal, barking bray) becomes the focal point for all harem members. Individuals which become separated from their group seek it with every sign of distress while the stallion too calls and searches until the group is reunited. Normally only harem stallions mate with harem mares but neighbours and bachelor groups show intense interest in any oestrous females. One foal (rarely 2) is born after a 12-month gestation. Foals suck milk for up to 6 months but begin to graze in the first month. They are sexually mature by 1½–3 years but females cycle without conceiving for a year or two and males seldom acquire harems before 5 years of age. Common Zebras are known to live for 40 years.

Equus q. quagga
E.q. burchelli
E.q. crawshayi
E.q. crawshayi x boehmi
E.q. boehmi
E.q. antiquorum
E.q. selousi

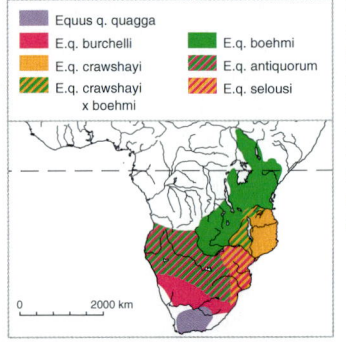

Subspecies: These form 3 regional foci with intermediate variable types coming from very extensive interzones. A fourth type, the Quagga, is extinct (possibly a distinct species). There are 4 major populations: (a) *E. q. quagga* (Cape, Karoo), extinct; (b) *E. q. burchelli* (NE Cape); (c) *E. q. crawshayi* (SE Africa), tropical; (d) *E. q. boehmi* (central and E Africa). Intermediate or variable populations: (b × d) *E. q. antiquorum* (subtropical SW Africa); (b × c) *E. q. selousi* (SE Africa), subtropical. Intermediates between c and d occur in Rukwa/Usangu area.

E. q. boehmi

Intermediate *crawshayi* × *boehmi* (from Rukwa/Usanga)

E. q. antiquorum

E. q. crawshayi

E. q. burchelli

E. q. selousi

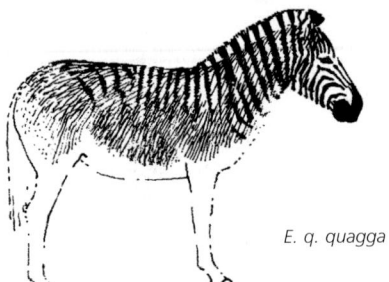

E. q. quagga

MOUNTAIN ZEBRA *Equus zebra* (possibly 2 species)

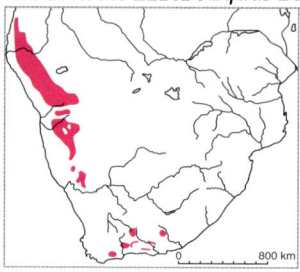

SIZE HB 220–260cm. T 40–55cm. SH 146cm (115–150cm). W 275kg (230–320kg) (female), 300kg (250–386kg) (male).
DESCRIPTION Evenly spaced, vertical, black and white stripes on neck and body with a sudden 'change of scale' to 3 or 4 very bold, horizontal stripes on hindquarters. The body stripes extend into an enclosed 'grid-iron' pattern on the rump and upper tail. The legs have fine, even, black and white striping. Black stripes on the face graduate to orange-brown on the bridge of the nose and around the mouth and nostrils (which are dark brown). The ears are moderately long and broad, their backs marked with bold black and white patches. Striping in the tall mane and over a dewlap enlarges the visual impact of the neck, especially in adult males (making them look 'front-heavy'). Hooves grow exceptionally fast, leaving a characteristic hard-edged, rounded spoor.

Subspecies: Cape Mountain Zebra, *E. z. zebra* (Cape and Karoo); Hartmann's Mountain Zebra, *E. z. hartmanni* (S Angola to Orange R.). The smaller Cape race averages 50kg lighter.

HABITAT Formerly widespread in bushy Karoo shrubland in uplands where extreme daytime drought in summer is offset by nocturnal dew and mist. Here the animals often occupied separate summer and winter ranges (up to 120km apart). They moved between pastures and water sources on well-worn traditional paths.

Where grazing permits, individual herds are seasonally residential (i.e. live within a 3–5km² range). Some local populations are less water-dependent than others; most prefer to drink daily and can dig into river beds with their hooves.

FOOD Almost exclusively grazers (but will browse acacias on occasion). Grasses tend to be either patchy or sparse throughout their range (except for seasonal desert flushes). Recorded preferences are for *Themeda, Heteropogon, Cymbopogon* and *Aristida* species. *Stipagrostis* and *Hyparhennia* are other common grasses growing on deeply drained sites. Both individual grazers and social units tend to disperse more widely under these conditions. (They may also be less constrained by large carnivores, which are generally rare in such habitats.) The timing and intensity of grazing is strongly influenced by temperature and season, with animals taking shelter and becoming inactive during the middle of the day in summer.

BEHAVIOUR Breeding-age females are coerced by the largest, most active males into 'harems' of several mothers accompanied by their latest offspring. Such harem groups average 5 animals and seldom exceed 12. Both harem structure and home ranges can become very stable and enduring. Elsewhere harems may be less permanent and highly mobile, with long daily or seasonal movements. Aggregations are temporary and seldom exceed 30. They rarely associate with other grazers. Non-breeding males, and occasionally young females, form small, unstable 'bachelor' groups. Mountain Zebras are less vocal than other zebras. Subordinate animals appease superiors with a high, whistling whinny. A 2-phase barking bray, most often made by the male, both alerts and draws his harem together. When dominant males meet, they circle and strut broadside. The enlarged stripe pattern on the rump is visible from a greater distance than the vertical body stripes. This may help the zebras to maintain visual contact over wider distances on sparse grazing. The 'grid-iron' of smaller stripes above the root of the tail appears to be the target for 'chinning'. This is a form of ritual social behaviour in which the zebra (usually a male, but of any age) approaches another and presses the chin very forcefully on the 'grid-iron'. Actual grooming is very rare among adults but much rubbing, leaning and circling (especially among adult males) may be accompanied by mouth-champing. This behaviour suggests an uneasy mix of social and anti-social impulses.

One foal is born after a 1-year gestation. The spacing of births varies. Nursing foals coerce their mothers to permit suckling by blocking her path and leaning against her chest. Most offspring have left or are chased out of the parental group by 2 years old. They live for at least 25 years.

Common Zebra
E. q. crawshayi
(see page 192)

Hartmann's
Mountain Zebra
adult male

Quagga
(see page 192)

Cape
Mountain
Zebra

Hartmann's
Mountain
Zebra
Juvenile

GREVY'S ZEBRA *Equus grevyi*

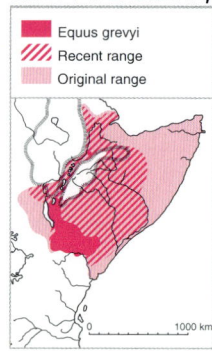

Equus grevyi
Recent range
Original range

SIZE HB 250–300cm. T 40–75cm. SH 140–160cm. W 385kg (350-400kg) (female), 430kg (380–450kg) (male).
DESCRIPTION A long-legged, long-faced zebra with broad, rather ovoid ears, a stripeless white belly and a white-margined spinal stripe. The stripes are very uniformly distributed over the body, head and limbs but overall widths vary so that there are lighter and darker individuals among the 'even' majority.
HABITAT Bush/grass mosaics with a preference for tracts of grassland growing on deep sand, hard-pans, sumplands and in areas where fire and elephants have degraded the dominant *Acacia/Commiphora* woodlands. Seasonally waterlogged plains are extensive in parts of its range and gatherings of thousands of zebras were seen on such grasslands in the past. It associates with giraffe, Oryx, Eland and, in the southern part of their range, with Common Zebra, Impala and Buffalo. An individual's long-term range covers many thousands of kilometres.
FOOD Benefits from the spread of a grassland type dominated by *Pennisetum schimperi*, a tough grass incompletely exploited by other grazers, but grazes many other genera as well.
BEHAVIOUR Grevy's Zebra has an open society in which females with their young and males on established territories (of up to 12km^2) are the stable foci. Females associate in nursing groups, males in bachelor groups and all classes may join up in large, mixed herds. Aggression is inconspicuous except that territorial males assert their mating prerogatives. The most successful males win grassy territories close to water. Grass and water are major attractions, especially for lactating females.
Resident stallions actively seek the company of visiting males. Dominance is asserted by a proud posture, with arched neck and high-stepping gait. Submission is signalled by a lowered head and raised tail. While courting and copulating the male utters a very loud bray followed by a long, strangulated squeak. Both males and females tend to appease the caller. A single foal is born after a variable but exceptionally long gestation of about 400 days. Males and females tend to breed in the wild at about 6 years. They live for at least 24 years.

WILD ASS *Equus africanus*

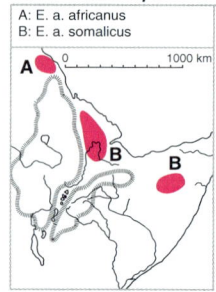

A: E. a. africanus
B: E. a. somalicus

SIZE HB est. 195–205cm. T 40–45cm. SH 115–125cm. W 270–280kg.
DESCRIPTION The wild ancestor of domestic donkeys, the Wild Ass is lean and muscular, fawn or grey, with a near-white belly and legs. It has a short, hairy black brush to the tail, a black mane and black margins to the long leaf-shaped ears. Hooves are exceptionally narrow. Formerly more widespread across northern Africa.
Subspecies: Nubian Wild Ass, *E. a. africanus*: grey with only shoulder striped. Somali Wild Ass, *E. a. somalicus*: fawn, with only legs striped.
HABITAT Semi-desert grasslands and dwarf shrublands (typified by aloes and euphorbias) where the asses tend to retreat into rocky hills and seek shade during the day. They are most active when the weather is cooler: at dusk, dawn and during the night. They are always within a 30km walk to water (but will tolerate brackish sources). They are able to go without water for about 3 days.
FOOD Grasses, notably *Eragrostis*, *Dactyloctenium* and *Chrysopogon*. Wild Asses are well adapted to graze the hardest of desert grasses, such as *Panicum* and *Lasiurus* species. They use their incisors and hooves to break open tussocks.
BEHAVIOUR Very small mother-offspring units are independent of each other but gather opportunistically in search of good grazing. Preferred range often within vast territories held by mature males. These may exceed 20km^2 and their boundaries with those of adjacent males are marked by dung piles. Other males tolerated within territory but all access to females monopolised by territory-holder. One foal born after a 330–365-day gestation. It can start grazing within weeks of birth but may suckle for as long as 6 months. Animals are known to live for 40 years in captivity.

Grevy's Zebra

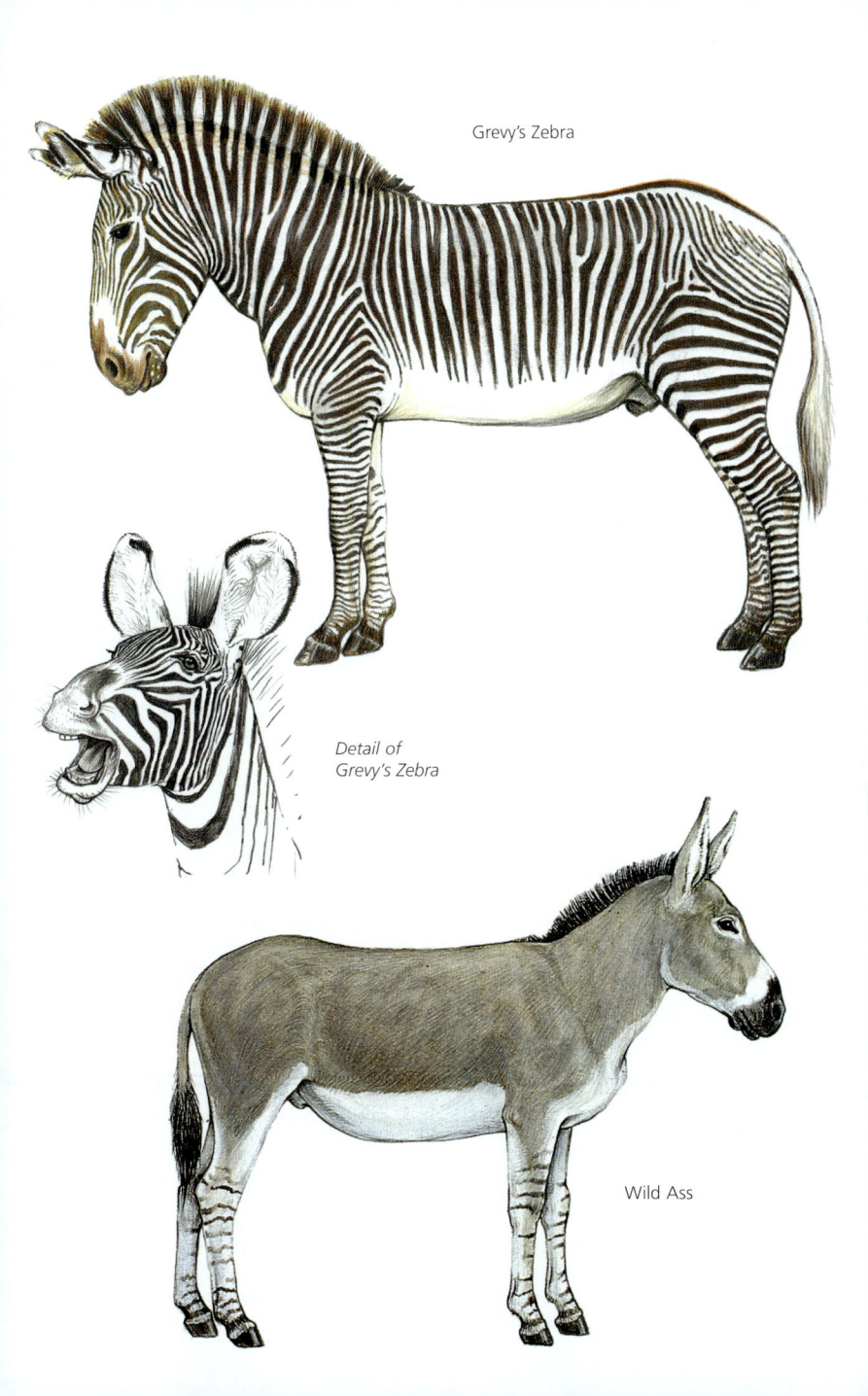

Detail of Grevy's Zebra

Wild Ass

RHINOCEROSES Rhinocerotidae

Once very abundant but now very scarce, rhinoceroses are the second largest land animals only surpassed by elephants in bulk and weight. They have relatively short, powerfully muscled legs, a short neck and a massive head, armed with a nasal horn or horns.

BLACK (BROWSE) RHINOCEROS *Diceros bicornis*

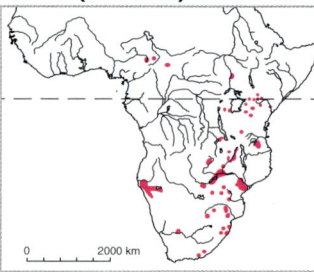

SIZE HB 290–375cm. T 60–70cm. SH 137–180cm. W 700–1,400kg.

DESCRIPTION Its thickest skin forms inflexible plates over the shoulders, haunches, sides, forehead and cheeks. Skin around the muzzle, eyes, ears, undersides and legs is thinner and more flexible. The head has a short forehead and a very muscular, mobile mouth ending in a sharply pointed upper lip. The 3 toes leave characteristic tracks. Other signs of the rhino's presence include rubbed trees, rocks and termitaries, well-scattered dung middens and habitually sprayed urine-posts.

Subspecies: Highly variable: 23 subspecies have been named.

HABITAT Favours edges of thickets and savannahs with areas of short woody regrowth and numerous shrubs and herbs.

FOOD Low-level browse (leaves, twigs and branches), typically in *Acacia*, thicket, hard-pan and riverine plant communities. Some 200 species from 50 families recorded. Salt a major attraction. Can go for up to 5 days without water if food is moist; otherwise always found within daily walking distance of water. Horns occasionally used to loosen soil around roots or to break branches above its reach.

BEHAVIOUR A female with her young is basic social unit. Adult females form temporary associations but aggression is elicited by total strangers. Home ranges can cover over 130km², but some are as small as 2.6km². Overtly territorial behaviour is also very variable. Males in high-density areas generally tolerant of neighbours. Males in low-density areas more likely to be aggressive.

WHITE (GRASS) RHINOCEROS *Ceratotherium simum*

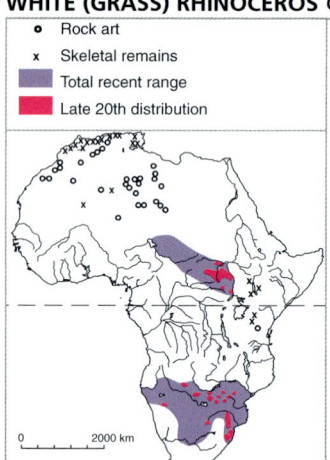

- ○ Rock art
- x Skeletal remains
- Total recent range
- Late 20th distribution

SIZE HB 360–420cm. T 80–100cm. SH 170–185cm. W 1,400–2,000kg (female), 2,000–3,600kg (male).

DESCRIPTION Of similar skin colour to the Browse Rhino. Head is long (especially the forehead); mouth very wide, flat-fronted and set low over the chin. Neck forms a prominent hump when the head is raised. Spoor elongate with prominent cleft at the back. Subspecies: Southern White Rhino, *C. s. simum* (southern savannahs); Northern White rhino, *C. s. cottoni* (northern savannahs).

HABITAT Preference for short-grass areas and undertakes seasonal movements to avoid waterlogged long grass. Where territories maintained by resident bulls their border-patrolling and scent-marking leave foot-scuffs, dung middens, urine sprays, rubbing posts and horned vegetation along boundaries.

FOOD Short grasses, typically *Cynodon, Digitaria, Heteropogon* and *Chloris* species in wet-season areas, are preferred. After dry-season fires, *Themeda, Hyparrhenia* and *Setaria*.

BEHAVIOUR Females and their immediate offspring occupy large (4–12km²) overlapping home ranges. Males defend territories but tolerance is related to population density. In Zululand parks male territories can be as small as 0.75–2.6km². White Rhinos are extremely vocal. Infantile squeaks and pantings become loud chirps, gasps and puffings (contact) or snarls and squeals of distress in adults. Dominant males grunt and bellow or court females with a low, pulsing cry.

Black (Browse) Rhinoceros

Detail of lip

White (Grass) Rhinoceros

Sketches of White Rhinoceros

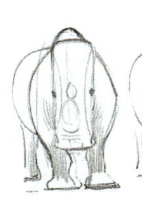

200 — PLATE 90 HIPPOS

EVEN-TOED UNGULATES Artiodactyla
HIPPOPOTAMUSES Hippopotamidae

Hippos resemble gigantic, amphibious pigs with enlarged lower jaw and canines, 4 large, blunt toes on each foot and a very rotund body build. Their shiny, naked skin is densely perforated by minute skin-conditioning mucus glands.

HIPPOPOTAMUS *Hippopotamus amphibius*

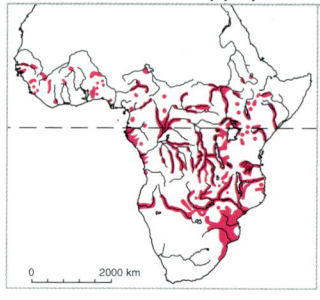

SIZE HB 280–350cm. T 35–50cm. SH 130–165cm. W 510–2,500kg (female), 650–3,200kg (male).
DESCRIPTION Eyes, ears and nostrils on top of head. Main colour of smooth, shiny hide purplish grey to blue-black. Underside, eye rims, ears and mouth show variable expanses of pink. Hide glands exude a blood-like fluid. Males have larger canines and incisor teeth set in massive jaws and skull and also a huge jowl and thickened neck.
HABITAT A silent, solitary grazer on land by night, a vocal, densely social and sedentary wallower by day. It is possible that large populations cause long-term vegetation cycles because their progressive degradation of the grazing encourages regeneration of thickets. Closely cropped lawns, paths radiating from the water and great accumulations of dung are characteristic signs of intensive use by hippos. 
FOOD Both creeping and tussock grasses are taken. Crops grass by using its leathery (not muscular) lips. Walks slowly, closing its lips over mouthfuls of grass and wrenching them away with a regular swinging of the head. Can ingest up to 60kg in less than 5 hours out of the water.
BEHAVIOUR Hippos have a very hierarchical society in which individuals must advertise their status and condition, especially to superiors.

Females accompanied by up to 4 successive offspring are only stable social unit. Degrees of sedentariness or nomadism highly variable. The largest males occupy narrow strips of water and land along the foreshore. Here they defend exclusive mating rights but tolerate most subordinate males. Aggregations range between 2 and 150. Large groups are very vocal, the main call being a reverberating nasal wheeze followed by a series of guttural honks. In the early morning this is associated with the return to water. It is the response to all disturbances. Males also wheeze-honk while copulating (the female lies prostrate).

PYGMY HIPPOPOTAMUS *Hexaprotodon liberiensis*

SIZE HB 150–177cm. T 15–21cm. SH 70–92cm. W 180–275kg (sexes are of similar size).
DESCRIPTION Rotund-bodied, thick-necked hippo with a similar rounded, toothy muzzle (but proportionately much smaller head) to the Common Hippo. Eyes, ears and nostrils do not protrude as much. Body is naked, sepia-brown. The toes, less webbed and more widely splayed than those of the Common Hippo, leave a distinctive 4-pronged spoor.
HABITAT Forested watercourses where it shelters by day in ponds, rivers and swamps. At night follows tunnel-like paths through dense riverine vegetation to graze in glades, or along grassy trails.
FOOD Graze consists of various green grasses and herbs, various sedges, herbaceous shoots and fallen fruits. Food is cropped by tearing the plant between the upper and lower lips.
BEHAVIOUR Only been recorded singly, in twos or, rarely, threes. Normally very silent but captive specimens have been recorded snorting, grunting, squeaking and hissing. They also make a much quieter groaning equivalent of the Common Hippo's honking call.

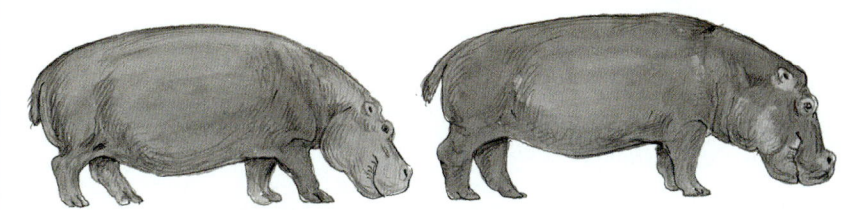

Hippopotamus

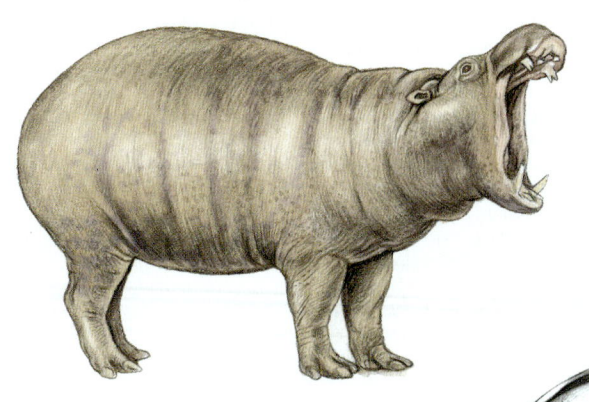

female

male

Pygmy Hippopotamus

Sketch of newborn
Pygmy Hippo

PIGS Suidae

Pigs are robust, large-headed animals with relatively short legs and a compact body build. The skulls of African pigs show striking adaptations to their preferred foods and to modes of tusk- or snout-fighting that are unique to each species.

WILD BOAR *Sus scrofa*

SIZE HB 85–130cm (female), 100–160cm (male). T 15–21cm. SH 60–90cm. W 30–80kg (female), 33–130kg (male).
DESCRIPTION Flat-sided, shaggy pig with long snout, large, leaf-shaped ears and short dorsal mane. Colour varies between dark grey-brown and dirty tawny colour. Tracks reveal 2 oval hoof-marks (with side hooves only imprinting in mud).
HABITAT In N Africa mainly oakwoods and scrub; also in tamarisk groves on desert margins.
FOOD Omnivorous, with acorns the main seasonal staple; also bulbs, roots, fallen fruits, snails, insect larvae and other invertebrates. Wild boars occasionally scavenge and eat small vertebrates.
BEHAVIOUR Females and their young form associations with one or more other mother families. These have loose, temporary associations with adult males in the vicinity. The animals tend to be sedentary but are quick to respond to disturbance or hunting with rapid movement and changes in behaviour. Thus mainly diurnal habits can change to nocturnal habits and distances of 20–30km may be covered. Home ranges are very variable, from 2 to 20km^2.

BUSH PIG *Potamochoerus larvatus* see map above

SIZE HB 100–177cm. T 30–45cm. H 55–100cm. W 45–150kg.
DESCRIPTION Compact, with slab-like, short-legged body, tapering into the head and snout with little indication of a neck. The dorsal crest and face are often white or grey. Body colour varies from blonde or red to grey, brown or black. Colour varies with sex, age, region or individual; 17 subspecies have been named.
HABITAT A wide range of forested and woodland habitats, with a distinct preference for valley bottoms with dense vegetation and soft soils.
FOOD Omnivorous and highly adaptive to local and seasonal conditions. Roots, tubers, bulbs and corms are the principal foods; also fallen fruits and herbage. In addition to fungi, takes various animals, rooting for larvae and beetles, snails, amphibians and reptiles. Occasionally scavenges.
BEHAVIOUR A female and her young are often accompanied by an adult male within a restricted area where trunk-slashing along paths, rubbing posts and latrines suggest that males, and perhaps females too, are territorial, if only seasonally. Larger associations are seen but only rarely. Home ranges of up to 10km^2 have been estimated and nightly foraging walks of up to 6km.

RED RIVER HOG *Potamochoerus porcus* see map above

SIZE HB 100–145cm. T 30–45cm. SH 55–80cm. W 45–115kg.
DESCRIPTION Bright russet with narrow white dorsal crest, white 'brows', cheek tufts and jaw-line. Ears leaf-shaped with long white tassel. Muzzle and forehead are black and the fur is sleek and short over most of the body (except jaws and flanks which have longer hair).
HABITAT Rarely outside rainforest. Marked preference for river courses and swamp-forest margins. Here it ploughs up extensive areas while excavating roots and invertebrates.
FOOD Omnivorous but with underground roots and tubers the main staple. Fallen fruits are of great importance locally and seasonally, as are invertebrates.
BEHAVIOUR Often found in small groups of up to 15 animals, occasionally gathers in very large but temporary assocations of up to 60 animals. During confrontations between males, both animals strut broadside, with bristling fur and erect crests. They champ jaws, grunt, paw the soil and whip their slender tails back and forth.

Wild Boar

Bush Pig

Red River Hog

GIANT HOG *Hylochoerus meinertzhageni*

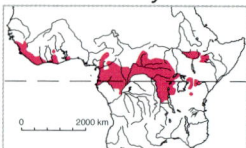

SIZE HB 130–210cm. T 25–45cm. SH 80–100cm. W 100–200kg (female), 140–275kg (male).
DESCRIPTION Heavily built, covered in long black hair. The rhinarium, or snout disc, may be over 50cm across and is very broad and swollen. Over the forehead is a dish-like depression surrounded by a circle of raised bone, tissue and bare skin. Mature males have grotesquely swollen preorbital glands.
HABITAT Mainly forest/grassland mosaics but range from subalpine areas and bamboo groves through montane to lowland and swamp forests, galleries, wooded savannahs and post-cultivation thickets.
FOOD Many species of grasses, sedges and herbs, which are cropped at various stages of growth. In some montane areas herbaceous growth may also be very important. Rootles less than other pigs; prefers to graze on mats of relatively short green grass.
BEHAVIOUR The basic social group is a mother and her offspring of up to 3 generations, but this unit may associate with a variety of neighbouring families. Sleeping-sites change frequently and are used by different permutations of neighbouring families. They are often very vocal, using close-contact quiet grunts in thick cover and a louder barking call to establish contact over a distance. Males make an extended grunting call that builds up to a trumpeting crescendo and then dies away.

DESERT WARTHOG *Phacochoerus aethiopicus*

Phacochoerus africanus
Phacochoerus aethiopicus delamerei
P. a. aethiopicus presumed range

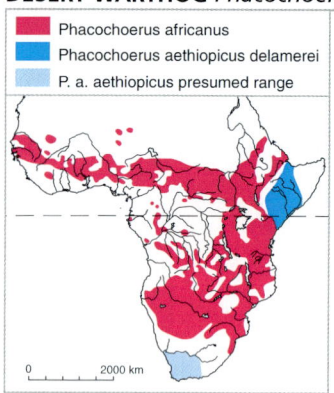

SIZE HB est. 100–150cm. T est. 35–45cm. SH est. 50–75cm. W 45–100kg.
DESCRIPTION Closely resembles Common Warthog but the dentition and the associated leverage for chewing have been modified and specialised, apparently toward more thorough mastication.
HABITAT The 2 subspecies now widely separated; it is likely that an 'arid corridor' once linked them, perhaps during last Ice Age (20,000 years ago). In modern Somalia survives under conditions that are drier than any currently tolerated by the Common Warthog. Extinct in Cape.
FOOD Grazes and ingests excavated roots and rhizomes with its hard, sharp-edged lips.

COMMON WARTHOG *Phacochoerus africanus*   *see* map above

SIZE HB 105–152cm. T 35–50cm. SH 55–85cm. W 45–75kg (female), 60–150kg (male).
DESCRIPTION Relatively long-legged but short-necked with prominent, curved tusks. The facial callosities, or 'warts', consist of 3 paired masses of thickened skin and connective tissue protecting the jaws, eyes and muzzle. Warthogs run at a high, jaunty trot, with back straight and the very narrow tail held vertically. The head is held high. Feeding animals drop to their knees and commonly graze in this position, with their hindquarters raised.
HABITAT Commonest on alluvial soils in lightly wooded country with a mosaic of vegetation types but well distributed throughout savannah and open-woodland areas of tropical Africa.
FOOD Grazing throughout the rains, warthogs favour mats of short species. They also strip growing grasses of their seedheads. In dry season turn to leaf bases and rhizomes that store nutrients. They unearth these with the sharp edge of the nose disc. Generally stay within walking distance of water.
BEHAVIOUR There are several social levels. Mothers and their female offspring retain the most enduring bonds. Thus a new family unit joins others that are probably also close relatives. These loose groupings live within 'clan areas' averaging about 4km^2.

Giant Hog

Common Warthog

Desert Warthog detail

Common Warthog detail

GIRAFFE *Giraffa camelopardalis*

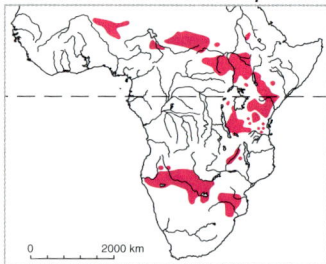

G. camelopardalis former range

SIZE HB 3.5–4.8m. T 76–110cm. Total height 3.5–4.7m (female), 3.9–5.2m (male). W 450–1,180kg (female), 1,800–1,930kg (male).

DESCRIPTION The length of a giraffe's neck is only matched by that of its legs and its slow-motion lope covers ground at a great rate (its Arabic-derived name means 'fast walker'). Giraffes can run at 60kph. Both young and old are able to outstrip most predators. The neck is fringed with a short, thick mane and both sexes develop three 'horns' above the eyes. The face is strongly tapered and a 45cm tongue is the principal means of gathering foliage in to the large, elastic mouth and lips. Colours vary greatly between individuals and from region to region (see plate).

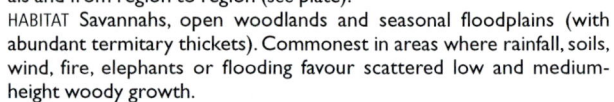

HABITAT Savannahs, open woodlands and seasonal floodplains (with abundant termitary thickets). Commonest in areas where rainfall, soils, wind, fire, elephants or flooding favour scattered low and medium-height woody growth.

FOOD Known to feed from over 100 species of plant but *Acacia*, *Commiphora* and *Terminalia* species are major staples. The wet season is a period of abundant, green deciduous growth, during which time Giraffes are widely dispersed. During the dry season they concentrate where evergreens survive. The amount that Giraffes eat in a day varies but is less than half the intake of typical grazers. It is the concentrated nutritional value of the foliage which they select and super-efficient digestion that makes modest feeding possible.

BEHAVIOUR Adult males may be vestigially territorial because mature bulls monopolise all matings and tend to be intolerant of other large males at the cores of their very variably sized home ranges (cores may be as large as 80km^2 but year-long movements are known to range from 5 to 654km^2 or more). Females have very unstable home ranges that may drift from year to year. These overlap those of very many other females with which they may associate (in mixed sex groups of up to 50 animals). Such associations are temporary. The only stable associations of a female giraffe's life are the year-long periods of motherhood and the traditional, highly localised, calving area to which she returns again and again to give birth. Newborn calves rise to their feet within 5 minutes and after a week or so may join up to 9 other very young calves also born in the vicinity. One or more mothers are often nearby, although they tend to leave the 'crèche' of youngsters on their own during the middle of the day (the time of day when they feed most intensively and when most predators are inactive). Between half and three-quarters of all Giraffes fail to survive their first year. The main cause of death is predation.

GIRAFFE POPULATIONS: Four major populations can be recognised and, within these, further regional varieties or subspecies are commonly recognised.

Population	Taxa	Region
Somali arid	*G. c. camelopardalis*	Eritrea, Blue Nile
	G. c. reticulata	N Kenya, Somalia
Saharan	*G. c. peralta*	Sahara
Northern savannah	*G. c. congoensis*	Cameroon to Uganda
	G. c. rothschildi	W Kenya, Uganda
Southern savannah	*G. c. tippelskirchi*	E Africa
	G. c. thornicrofti	Luangwa valley, Zambia
	G. c. angolensis	S Angola
	G. c. giraffa	S Africa

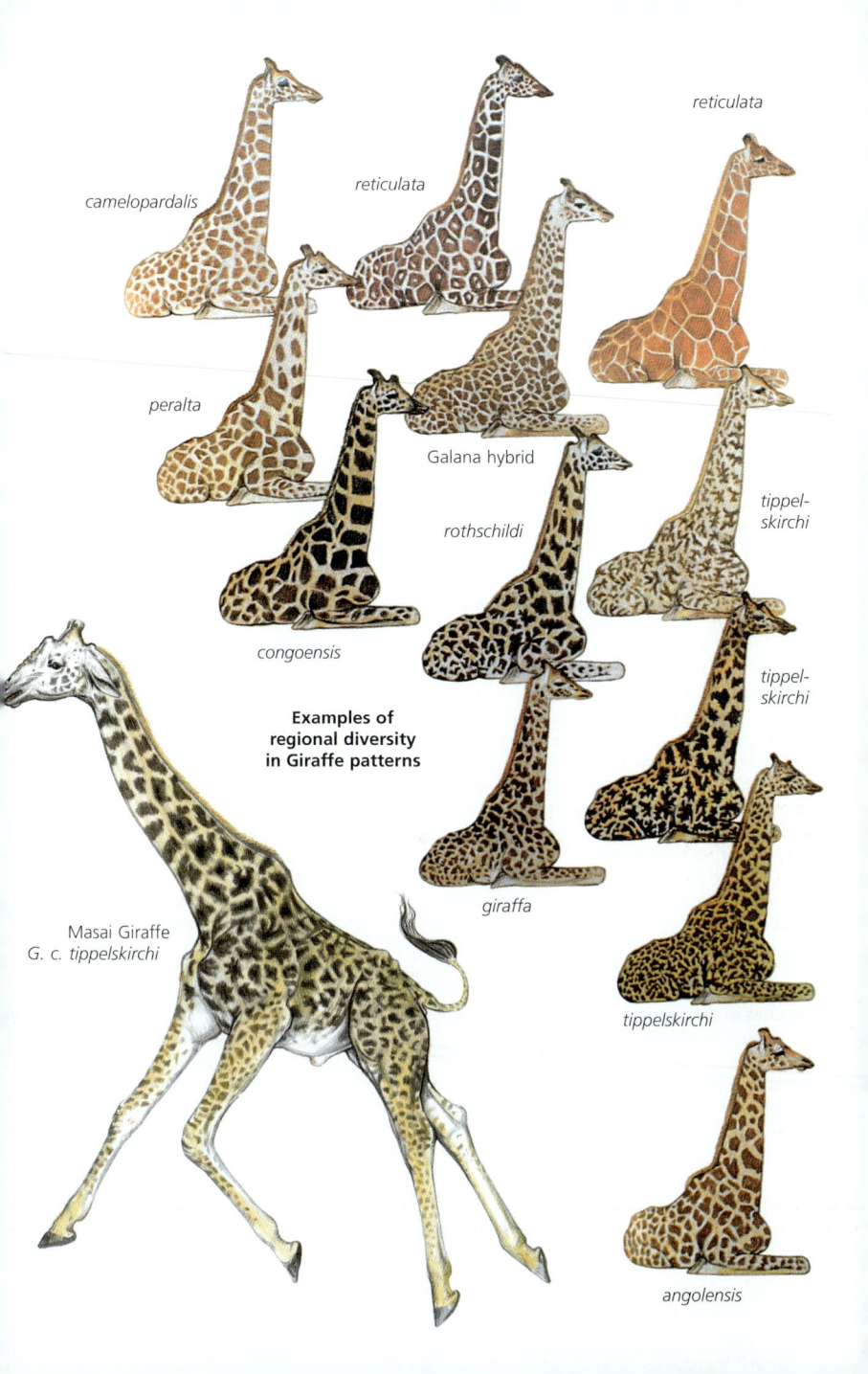

Examples of regional diversity in Giraffe patterns

BOVIDS or HORNED UNGULATES Bovidae
Horned ungulates are long-legged, hooved herbivores that range in size from the 2kg Pygmy Antelope to the almost 1,000kg Eland. The males of most species, and the females of some species, are horned with true keratinous horn sheaths over bony cores. All horned ungulates ruminate but food preferences vary widely.

BOVINES Bovinae
These animals are distinguished from antelopes by their generally larger size, an absence of facial or pedal glands and smooth or keeled rather than annulated horns.

OXEN Bovini

AFRICAN BUFFALO *Syncerus caffer*

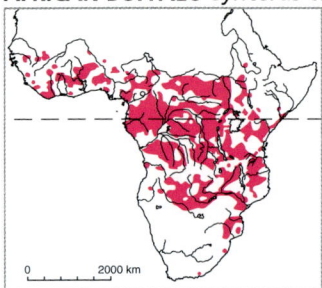

SIZE HB 170–340cm. T 50–80cm. H 100–170cm. W 250–850kg.

DESCRIPTION Large ox with thick, bossed horns and tasselled ears. The coat is short, often sparse and coloured from a rich red to black. The underside and chin of the Buffalo is often pale (even creamy white) and patches of contrasting colour appear on the face and legs. The differences between Forest and Savannah Buffaloes are very great but there are intermediate and mixed types.

Subspecies: Forest Buffalo, *S. c. nanus*; Western Buffalo, *S. c. brachyceros*; Cape Buffalo, *S. c. caffer*; plus the possible relict 'Mountain Buffalo', *S. c. mathewsi*.

Forest Buffaloes are generally below 120cm in height and 320kg in weight; savannah forms are larger.

HABITAT The Forest Buffalo depends on low-level browse and an undetermined minimum of grass in its diet, limiting it to grassy glades, watercourses and waterlogged basins. The humid climate ensures continuous plant growth, which ensures that small areas will support Buffaloes throughout the year. Heavy browsing and grazing in 'buffalo glades' helps to limit or delay plant growth. Savannah Buffaloes also seek out forests and valley bottoms where possible but can stay in the open and resist overheating and desiccation by becoming immobile or by lying in wallows. Their need for water and dense cover, as well as grass, makes them favour mosaics and savannahs with patches of thicket, reeds or forest. They retain strong attachments to traditional ranges even when conditions change.

FOOD Grazing, breaking and trampling by Buffaloes favours rapid grass regrowth, which encourages intense and repeated foraging. Particularly favoured grasses are *Cynodon*, *Sporobolus*, *Digitaria*, *Panicum*, *Heteropogon* and *Cenchrus* species, but a wide choice of swamp vegetation is eaten. Grazing is quickly influenced by disturbance or human predation, with animals switching from continuous grazing to dawn, dusk and night-time grazing.

BEHAVIOUR The Forest Buffalo forms small groups of up to 12 animals with related females and their offspring as the core and 1 or more attendant males. Other males are solitary or form small bachelor parties. Savannah Buffaloes can assemble in much larger aggregations but similar 'family' clusters amplified into regular clan-like associations are also attended by bulls. Within these clans adults of both sexes develop hierarchical rank orders. They have well-marked seasonal breeding peaks and the dry 'off-season' sees many males breaking away from female families or clans. Gatherings of as many as 2,000 animals are only possible during the rains or on major patches of rich pasture.

Female receptivity is preceded by signs of oestrus that attract many bulls. Here the effects of male rank come into play, with the top bull or bulls having priority. Nonetheless fights are common and collisions after head-to-head charges have ended in one bull cartwheeling into the air to land on his back. Gestation lasts about 11 months and birth intervals of 2 years are normal. The cow–calf bond is very strong and exclusive but the female attachment to her herd is also close. Thus, all adults respond to distress calls and even bulls wounded by other bulls seek refuge in the herd. Vision, a dominant sense in most open-country animals, is less important than sound. Quiet lowing is the preferred way of keeping in touch, especially in dark forests. This allows even blind buffaloes to remain safe in the herd.

African Buffalo
S. c. caffer, male

Female Savanna Buffalo facial detail

African Buffalo
S. c. nanus, female

Female Forest Buffalo facial detail

: PLATE 96 SPIRAL-HORNED BOVINES

SPIRAL-HORNED BOVINES Tragelaphini

Medium-sized to large bovines with a deep body and a narrow head with big ears and twisted or spiral horns in the males. Teeth and digestion are adapted to a diet of young, nutritious vegetation.

BUSHBUCK *Tragelaphus scriptus*

SIZE HB 105–150cm. T 19–25cm. SH 61–100cm. W 24–60kg (female), 30–80kg (male).
DESCRIPTION A small bovine. Females and young are mainly red and males become progressively darker with sexual maturity and age. The undersides are white, there are white flashes above black hooves and white markings on face and ears. Western forest forms ('harnessed') have vertical and horizontal white stripes on flanks. Eastern and southern populations ('sylvan' forms) are sometimes plain and often sparsely marked with a few light spots or streaks on flanks or haunches. Up to 27 subspecies listed. Male has horns 25–57cm long.
HABITAT Dependent on thick cover. Can subsist on dew. Sometimes lives in reedbeds.
FOOD Largely shrubs, leguminous herbs and growing grass, also pods, fruits of many species. Feeding patterns strongly influenced by disturbance and predators. Rests and ruminates frequently.
BEHAVIOUR Lives at very variable densities. Not territorial, but solitary when feeding.

BONGO *Tragelaphus euryceros*

SIZE HB 170–250cm. T 24–65cm. SH 110–130cm. W 210–253kg (female), 240–405kg (male).
DESCRIPTION Long-bodied, muscular bovine, deep russet-red, with 10–16 vivid white stripes on each side. Both sexes have spiral horns. Males have a vestigial dorsal crest and bold, black and white markings on the legs and face. Males become heavier and darker with age. Subspecies: Lowland Bongo *T. e. euryceros* (W and C Africa), Mountain Bongo *T. e. isaaci* (Kenya).
HABITAT Landslides, floods, fires, treefalls, elephant-browsing, logging and fallow all favour regrowth of the low-level fresh greenery that this species needs. In montane areas mass die-offs of bamboo suits it. Active at night but stays close to refuges in undergrowth or thickets.
FOOD Foliage of shrubs and young trees, herbs, young grass and especially vines that are dragged down off trees or pulled up from the ground. Over 80 food plants known.
BEHAVIOUR Individuals do not form permanent links with others, but lactating mothers form large nursery herds after the young are beyond the concealment phase.

SITATUNGA *Tragelaphus spekei*

SIZE HB 115–155cm (female), 150–170cm (male). T 18–30cm. SH 75–105cm (female), 85–125cm (male). W 40–85kg (female), 80–130kg (male).
DESCRIPTION Shaggy, long-legged bovine, distinguished by spread-eagled stance and long, splayed hooves. Females hornless, rufous with 8 or 10 dorsal white stripes. Males larger and darker, with heavy, sharply keeled horns to 45–92cm. Subspecies: Nile Sitatunga *T. s. spekei* (Nile), Zaïre Sitatunga *T. s. gratus* (W and C Africa), Southern Sitatunga *T. s. selousi* (S Africa).
HABITAT Shrubby growth bordering forest waterways.
FOOD Shrubs, herbs and grasses with strong regional biases.
BEHAVIOUR Most active from 18.00–10.00h. A rich, year-round supply of greenery permits exceptionally small home ranges and potentially high densities. Females are especially prone to gather in high-density areas and may be accompanied by more than one generation of calves. They have a clumsy gait but are quiet and deliberate in their movements.

Bushbuck

Bongo *female*

Bongo *male*

Sitatunga *female*

Sitatunga *male*

NYALA *Tragelaphus angasi*

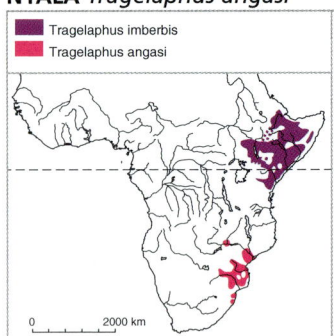

Tragelaphus imberbis
Tragelaphus angasi

SIZE HB 135–145cm (female), 150–195cm (male). T 36–55cm. SH 80–105cm (female), 100–121cm (male). W 62–90kg (female), 100–140kg (male).
DESCRIPTION Females are slender and russet with up to 18 bold white stripes down their sides. Males begin with similar colouring but pass through a prolonged metamorphosis as they mature. First they turn sandy-grey and grow tufts on the chin, throat and belly. As the horns lengthen, the dorsal crest and continuous fringes of hair also grow in length. The colour darkens and the pale vertical stripes fade and may disappear altogether. The timing of these developments varies individually and in some cases crests and colours remain relatively or absolutely undeveloped. The 'false' or side hooves are fringed with glands. Nyala lack inguinal glands in the groin. Male horns range from 40 to 83.5cm in length. Chunky hooves leave a distinctive spoor, with a compact, rounded margin.
HABITAT A mosaic of dense mopane (*Colophospermum mopane*) thickets and more open woodlands, pans and scrub. Grass in the open areas tends to be ephemeral growth during the summer rains. Uses the thickets for browsing and shelter but emerges into more open areas at night, especially during wet season.
FOOD Favoured browse species are *Acacia*, toothbrush trees (*Salvadora*), buffalo thorn (*Ziziphus*) and monkey apple (*Strychnos*). Picks up fallen leaves, herbs, cucurbits and various small legumes.
BEHAVIOUR Up to 50 animals can gather on a flush of fresh growth while oestrous females can attract much smaller aggregations. Essentially independent animals will readily meet and part with a frequency that depends on local densities. Home ranges vary from 33 to 360ha, with an average of about 75ha.

LESSER KUDU *Tragelaphus imberbis* see map above
SIZE HB 110–175cm. T 25–40cm. SH 90–110cm. W 56–70kg (female), 92–108kg (male).
DESCRIPTION Females and young are bright russet, with 11–15 vertical white stripes. They have a long, narrow head and resemble Nyala very closely, except for slightly longer legs and neck. Yearling males acquire sandy-grey colouring that is almost identical to that of similarly aged Nyala males. The black and white markings on face, tail, and tawny-orange legs are also extremely similar in both species, with the greatest contrast in males. Lesser Kudu remain well-camouflaged by their colouring. The short and sparsely haired neck has geometric white markings on throat and chest. There are inguinal glands in the groin and secretions around the false hooves.
Subspecies: Two described: *T. i. imberbis* (Horn of Africa), *T. i. australis* (E Africa).
HABITAT Deciduous bushlands and thickets dominated by *Acacia* and *Commiphora*. Residents display some seasonal movement from the more deciduous upper slopes in the wet season to low-lying evergreen belts in the dry season.
FOOD Browsers of foliage and herbage with a strong reliance on a few evergreen species during the dry season, notably the succulents (*Calyptrotheca* and *Euphorbia*) and the toothbrush tree (*Salvadora persica*). Over 100 species of plants have been recorded, including sprouts (especially *Combretum* and *Cordia*), buds, leaves and pods of various *Acacia* species, flowers and fruits. Grasses are taken sparingly while green and fresh.
BEHAVIOUR Highly residential but non-territorial animals. Females tend to aggregate most (up to 24 in a group) and occasionally 2 or 3 females (presumably close relatives) sustain long-term companionships. Hierarchies have not been observed and all classes meet and part casually. Older males actively avoid each other except in the presence of oestrous females. Females are the most residential, with home ranges of about 60–500ha. Newly independent males move over a larger area (up to 670ha) but gradually settle into a smaller home range. The normal gait is a level walk but animals can leap 2m when fleeing, throwing tail and hindquarters in the air and sometimes uttering a harsh bark as they go. Both sexes bark but this mainly serves avoidance and orientation rather than signalling alarm.

Nyala *male*

Nyala *subadult male*

Nyala *female*

Lesser Kudu *male*

Detail of Kudu markings

MOUNTAIN NYALA (GEDEMSA) *Tragelaphus buxtoni*

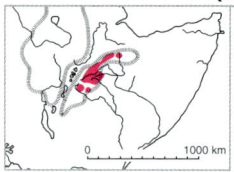

SIZE HB 190–200cm (female), 240–260cm (male). T 20–25cm. SH 90–100cm (female), 120–135cm (male). W 150–200kg (female), 180–300kg (male).
DESCRIPTION Hornless females resemble Red Deer hinds. Adult males nearly twice as heavy with deep chests, a dorsal crest and body colour of sepia brown that slowly gets darker with age. This throws white markings on the ears, face, throat, chest and forelegs into strong relief. They can be smooth and glossy or can become quite shaggy during the cold season. The tightness of the horns' spiral, and their thickness and length, vary; they can measure up to 118cm along the curve.
HABITAT Mosaics of high-altitude woodland, bush, heath, moorland and valley-bottom grassland. The woodlands (mostly juniper and *Hagenia*), heath and bush (dominated by sage brush, *Artemesia* and everlasting, *Helichrysum*) provide dry-season refuge. During rains may move to pasture at lower levels. Formerly ranged over SE highlands of Ethiopia, now restricted to Bale massif.
FOOD Herbs and shrubs with occasional grass, lichens and ferns. Most frequent browse are Solanaceae, St John's wort (*Hypericum*), lady's mantle (*Alchemilla*) and goosegrass (*Galium*).
BEHAVIOUR Females accompanied by one or two generations of young form frequent but impermanent associations with other mother-young groups numbering up to 13. Regularly joined by adult males. Groups smaller in dry season when they range widely. Females restrict their movements in the rains to about 5km². Males range as widely as 20km². Young males are more mobile and less solitary. Mating peak in December and single young born after an 8–9-month gestation, at the end of the wet season. Ancestors had a wider span of habitats (before the evolution of Greater Kudu) but have now become montane specialists in their diet and physiology.

GREATER KUDU *Tragelaphus strepsiceros*

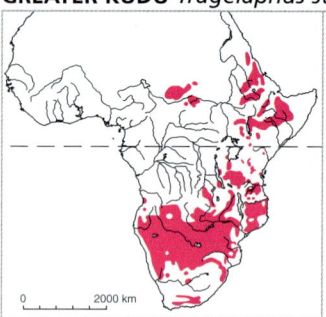

SIZE HB 185–235cm (female), 195–245cm (male). T 30–55cm. SH 100–140cm (female), 122–150cm (male). W 120–215kg (female); 190–315kg (male).
DESCRIPTION Tall, dun-coloured, with 4–12 pale stripes. Spiral horns reach record length of 181cm (along curve) in males. Both sexes have crest and mane. Males have a tessellated neck. Females normally hornless. Both sexes have very large, rounded ears. All living forms are substantially smaller than pleistocene greater kudus. Subspecies: *T. s. strepsiceros* (S and E Africa), *T. s. chora* (NE Africa), *T. s. cottoni* (Chad to W Sudan).
HABITAT Originally throughout the drier areas of E and S Africa, wherever thickets and dense woodlands provide browse and shelter. Now increasingly restricted to stony, hilly country; thickets and evergreen forests along watercourses and on cloudy heights provide dry-season refuges. In wet season disperses through deciduous woodlands and may emerge at night to graze off herbs and grass on open *Acacia/Commiphora* pans.
FOOD Very wide range of foliage, herbs, vines, flowers, fruits, succulents and grass. There are striking seasonal changes in diet, with choices much more restricted in the dry season, though the slow leaf-fall of bush willows (*Combetrum*) provides browse during this time.
BEHAVIOUR Wide dispersion during rains tends to separate sexes, but mating peak during the dry season draws animals back to the core of their range in valley thickets. Groups of 2–25 typically include several adult females with offspring of both sexes. Adults utter very loud and startling barks; males grunt when fighting or during confrontations; a hooting bleat signifies distress. Gestation lasts 9 months; the young lies up about 3 weeks and is weaned and fairly independent by 6 months. Greater Kudus have lived for 23 years in captivity.

Mountain Nyala
male

Mountain Nyala
female

Greater Kudu
male

DERBY'S ELAND *Taurotragus derbianus*

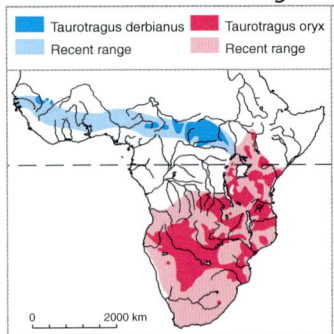

Taurotragus derbianus — Recent range
Taurotragus oryx — Recent range

0 — 2000 km

SIZE HB est. 210–240cm (female), est. 240–320cm (male). T 55–78cm. SH est. 140–160cm (female), 150–176cm (male). W est. 300–500kg (female), 450–907kg (male).
DESCRIPTION Very large bovine with 8–12 vertical white stripes on sandy-grey or rufous body. Both sexes have horns; those of males are longer (up to 123cm), more widely splayed and have a looser spiral than in the Common Eland. Mature males have a black neck and a pendulous dewlap from chin to chest. Ears broad, rounded and prominently marked, as are the hocks. Subspecies: *T. d. derbianus* (W of R Niger), rufous, average 15 stripes; *T. d. gigas* (E of R Niger), sandy-grey, average 12 stripes.
HABITAT Narrow and increasingly fragmented belt of *Isoberlinia* woodland stretching from Senegal to the Nile and sandwiched between cultivated savannahs of the Sudanian zone and wetter mosaics of forests and grasslands to the south.
FOOD Browse consists of dominant leguminous trees, notably *Isoberlinia*, *Julbernardia* and some young grasses and herbs in the wet season.
BEHAVIOUR Highly nomadic, with very large ranges and distinct seasonal movements. Males often solitary and contact with females ranges from a few hours to several weeks. Large herds in both wet and dry seasons suggest that security of the young, or social rather than ecological factors, influence female gregariousness.

ELAND *Taurotragus oryx*   see map above

SIZE HB 200–280cm (female), 240–345cm (male). T 50–90cm. SH 125–160cm (female), 135–178cm (male). W 300–600kg (female), 400–942kg (male).
DESCRIPTION Very large, tan bovine in which both sexes have horns and dewlap. Long tail with tufted tip and narrow, relatively small ears. Males tend to increase in weight throughout their life, neck and shoulders darken from tan to grey and dewlap enlarges until it hangs below the level of the knees. Hair on males' forehead also changes, becoming more and more bushy. Mouth and muzzle small and pointed in comparison to those of buffaloes and cattle. Subspecies: Cape Eland, *T. o. oryx* (S and SW Africa), tawny, adults lose stripes; Livingstone's Eland *T. o. livingstonii* (central woodlands), brown, up to 12 stripes; East African Eland *T. o. pattersoni* (E Africa), rufous tinge, up to 12 stripes.
HABITAT Primarily animals of the woodlands and woodland–savannah. In South Africa they have extended their range into temperate Highveldt and the Karoo. Elands gather in larger herds during and after the rains, and scatter into smaller groups in the dry season. Originally distributed from Cape of Good Hope to Nile floodplain and arid N Kenya.
FOOD Browse foliage and herbs. In dry season myrrh (*Commiphora*) and bush willows (*Combretum*) become major foods in many localities. Marula fruit and *Acacia* seeds are eaten in quantities in the dry season.
BEHAVIOUR Gregarious but with fluid and open system. Mutual attraction among calves leads to temporary isolated groups of up to 50 animals, all juvenile. Calf assemblies provide nucleus for female herds and hierarchies within these juvenile herds and the principle of 'rank by age and size' remain typical of all ages of Elands and both sexes. Temporary congregations of up to 1,000 recorded on flushes of green growth. Young animals, especially females, highly nomadic, older animals, especially males, more residential. Home ranges recorded up to 1,500 km^2. More matings recorded in rains, birth peaks nearly 9 months later at the end of dry season. Young have brief lying-out period before joining the 'crèches'. Growth exceptionally fast, due in part to the extreme richness of Eland milk. Known to have lived for up to 25 years.

Derby's Eland
male

Eland
female

Eland
male

ANTELOPES Antilopinae
Ranging from less than 2kg to over 400kg, the very diversity of antelopes typifies them.

DUIKERS Cephalophini
Forest antelopes with compact body and head. Short, wedge-shaped head with horns.

BUSH DUIKER *Sylvicapra grimmia*
SIZE HB 90–115cm (female), 70–105cm (male). T 7–19.5cm. H 45–70cm. W 12–25.5kg (female), 11–21.5kg (male).
DESCRIPTION Longer legged and larger eared than forest duikers. Colour varies regionally. Over 40 subspecies listed, in 8 regional groupings. Straight, upright horns in male only.
HABITAT Flourishes in a wide range of habitats.
FOOD Leaves and shoots of numerous dominant bush plants. Fruits are also very important seasonally. Do not need water.
BEHAVIOUR Males defend territories with little or no overlap in range.

BLUE DUIKER *Cephalophus monticola*
Cephalophus maxwelli
Cephalophus monticola

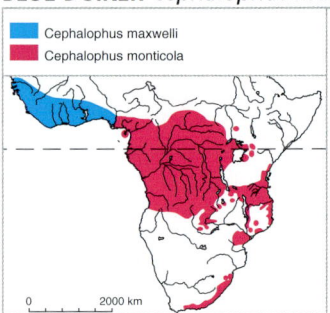

SIZE HB 55–90cm. T 7–13cm. H 32–41cm. W 3.5–9kg.
DESCRIPTION Small grey or brown antelope. Tail has underside and fringe with white hairs that reflect light. Subspecies: 26 named. Seven main populations.
HABITAT Lowland and montane rainforests, riverine and littoral forests and moist thickets.
FOOD Up to 80% of the diet may be fruit. Also foliage, traces of gum and animal matter.
BEHAVIOUR Bonded pairs on a small and regularly traversed territory (as little as 2.5–4ha).

MAXWELL'S DUIKER *Cephalophus maxwelli*
SIZE HB 63–76cm. T 12–15cm. H 35–42cm. W 6–10kg.
DESCRIPTION Strongly marked and more angular head. Grey-brown with paler underparts.
HABITAT Rainforest or derived savannahs.
FOOD Fallen fruits, herbs, shrubs and new growth; probably some animal matter.
BEHAVIOUR Pairs share a small common territory defended against others of the same sex.

ADER'S DUIKER *Cephalophus adersi*   no map
SIZE HB 66–72cm. T 9–12cm. H 30–32cm. W 6.5–12kg.
DESCRIPTION Washed-out, tawny red ground colour with a bold white band across the buttocks. Muzzle is pointed, with a rather flat front to the nose. Genetically at the root of duiker radiation.
HABITAT In Zanzibar has become almost entirely restricted to tall thicket forest growing on waterless coral rag. Probably extinct on mainland. Zanzibar policies likely to result in extinction of this species.
FOOD Fallen flowers, fruits and leaves.
BEHAVIOUR Pairs live in territories and breed throughout the year.

ZEBRA DUIKER *Cephalophus zebra*
Cephalophus zebra
Supposed former ranges

SIZE HB 70–90cm. T 10–15cm. H 40–50cm. W 15–20kg.
DESCRIPTION Head, shoulders, lower legs russet red. Hocks, muzzle and leg joints black. Back striped.
HABITAT Primary forests and margins.
FOOD Fruits and foliage.
BEHAVIOUR Because both sexes have horns and a thickened skull, it is likely that pairs share defence of home range.

Bush Duiker

Studies of Bush Duikers

Blue Duiker
C. m. aequatorialis

Maxwell's Duiker

Ader's Duiker

Zebra Duiker

PLATE 101 DUIKERS

NATAL DUIKER *Cephalophus natalensis*

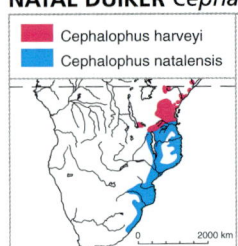

Cephalophus harveyi
Cephalophus natalensis

SIZE HB 75–87cm. T 9–14cm. H 40–43cm. W 12–14kg.
DESCRIPTION Small with red body, legs and frontal tuft. Margins of ears, chin, throat and underside of the tail are white. Upperside of tail, ears and muzzle black.
HABITAT From central Natal to the R. Rufiji valley, inhabiting coastal forests and thickets, low-lying riverine growth, escarpment and montane forests east of L. Malawi and the R. Shire.
FOOD Opportunistic; fruits, flowers and foliage. All feeding normally diurnal. Nocturnal in disturbed areas.

HARVEY'S DUIKER *Cephalophus harveyi*   see map above
SZE HB 85–95cm. T 11–15cm. H 44–50cm. W 13–16kg.
DESCRIPTION Rich red with a black line down the centre of the face and nape. The white, tufted ears are black-tipped.
HABITAT From coastal thickets to montane forests, riverine gallery and secondary forests wherever there is a variety of fruiting and flowering trees and shrubs.
FOOD Fruits, flowers and foliage from the forest floor. Diurnal.

RUWENZORI RED DUIKER *Cephalophus rubidus*   no map
SIZE HB 75cm. T av. 10cm. H av. 45cm. W est. 15kg.
DESCRIPTION Stocky. Glossy rufous coat, long, coarse hair on neck. Dense, soft fur over hindquarters.
HABITAT Afro-alpine, subalpine and woodland zones of Ruwenzori mountains.
FOOD Browse in a pasture of herbs. Mainly diurnal but activity periods influenced by rain.

RED-FLANKED DUIKER *Cephalophus rufilatus*

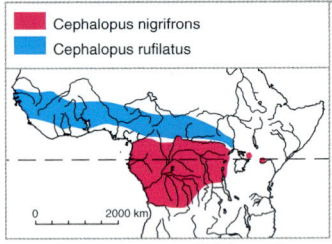

Cephalopus nigrifrons
Cephalopus rufilatus

SIZE HB 60–80cm. T 7–10cm. H 30–38cm. W 6–14kg.
DESCRIPTION Bright orange red on face, neck and flanks, brown or blue-grey gauntlets on limbs and brown or grey dorsal patch. Black nose and lower lip contrast strongly with white jaws and upper lip. Subspecies: *C. r. rufilatus* (Senegal to Chari valley), *C. r. rubidor* (Chari to Nile Valley).
HABITAT Resident, territorial species living in forest relicts and riverine thickets within the savannah along a broad band of country from Senegal to NW Uganda.
FOOD Fruits, flowers and foliage from numerous riverine species of trees, shrubs and herbs.

BLACK-FRONTED DUIKER *Cephalophus nigrifrons*   see map above
SIZE HB 80–107cm. T 7.5–15cm. H 45–58cm. W 14–18kg.
DESCRIPTION Long-legged, long-hooved duiker. Glossy red coat plain and thin in lowlands, thicker, darker and more grizzled in montane forest. Pale 'brow' below black forehead. Subspecies: *C. n. nigrifrons* (lowland forest from Cameroon to E Zaïre), *C. n. kivuensis* (W Rift mountains), *C. n. fosteri* (Mt Elgon), *C. n. hooki* (Mt Kenya).
HABITAT From Cameroon to Mt Kenya. Adapted to swamp forest and marshes at altitudes up to 3,500m. Territories marked with face glands and loud call.
FOOD Variety of fruits and succulent vegetation. A ratio of 72% fruits to 28% foliage recorded in fruit-rich Gabonese forest.

Natal Duiker

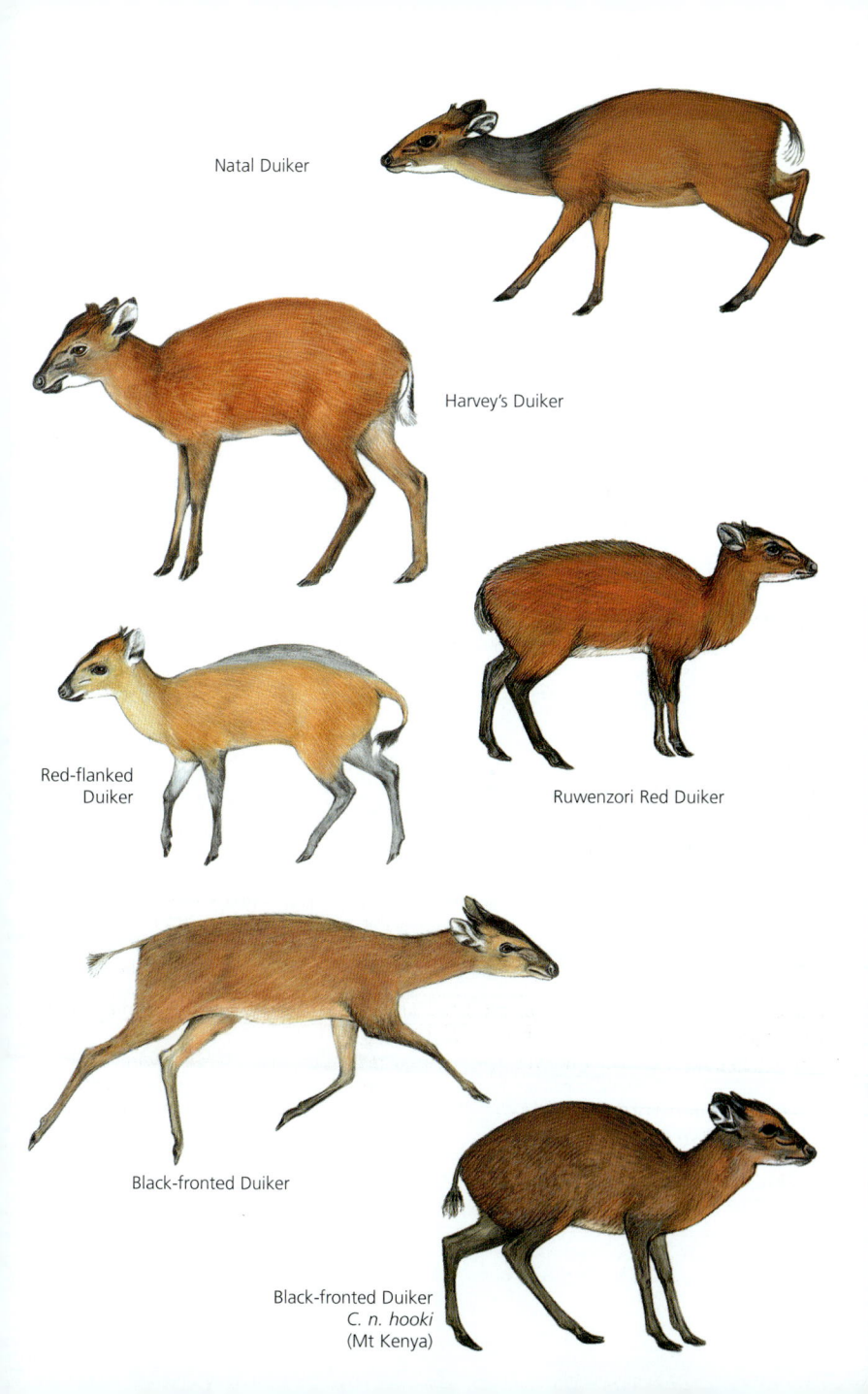

Harvey's Duiker

Red-flanked Duiker

Ruwenzori Red Duiker

Black-fronted Duiker

Black-fronted Duiker
C. n. hooki
(Mt Kenya)

WHITE-BELLIED DUIKER *Cephalophus leucogaster*

SIZE HB 78–100cm. T 8–15cm. H 42–51cm. W 15–20kg.
DESCRIPTION Pale with warm, sandy-brown forequarters, graduating towards grey near the black dorsal line. Fluffy, black and white-tipped tail.
HABITAT Sparsely and intermittently distributed from the R. Sanaga to W Rift, but only north of R. Zaïre. Only known to be common in a few highly localised places (notably N Gabon and Congo).
FOOD A ratio of 75% fruits to 25% foliage (and a marked taste for flowers) recorded in Gabon. Hard-shelled fruits (among them mututu, *Klainedoxa*) in diet implies ability to smash them open (probably with the forehead).

PETERS'S DUIKER *Cephalophus callipygus*

Cephalophus niger
Cephalophus callipygus

SIZE HB 80–115cm. T 8–16cm. H 45–60cm. W 16–23kg.
DESCRIPTION Very variable colouring, from pale tawny to rich russet or dark brown. Russet frontal tuft. Forehead heavily reinforced. Four subspecies described.
HABITAT Ranges through equatorial forest zone from Cameroon to W Kenya.
FOOD 83% fruits and only 16% leaves (at Makoku, Gabon).

BLACK DUIKER *Cephalophus niger* see map above

SIZE HB 80–100cm. T 7–14cm. H 45–55cm. W 16–24kg.
DESCRIPTION Glossy black, with swollen nostrils and short, stocky legs. Short horns, normally present in both sexes, hidden in coronal tuft of dense reddish hair.
HABITAT Rainforest from Sierra Leone to SW Nigeria.
FOOD Fruits and flowers, leaves and herbs. Dependent on year-round fruit fall.

ABBOTT'S DUIKER *Cephalophus spadix*

Cephalophus spadix
Cephalophus silvicultor

SIZE HB 97–140cm. T 8–13cm. H 66–74cm. W 50–60kg.
DESCRIPTION Glossy, nearly black, with a paler grey face, a very prominent russet tuft between the horns and a reddish tinge to the belly and lower flanks. The wedge-shaped head ends with a broad, flat-fronted nostril pad that overhangs the mouth.
HABITAT Montane forest duiker restricted to wetter (and therefore mainly eastern) sides of a few isolated massifs in E and S Tanzania. It is commonest in the Kilimanjaro National Park and Forest Reserve between 1,300 and 2,700m in forest and high-altitude swamps.
FOOD Fruits, flowers, green shoots and herbage; recorded browsing balsam (*Impatiens*).

YELLOW-BACKED DUIKER *Cephalophus silvicultor* see map above

SIZE HB 125–190cm. T 11–20cm. H 65–87cm. W 45–80kg.
DESCRIPTION Greyish brown with vivid cream-coloured patch on back. Long, wedge-shaped head has light grey muzzle and cheeks ending in a shiny black rhinarium.
HABITAT Rainforest, montane forests and many permutations of forest–savannah mosaics, from narrow riverine strips to fragmented woods. Attracted to salt-licks.
FOOD Fallen seeds, fruits, berries and bark of shrubs, fungi, ground moss and many herbs.
BEHAVIOUR Mainly solitary and spaced out in territories (probably shared by a male and female).

White-bellied Duiker

Peters's Duiker
C. c. weynsi

Black Duiker

Abbott's Duiker

Yellow-backed Duiker

OGILBY'S DUIKER *Cephalophus ogilbyi*

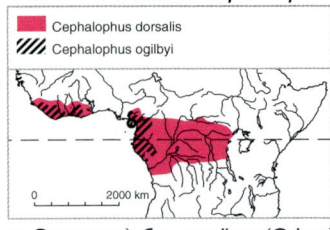

Cephalophus dorsalis
Cephalophus ogilbyi

SIZE HB 85–115cm. T 12–15cm. H 55–56cm. W 14–20kg.
DESCRIPTION Orange to mahogany-coloured with a very red rump, a paler underside, and a black dorsal line (of variable extent). Face has marked brows and short but peculiarly curved horns with strong corrugations (in both sexes). In common with the Bay Duiker and Jentink's Duiker, this species has massive hindquarters and a deep, slab-sided body but, unlike them, has long, slender legs. Subspecies: *C. o. ogilby* (Bioko), *C. o. brookei* (Sierra Leone to Cameroon), *C. o. crusalbum* (Gabon).
HABITAT Primarily forests close to the W African coast, where it is rare and patchily distributed. On Bioko I. it is a common and dominant species. The absence of other large duikers (especially the Bay Duiker) is clearly a factor.
FOOD Mainly fallen fruits, with the large, hard fruits of mututu (*Klainedoxa*) noted. Distribution might be influenced by a superabundance of fibrous fruits and numerous primates, which contribute to the fruit-fall.

BAY DUIKER *Cephalophus dorsalis*   see map above

SIZE HB 70–100cm. T 8–15cm. H 40–56cm. W 15–24kg.
DESCRIPTION Heavily built with a red or yellowish brown coat, black or dark brown legs and a black midline along back and belly (definition varies individually). Fur coarse. Muzzle extremely reduced, strongly tapered. Eyes larger and higher in the head and head is broader and flatter than in any other duiker. Subspecies: *C. d. dorsalis* (Senegal to Togo), *C. d. castaneus* (E Nigeria to E Zaïre).
HABITAT The entire equatorial lowland rainforest block from Senegal to L. Tanganyika, with a preference for high primary rainforest. Also patches within savannah mosaics (if undisturbed). May visit edges of clearings and prefers well-diversified zones with both dry and waterlogged areas. Shelters in hollow trees, between buttresses, under fallen trunks and in dark, dense thickets, only emerging to feed at night. Lives at low density; 2 or 3 animals inhabit 12–20ha.
FOOD Hard or fibrous fruits, such as wild mango (*Irvingia*), mututu apples (*Klainedoxa*), African breadfruit (*Treculia*), and white star apple (*Chrysophyllum*), have been recorded; also less difficult fruits, such as monkey orange (*Strychnos*) and yellow mulberry (*Myrianthus*). Also known to stalk, kill and eat birds but fruits accounted for 73%, and foliage 27%, in a Gabon sample.

JENTINK'S DUIKER *Cephalophus jentinki*

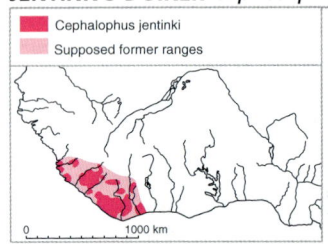

Cephalophus jentinki
Supposed former ranges

SIZE HB est. 130–150cm. T est. 12–16cm. H est. 75–100cm. W est. 55–80kg.
DESCRIPTION A long-horned (up to 17cm), very robust, short-legged duiker with a bold pattern of black, white and grey. The nearly black head and neck are offset by a vivid white halter over the shoulders and lower chest and a white border surrounds mouth and nose. This colouring involves both skin and fur, the latter being extremely short and fine. In contrast to the fore-end the hindquarters are grey agouti.
HABITAT Only found in the high primary forest zone between Sierra Leone and the R. Niouniourou, a distribution that broadly coincides with many monkey populations and also that of the Zebra Duiker. Within this zone it enters secondary growth, scrub, farms, plantations and is even known to visit the seashore, presumably for salt. It is a 'hider', choosing hollow trees, fallen trunks and the buttress bays of kapok (*Ceiba*), *Bombax*, and mututu trees (*Klainedoxa*) for shelter. Unusually for duikers they sometimes lie up in pairs. Like the Bay Duiker it bolts from these daytime refuges with great speed if discovered, but has no stamina and does not go far.
FOOD Known to enter plantations to eat palm nuts, mangoes and cocoa pods. The growing stems of tree seedlings are eaten (African teak, *Chlorophora*, has been identified).

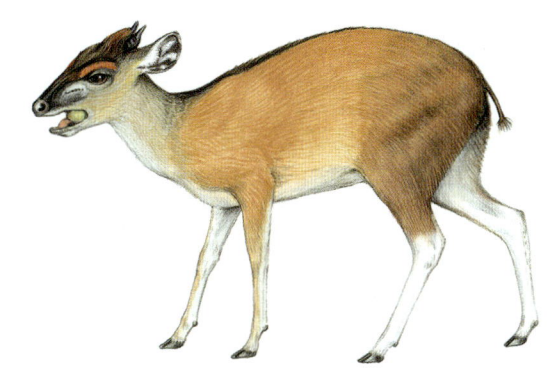

Ogilby's Duiker

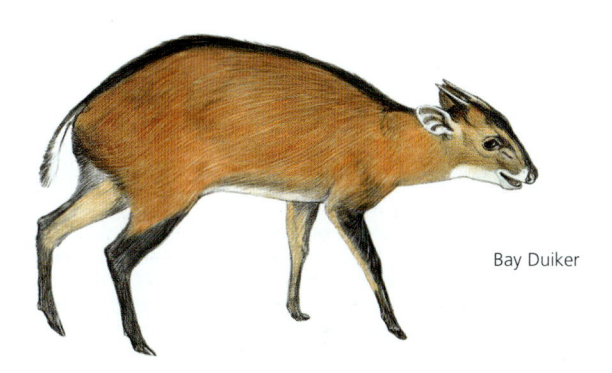

Bay Duiker

Jentink's Duiker

DWARF ANTELOPES Neotragini

A taxonomic 'basket' for living survivors of a bovid root stock. They have slender legs, longish neck, large eyes, large preorbital glands and simple spike horns in males.

ROYAL ANTELOPE *Neotragus pygmaeus*

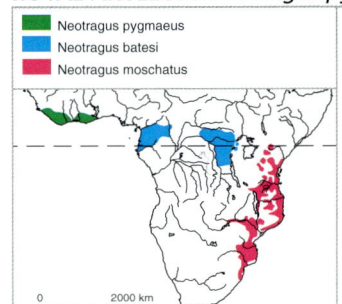

- Neotragus pygmaeus
- Neotragus batesi
- Neotragus moschatus

SIZE HB 38–51cm. T 5–8cm. H 24–26cm. W 1.5–3kg.
DESCRIPTION Reddish or golden brown, white belly, chin and chest. Tiny, conical horns. Gait high-stepping under bunched, compact body but it can slip away in a ground-hugging scamper or fast, high jumps.
HABITAT Dense undergrowth along forest edges, in clearings, road verges and cultivation, in moist forest belt and galleries in forest–savannah mosaics.
FOOD Fresh greenery, buds, leaves, fruits and fungi.

DWARF ANTELOPE *Neotragus batesi*

SIZE HB 50–57.5cm. T 4.5–8cm. H 24–33cm. W 2–5.5kg. (female averages 0.6kg heavier).
DESCRIPTION Soft mahogany-brown fur has a shiny gloss. White markings are conspicuous. The smaller male has very short conical horns. Subspecies: *N. b. batesi* (R Niger – R Zaïre), *N. b. harrisoni* (NE Zaïre, W Uganda).
HABITAT Dense, low undergrowth near watercourses, roads, gardens and chablis (tree falls).
FOOD Browses leaves and shoots.

SUNI *Neotragus moschatus*   see map above

SIZE HB 57–62cm. T 8–13cm. H 30–41cm. W 4–6kg.
DESCRIPTION Compact stance and disproportionately broad head on a short neck. Males have finely annulated horns; 13cm maximum. Enormous facial glands, especially in males. Tail has a white underside and is flashed from side to side (rather than flipped up and down as Blue Duiker). Subspecies: *N. m. moschatus* (Zanzibar), *N. m. livingstonianus* (East African mainland), *N. m. zuluensis* (S Africa).
HABITAT Coastal forests and thickets wherever there is thick undergrowth and regenerating fallow.
FOOD A variety of leaves, shoots and herbs and, more rarely, grass roots and mushrooms.

CAPE GRYSBOK *Raphicerus melanotis*

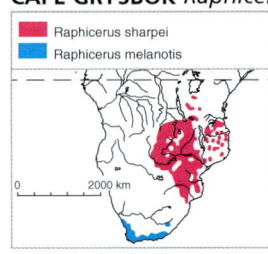

- Raphicerus sharpei
- Raphicerus melanotis

SIZE HB 65–80cm. T 4–8cm. H 45–55cm. W 8–12kg (female 0.5kg heavier).
DESCRIPTION Thick-coated, chunky. Strawberry roan in colour. Ears very large and lined with white hair. Males have short, smooth, widely spaced horns. Rump fur can be fluffed out. Tail short and inconspicuous.
HABITAT Scrub thickets bordering hills, gorges and dunes.
FOOD Browses thicket and shrubby growth. Feeds mainly at night.

SHARPE'S GRYSBOK *Raphicerus sharpei*   see map above

SIZE HB 61–75cm. T 5–7cm. H 45–60cm. W 7–11.5kg.
DESCRIPTION 'Skirt' of elongated fur over the hindquarters. The reddish fawn fur densely interspersed with white hairs. Horns present in males only.
HABITAT L. Victoria to Transvaal, Zambezi valley bounds western limits. Generally scarce and localised.
FOOD Browses leaves, buds, herbs and fruits including tough dry material.

Royal Antelope

Dwarf Antelope

Suni

Cape Grysbok

Sharpe's Grysbok

STEINBUCK *Raphicerus campestris*

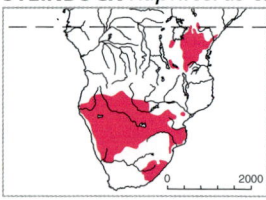

SIZE HB 70–95cm. T 4–6cm. H 45–60cm. W 7–16kg.
DESCRIPTION Can be mistaken for Bush Duiker or Oribi but has rounded hauches without visible tail, very large, white-lined ears, a retroussé, black-bridged nose and big, black-rimmed eyes encircled by white. Males have upright, spiked horns. Subspecies: *R. c. campestris* (S Africa), *R. c. neumanni* (E Africa).
HABITAT In S Africa mainly open plains. In E Africa common in stony savannahs and among *Acacia*–grassland mosaics.
FOOD Browses at or near ground level and adept at scraping up selected roots and tubers. Favours shoots of dominant shrub and tree species.
BEHAVIOUR Pairs live for long periods with same partner on same territory (4ha to 1km^2).

ORIBI *Ourebia ourebi*

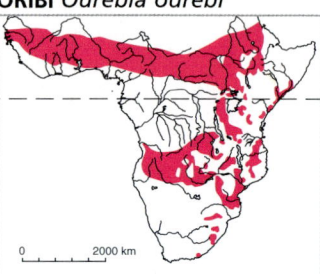

SIZE HB 92–140cm. T 6–15cm. H 50–67cm. W 12–22kg. (female averages 2kg heavier).
DESCRIPTION Tall, slender, sandy body colour, with white undersides, upper throat, mouth and ear linings. Light-coloured muzzle deflects down sharply from the forehead. Alert and shy, utters piercing whistle as it flees with rocking-horse gait. 7 subspecies listed.
HABITAT Grasslands. Prefers flats or gentle slopes. Commonest on lawns of short grass.
FOOD Mainly fresh green grass typical of fire-climax communities.
BEHAVIOUR Females larger than males and independent in their movements but, as the object of continuous attention from a single male, each adult female determines the area within which he is intolerant of other males. Whistle may serve as both alarm and also to advertise shifting positions and movement.

KLIPSPRINGER *Oreotragus oreotragus*

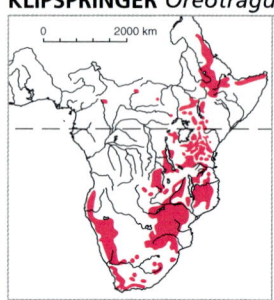

SIZE HB 75–115cm. T 6.5–10.5cm. H 43–60cm. W 8–18kg (av. weights vary regionally 10–15kg).
DESCRIPTION Unique for walking on the tips of its hooves and for its dense cloak of lightweight fur, which is brittle, coarse and rustles when shaken or touched. Short, wedge-shaped face. 7 subspecies listed.
HABITAT Varied. Two features in common: rocky, stony ground and abundant short vegetation.
FOOD Herbs and low foliage. Grass a wet-season food.
BEHAVIOUR Female generally attended by a male. Young or an adult offspring with her or nearby. 'Duets' of whistling are a means of regaining contact after disturbance.

BEIRA *Dorcatragus megalotis*

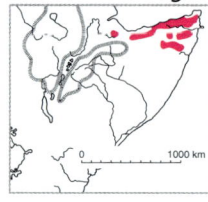

SIZE HB 76–87cm. T 5–8cm. H 50–76cm. W 9–12kg.
DESCRIPTION Long-legged, long-necked antelope with enormous ears, vertical, upright horns (9–13cm) in the males only, and goat-like hooves. Intensely black eyelids contrast strongly with surrounding brilliant white fur.
HABITAT Usually close to stony ridges, gorges and plateau margins.
FOOD Herbs and browsed leaves and buds.
BEHAVIOUR Pairs or parties with single male. Groups of up to 12 probably associations of 2 neighbouring families.

Steinbuck

Steinbuck detail

Oribi

Klipspringer

Beira

Klipspringer detail

DIKDIKS *Madoqua*

A radiation of very small, long-legged antelopes with a fine, soft, grizzled (sometimes colourful) coat. Relatively large eyes and ears, a prominent crest and a fur-covered nose that is enlarged into a proboscis in several species.

SALT'S DIKDIK *Madoqua saltiana*

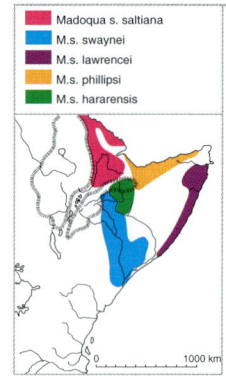

- Madoqua s. saltiana
- M.s. swaynei
- M.s. lawrencei
- M.s. phillipsi
- M.s. hararensis

SIZE HB 52–67cm. T 3–4.5cm. H 33–40.5cm. W 2.5–4kg.
DESCRIPTION Small, with short, squared-off, furry nose. Short male horns up to 9cm. Coat agouti-freckled and legs sandy or reddish. 5 subspecies (see map).
HABITAT Evergreen and semi-deciduous bushlands and thickets in Horn of Africa.
FOOD Herbs, foliage and shoots, especially *Acacia*.
BEHAVIOUR Predominantly nocturnal and crepuscular. Subordinates (of both sexes) lower forequarters and expose greyer backs. Dominant animals flare crests and strut in side-on displays of red or yellow limbs and flanks.

SILVER DIKDIK *Madoqua piacentinii* see map below

SIZE HB 45–50cm. T est. 3–4cm. H 30–33cm. W est. 2–3kg.
DESCRIPTION Soft, fine fur, back and sides uniform silvery grizzle. Limbs, ears and muzzle sandy ochre. Bridge of nose often a vivid russet.
HABITAT Low, dense thickets growing along Obbia coast.
FOOD Shoots and foliage of shrubs and herbs in undergrowth.

KIRK'S DIKDIK complex *Madoqua (kirkii)* (4 species)

- Madoqua saltiana
- Madoqua kirkii complex
- Madoqua guentheri
- Madoqua piacentinii

SIZE HB 55–72cm. T 4–6cm. H 35–45cm. W 3.8–7.2kg.
DESCRIPTION Very slender, small-snouted dikdiks with grizzled or salt-and-pepper grey coats more or less suffused with yellowish ochre tints. Eyes bordered with white; ear lining, chin and belly also white. 4 genetically distinct forms very similar in appearance. *M. (k.) kirkii* Somali–Kenya coast. *M. (k.) cavendishi* E. African uplands. *M. (k.) thomasi* central Tanzania. *M. (k.) damarensis* SW Africa.
HABITAT Each taxon occupies a distinct geographic region of bushland.
FOOD Evergreen shoots and foliage of herbs and shrubs.
BEHAVIOUR Diurnal/nocturnal. Similar habits to other dikdiks.

GÜNTHER'S DIKDIK *Madoqua guentheri* see map above

SIZE HB 55–65cm. T 3–5cm. H 34–38cm. W 3.7–5.5kg.
DESCRIPTION Small, slender, grizzled grey with brown or reddish flushes on sides and neck, reddish fawn legs, nose and back of ears. Belly, chin, fur in the ear and around the eye are white. Nose is longer and more elastic than any other dikdik but capacity to extend, shorten, 'empty' or inflate the proboscis makes it a difficult characteristic for distinguishing *M. guentheri* in the field.
HABITAT Of all dikdiks, live in the driest, hottest desert and subdesert scrub.
FOOD Green (and wilted) foliage, buds, shoots and bark of dwarf shrubs and herbs.

Silver Dikdik

Salt's Dikdik

Kirk's Dikdik
female

Günther's Dikdik
male

RHEBOK Peleini
A taxon to accommodate the enigmatic Rhebok.

RHEBOK *Pelea capreolus*

SIZE HB 105–125cm. T 10–20cm. SH 70–80cm. W 18–30kg.
DESCRIPTION Woolly, tawny grey coat rounds the body contours. Blunt, swollen nose. Ears very long and pointed; black-lidded eyes. Males have vertical spike horns up to 29cm.
HABITAT Highveld, 'sourvelt' and secondary grasslands, mainly on plateaus and mountains.
FOOD Mainly a grazer. Independent of water.
BEHAVIOUR A female and her female offspring provide a basic social unit of up to 14.

REEDBUCKS and KOBS Reduncini
Medium-sized to large antelopes, well-muscled bodies, thick neck (especially in males). Largest species shaggy; smaller ones sleek. Restricted to well-watered areas.

MOUNTAIN REEDBUCK *Redunca fulvorufula*

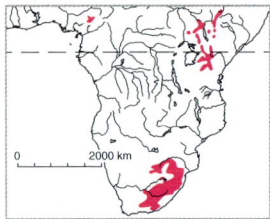

SIZE HB 110–136cm. T 17–26cm. SH 60–80cm. W 19–35kg (female), 22–38kg (male).
DESCRIPTION Soft, fleecy fur tawny grey, white underparts and underside to the tail. Eyes prominent and, in males, short, forward-curved black horns. 3 disjunct subspecies: *R. f. fulvorufula* (S Africa), *R. f. chanleri* (E and NE Africa), *R. f. adamuae* (N Cameroon).
HABITAT Prefers grassy ridges in broken rocky country.
FOOD Grazers; *Themeda*, *Hyparrhenia* and *Cymbopogon* recorded.
BEHAVIOUR Two to 8 females with young but temporary aggregations of up to 50 can form.

BOHOR REEDBUCK *Redunca redunca*

Redunca redunca
Redunca arundinum

SIZE HB 100–135cm. T 18–20cm. SH 65–89cm. W 35–45kg (female), 43–65kg (male).
DESCRIPTION Slender proportions of females contrast with the thick-necked, horned males. Black patches below ears. Loud whistles (mainly uttered at night). 4 subspecies listed.
HABITAT Mostly large-scale sump grasslands with extensive annual flooding, drought and fires.
FOOD Exclusively grazers with a recorded preference for typically dominant species. Feed mainly after dark.
BEHAVIOUR Females disperse into discrete home ranges during the wet season (when most young are born). Males also scattered at this time.

SOUTHERN REEDBUCK *Redunca arundinum* see map above

SIZE HB 120–160cm. T 18–30cm. SH 65–105cm. W 50–85kg (female), 60–95kg (male).
DESCRIPTION Largest reedbuck with fine, almost woolly coat. Black and white markings on the front of the forelegs prominent. The horns, only on males, grow up to 45cm long. Subspecies: *R. a. arundinum* (south of Zambezi), *R. a. occidentalis* (tropical Africa).
HABITAT Widely distributed in grass valleys and glades within Miombo (*Brachystegia*) woodlands. Adapted to mosaics of scrub and grass.
FOOD Favourites are dominants in their habitat, i.e. *Hyparrhenia*, *Panicum* and *Leersia*.
BEHAVIOUR Converge on water sources in the dry season. Disperse widely when grass tall.

Rhebok

Mountain Reedbuck

Bohor Reedbuck

Southern Reedbuck

KOB *Kobus kob*

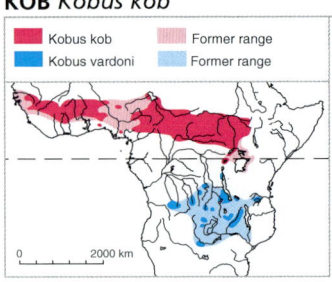

SIZE HB 160–180cm. T 10–15cm. SH 82–92cm (female), 90–100cm (male). W 60–77kg (female), 85–121kg (male).
DESCRIPTION Males have thick, lyrate horns; colouring varies from rufous, or pale brown, to black and white in the Sudd floodplain. Subspecies: Western Kob, *K. k. kob* (northern savannahs), Uganda Kob, *K. k. thomasi* (E Africa and NE Zaïre), White-eared Kob, *K. k. leucotis* (Sudd floodplain).
HABITAT Flats or gently rolling country close to water.
FOOD Grazers of the commonest grasses.
BEHAVIOUR Resident populations move daily between habitual grazing grounds and watering places.

PUKU *Kobus vardoni* (genetically close to Kob)   see map above

SIZE HB 126–142cm. T 28–32cm. H 77–83cm. W 48–78kg (female), 67–91kg (male).
DESCRIPTION Has heavier proportions, a coarser coat and shorter horns than the Kob.
HABITAT More tolerant of narrow grasslands and park-like woodlands than the Kob.
FOOD Preferred grasses are *Brachiaria*, *Eragrostis*, and *Vossia* shoots.

LECHWE *Kobus leche*

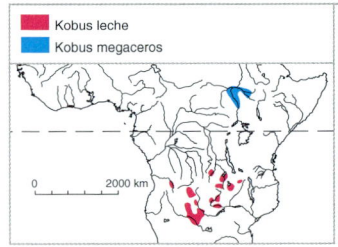

SIZE HB 130–170cm (female), 160–180cm (male). T 30–45cm. SH 85–95cm (female), 85–110cm (male). W 60–95kg (female), 85–130kg (male).
DESCRIPTION Heavily built, with elevated haunches. Splayed, elongated hooves. In males, long annulated horns. Subspecies: Red Lechwe, *K. l. lechwe* (NW Zambia, Zaïre, Angola, Botswana), Kafue Lechwe, *K. l. kafuensis* (Kafue flats), Black Lechwe, *K. l. smithemani* (Bengweulu basin).
HABITAT Margins between swamps and floodplains.
FOOD Grasses and shoots of trampled reeds.
BEHAVIOUR Females concentrate where best grazing is localised, dispersing when it is widespread.

NILE LECHWE *Kobus megaceros*   see map above

SIZE HB est. 130–170cm (female), est. 160–180cm (male). T 45–50cm. SH est. 80–85cm (female), est. 100–105cm (male). W est. 60–90kg (female), est. 90–120kg (male).
DESCRIPTION Short face. Hooves exceptionally elongated. Males have lyrate horns and slowly darken over several years. Upper shoulder creamy white.
HABITAT Grasslands between deep swamp and rain-flooded grasslands (Sudd region of White Nile).
FOOD *Oryza* in early flood season but mainly *Leersia*, *Echinochloa* and *Vossia* as floods recede.
BEHAVIOUR Females determine movements. Adult males drive other males away from female groups.

WATERBUCK *Kobus ellipsiprymnus*

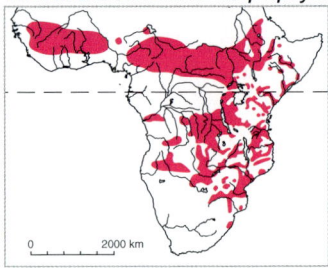

SIZE HB 177–235cm. T 33–40cm. SH 120–136cm. W 160–200kg (female), 200–300kg (male).
DESCRIPTION Variable in colour. Grey and rufous individuals in mixed groups. Male has long horns (50–99cm). Subspecies: *K. e. ellipsiprymnus* (SE Africa), rump crescent; *K. e. defassa* (NE, central and W Africa), white under tail.
HABITAT Sedentary in savannahs, woodlands and mosaics close to permanent water.
FOOD Many grass species, including reeds and rushes.
BEHAVIOUR Both sexes remain for up to 8 years on same home range.

Kob
K. k. thomasi

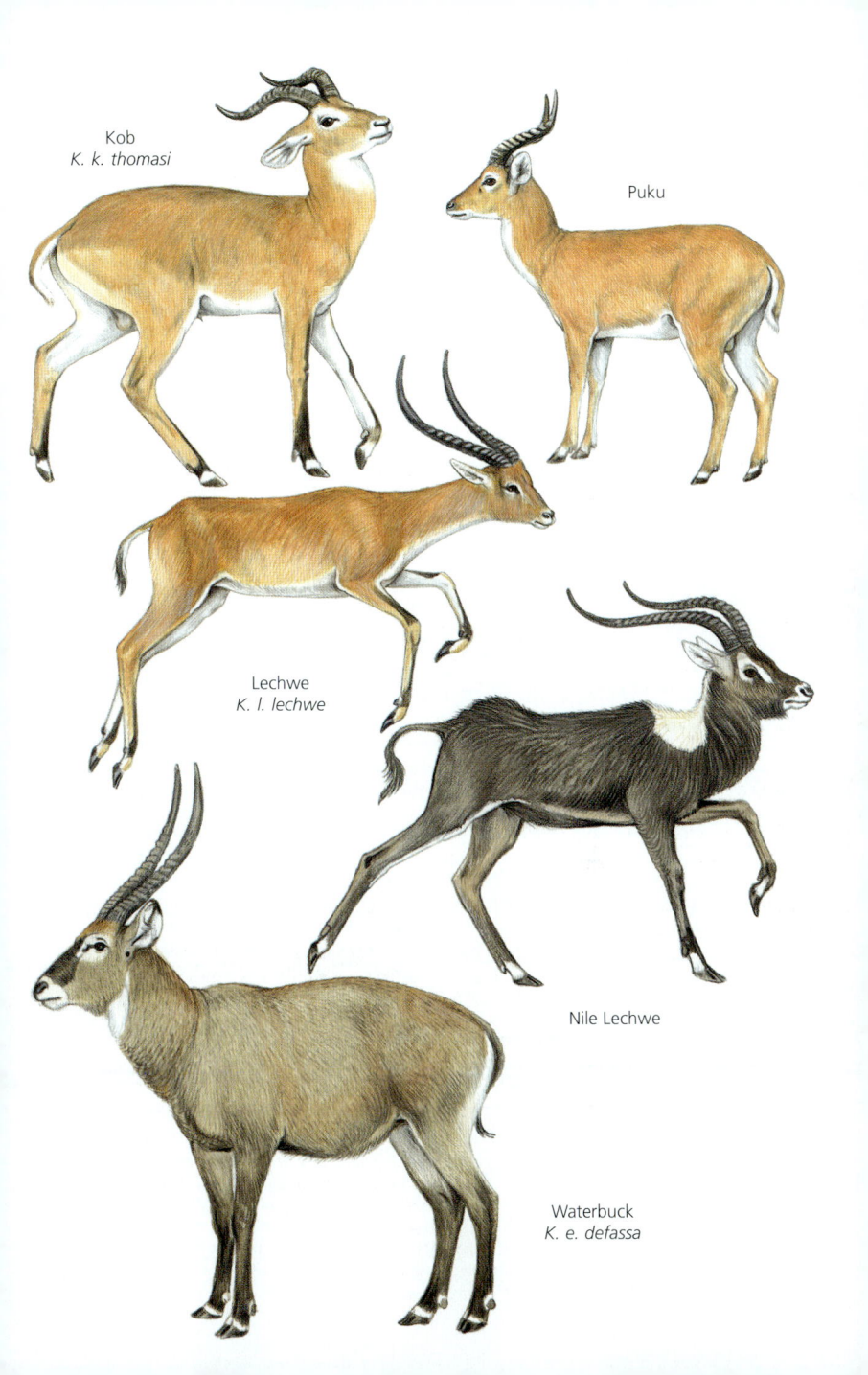

Puku

Lechwe
K. l. lechwe

Nile Lechwe

Waterbuck
K. e. defassa

GAZELLINE ANTELOPES Antilopini

Long-legged, long-necked antelopes with light-coloured coat, large sensitive eyes and ears, a small mouth and, in some species, preorbital glands. Alert to both sound and movement.

GAZELLES *Gazella*

Slender, fawn or rufous antelopes; often with dark flank-mark separating body colour from white underparts. Divided into small and large desert gazelles, gleaners, and cold-adapted gazelles.

DORCAS GAZELLE *Gazella dorcas*   *see also* map below

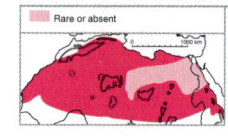

SIZE HB 90–110cm. T 15–20cm. SH 55–65cm. W 15–20kg.
DESCRIPTION Smallest gazelle but proportionally longest limbed. Very long ears. Lyre-shaped horns, on both sexes. 5 subspecies listed.
HABITAT N and NE Africa in subdeserts with sparse vegetation.
FOOD Herbs, succulents and shoots of shrubs.

SPEKE'S GAZELLE *Gazella spekei*

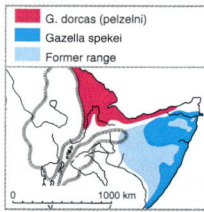

SIZE HB 95–105cm. T 15–20cm. SH 50–60cm. W 15–25kg.
DESCRIPTION Small, with inflatable nasal region. Fawn with black flank stripe, white buttocks with dark margins. A pale face.
HABITAT Ocean littoral of Somalia in stony semi-desert dominated by stunted shrubs and sparse desert grasses.
FOOD Grass, herbs, shrubs and succulents.

THOMSON'S (RED-FRONTED) GAZELLE *Gazella rufifrons*

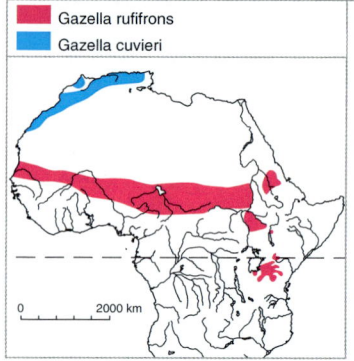

SIZE HB 80–120cm. T 15–27cm. H 55–82cm. W 15–25kg (female), 20–35kg (male).
DESCRIPTION Reddish back and white underparts separated by black flank band. White buttocks have black marginal stripes. Subspecies: Red-fronted Gazelle (*rufifrons, laevipes, kanuri*), Sahel; Eritrean Gazelle (*tilonura*), Eritrea; Mongalla Gazelle (*albonotata*), Sudd, east of Nile; Thomson's Gazelle (*thomsoni, nasalis*), E and W of Rift Valley; Red Gazelle (*rufina*), Algeria, extinct?
HABITAT Dry grasslands and shrubby steppes of Sahel. Similar (but moister) habitats in E Africa.
FOOD Mainly growing green grass in rains but switches to herbs, foliage of shrubs and seeds in dry season.

CUVIER'S GAZELLE *Gazella cuvieri*

SIZE HB 95–105cm. T 15–20cm. SH 60–69cm. W 15–20kg (female), 20–35kg (male).
DESCRIPTION Grey-brown in colour. Nose has prominent black spot. Horns rise vertically before diverging out and back; smooth tips curving in and forwards.
HABITAT From Morocco to Algeria in maquis scrub, open parkland of pines, oak thickets and rushes.
FOOD Grass, herbs and shrubs; often visits cultivated fields.

RHIM GAZELLE *Gazella leptoceros*

SIZE HB 100–110cm. T 15–20cm. SH 65–72cm. W est. 14–18kg.
DESCRIPTION Pale yellowish grey, faintly marked with face and flank stripes. Ears long and narrow. Long, nearly straight horns.
HABITAT Confined to great sand deserts of E Sahara from Algeria to Egypt.
FOOD Feather grass (*Aristida pungens*, or 'drinn'); also succulents, herbs and foliage of shrubs.

- Dorcas Gazelle
- Speke's Gazelle
- Thomson's Gazelle
- Cuvier's Gazelle
- Rhim Gazelle

GRANT'S GAZELLE complex *Gazella (granti)* (3 species)

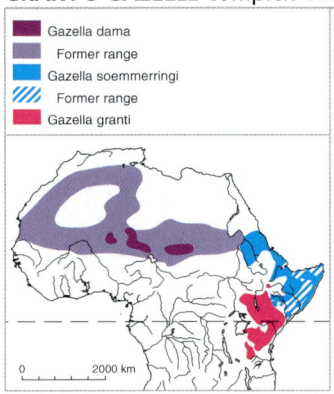

Gazella dama
Former range
Gazella soemmerringi
Former range
Gazella granti

SIZE HB 140–166cm. T 20–28cm. SH 78–83cm (female), 85–91cm (male). W 38–67kg (female), 60–81.5kg (male).
DESCRIPTION Large pale gazelles with upright stems to the long horns above relatively small eyes set in characteristic, leaf-shaped eye patches, or 'masks', of jet-black skin. Above nostrils a slightly inflatable nasal sac. Mouth proportionately large for a gazelle. Tail markedly tapered and carries a wispy fringe. Rectangular white buttock patch emphasised by dark vertical stripe down each thigh.
Species: Grant's Gazelle, *G. (g.) granti* (Mt Kenya to Ruaha valley); Bright's Gazelle, *G. (g.) notata* (north of Mt Kenya); Tana Gazelle, *G. (g.) petersi* (lower Tana valley).
HABITAT Distribution spills over from the central axis or 'spine' of the E Rift. This upland distribution coincides with rain-shadows and with an arid corridor of unstable climate across the E African plateau. The Tana species lives in the lower Tana valley, and west of the R. Juba in Somalia. Here the gazelles live on very flat plains that are briefly flooded during occasional and unpredictable rains. Where their range becomes dense bush the gazelles are restricted to glades or open, scrubby valleys. They do not tolerate soft soils but will live in bush and tall grass more readily than any other types of gazelle.
FOOD Herbs and shrub foliage during later wet and dry seasons; grass grazed while green.
BEHAVIOUR Fighting and territorial displays, characterised by flicking of raised head on bulging neck and slow, stiff circling, during biannual mating peaks.

SOEMMERRING'S GAZELLE *Gazella soemmerringi* see map above

SIZE HB 125–150cm. T 18–23cm. SH 81–90cm. W 38–46kg.
DESCRIPTION Large, generally pale gazelle with extensive white on rump, strongly marked facial blazes. Lyrate, backwardly swept horns have in-pointed hooked tips. Subspecies: *G. s. soemmerringi* (Sudan): brown face, shorter horns. *G. s. berberana* (Somalia): black face, longer horns. *G. s. butteri* (S Ethiopia): dark flank, thigh stripes.
HABITAT Endemic to Horn of Africa. Favours rough, hilly country with scattered evergreen thickets and *Acacia/Commiphora* steppe, as well as open, short-grass plains.
BEHAVIOUR Seldom seen in herds larger than about 15. Like Grant's Gazelle, males flick their heads during confrontations. Yank hookevalley); Bright's Gazelle, *G. (g.) notata* (north of Mt Kenya); Tana Gazelle, *G. (g.) petersi* (lower Tana valley).d horns sideways during fights in efforts to destabilise opponent.

DAMA GAZELLE *Gazella dama* see map above

SIZE HB 140–165cm. T 25–35cm. SH 90–120cm. W 40–75kg.
DESCRIPTION Largest gazelle, with long legs and neck, and short, compact, double-curved horns. The face and underparts are white in all forms; extent of rufous on upperparts varies according to population. Subspecies: Mhorr Gazelle, *G. d. dama* (W Sahara); Nubian Gazelle, *G. d. ruficollis* (Sahara west of the Nile).
HABITAT Until recently one of the most widespread and common of Sahara gazelles, making mass movements between its wet-season pastures deep in the Sahara and dry-season range in the semi-deserts and open bushlands of the Sahel.
FOOD Mainly herbs, succulents and shrubs (notably *Acacia*).
BEHAVIOUR Herds of many hundreds used to be seen on the move before dispersing into smaller groups numbering up to about 15.

Grant's Gazelle
G. (g.) granti

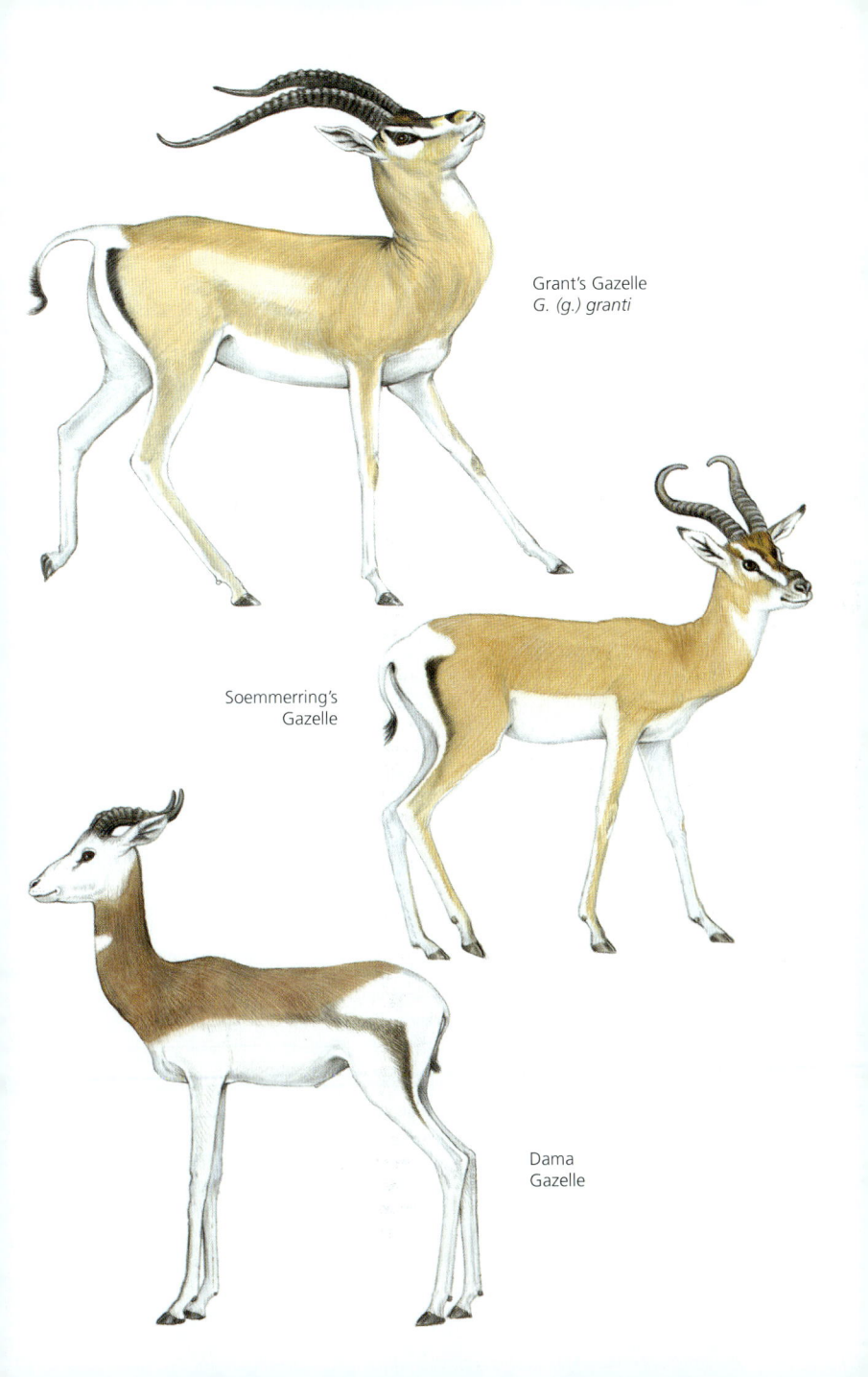

Soemmerring's Gazelle

Dama Gazelle

DIBATAG *Ammodorcas clarkei*

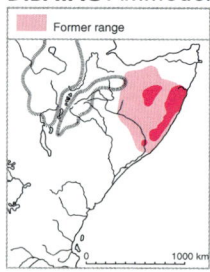

SIZE HB 152–168cm. T 30–36cm. SH 80–88cm. W 22–29kg.
DESCRIPTION Males have shortish horns with heavy bases and tips sharply angled forward. Tail, carried like a waggling baton, is conspicuous. During flight, tail and head held erect.
HABITAT Camel-brush or 'gedguwa', an *Acacia/Commiphora* deciduous bushland in central Somalia and the Ogaden (Ethiopia). Avoids dense thickets.
FOOD Foliage of *Acacia*, *Commiphora* and other shrubs.
BEHAVIOUR Males territorial, visiting latrines daily. Also reported to make periodic small-scale shifts in range. Up to 5 females and young seen with single adult males but singles or twos commoner. Fighting males tuck muzzle between forelegs for protection and clash horns along back surfaces.

GERENUK *Litocranius walleri*

SIZE HB 140–160cm. T 22–35cm. SH 80–105cm. W 28–45kg (female), 31–52kg (male).
DESCRIPTION Two-toned chestnut back, light fawn sides and white underparts. Dainty muzzle protrudes from a heavily reinforced brain-case. Males' horns have thick, diverging shafts, rising in a bold arc and then curling forward in a tight hook towards the tip.
HABITAT Dependent on an abundance of bushes and small trees, including evergreens. Avoids true, dense thickets and is commonest on flats where *Acacia*, *Commiphora* and other bushland species are well spaced or in small clumps.
FOOD Almost exclusively a tree-foliage browser (creepers and vines being the main exception). Acacias, with their very small, nutritious leaflets, are the major staple.
BEHAVIOUR Habitually rises on its hindlegs to reach a zone over 2m high. Normally very residential, living in well-spaced home ranges of 3–6km². Here single adult males exclude other adult males but regularly associate with females and their offspring. Males fight by clashing horns with violent downward nods of the head. The contact call is a frog-like humming grunt.

SPRINGBUCK *Antidorcas marsupialis*

SIZE HB 120–150cm. T 14–28cm. SH 68–90cm. W 20–43kg (female), 30–59kg (male).
DESCRIPTION A gazelle-like antelope with white underparts extending well up the sides, rump and dorsal midline. Head also white but marked from crown to mouth with brown streaks (which conceal very protuberant eyes). Upperparts cinnamon fawn above an arc of black or brown on the flanks. Differs from gazelles in having longer, broader and less flexible bridge to nose, deeper, more muscular cheeks, and horns that sweep backwards and hook inwards from peculiarly swollen bases. White dorsal crest normally hidden but can be erected (as can the white hair on the buttocks) to create an eye-catching signal.
HABITAT Dry, open plains with a marked preference for flat drainage lines and the fringes of pans where soil conditions or overgrazing keep grasses and herbs low.
FOOD Broadly a summer grazer and winter browser. Can survive on the residual moisture in plants.
BEHAVIOUR Females highly mobile, moving independently of one another (but with current offspring). Because they form no close attachment to others or to territory, less is known of them than males which comprise 3 main classes: immatures; unattached, non-breeding 'bachelors'; and territorial, breeding males. Juveniles and subadults have a habit of hunch-backed bouncing, 'pronking', conspicuously.

Dibatag

Gerenuk *male*

Gerenuk *female*

Springbuck

IMPALA Aepycerotinae

A taxon to accommodate the unique Impala. Previously thought to derive from a primitive Alcelaphine.

IMPALA *Aepyceros melampus*

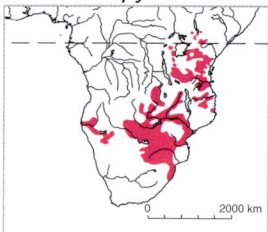

SIZE HB 120–160cm. T 30–45cm. SH 75–95cm. W 40–60kg (female), 45–80kg (male).

DESCRIPTION Gazelle-like with brown or yellowish brown back, lighter on haunches, shoulder, neck and head, and sharply lighter on flanks. Underside, chin, mouth and ear linings are white. Ear tips, thigh stripes, midline of tail and bushy fetlock glands are black. Adult males have long, narrow horns, with shallow, well-spaced annulations, that arch up and out then back and up.

Subspecies: Common Impala, *A. m. melampus* (SE Africa). Black-faced Impala, *A. m. petersi* (SW Africa).

HABITAT 'Edges' between grassland and denser woodlands are preferred. Require high-quality fodder (whether grass or leaves), moisture, shade and cover. In favourable localities numbers can reach over 200 per km^2. Grassland occupied during rains, woodland more in dry season.

FOOD Almost wholly grazers during the rains. Amount of grass in diet drops to about 30% in dry season when Impalas mostly in woodlands, browsing on shrubs, herbs, pods and seeds. Feeding usually in 2 major bouts (around dawn and dusk) and 2 minor bouts (midnight and early afternoon), with shading and ruminating in between.

BEHAVIOUR Females form 'clans' of 30–120 animals with home ranges radiating out from fairly stable centres but extensively overlapping ranges of neighbouring female clans. Year-round movements may extend for about 1km but core ranges estimated at 80–180ha. Although gregarious, neither females nor males form lasting associations (not even with their young). Most healthy adults males intolerant in presence of oestrus females, so fights very common during the rut.

ALCELAPHINES Alcelaphinae

Alcelaphines have long faces and legs, double-curved, hollow horns, fast gaits and a part or wholly grass diet. They are adapted to live at high densities on rich but unstable pastures.

HIROLA (HUNTER'S HARTEBEEST) *Beatragus hunteri*

SIZE HB 120–200cm. T 30–45cm. SH 100–125cm. W est. 80–118kg.

DESCRIPTION Of medium weight, with long legs and a long body but a relatively short neck and long face. Lyrate horns not unlike those of Impala but have less flare and much heavier bases with pronounced annulations. Uniform sandy colouring gives way to slaty grey in older males. Long tail and black-tipped ears startlingly white, as are 'spectacles' around eyes.

HABITAT A narrow strip of seasonally arid, grassy plains sandwiched between the waterless *Acacia* bush of the hinterland and forest–savannah mosaic on the coast. Northern margins of its range coincide with a type of very dry *Acacia* scrub where the grass cover becomes very much sparser.

FOOD Strictly a grazer, feeding on the dominant grasses, notably species of Chloris, Cenchrus and Digitaria. Feeds most intensively early morning and evening. Able to go without drinking, also survives drought by laying down fat and avoiding energetic activity.

BEHAVIOUR Females with young form groups numbering between 5 and 40, often attended by single territorial male. All-male groups common. Herds relatively sedentary and solitary males particularly so. Such males posture on habitual stamping grounds, which they scrape with the feet and mark with accumulations of dung. Posturing includes head-flagging. Most calves born at beginning of short rains (October–November), suggesting a mating peak at the start of the main rains in March–April. Calves are vulnerable to many predators.

Impala

Hirola

BONTEBOK, BLESBOK *Damaliscus dorcas*

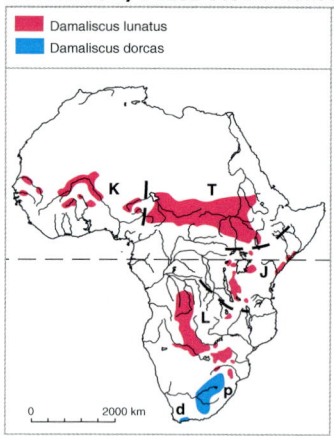

Damaliscus lunatus
Damaliscus dorcas

SIZE HB 140–160cm. T 30–45cm. SH 85–100cm. W 55–70kg (female), 65–80kg (male). Bontebok an average 8kg lighter.
DESCRIPTION Smaller southern cousins of the Topi, with very strong contrasts of colour in adults but young are fawn colour. Compact body, short neck and long nose with an expanded muzzle. Horns resemble enlarged gazelle horns. Subspecies: Bontebok, *D. d. dorcas* (W Cape): glossy dark purplish brown with white buttocks and 'stockings'. Blesbok, *D. d. phillipsi* (Highveld): dull reddish brown with ill-defined off-white buttocks and off-white lower legs.
HABITAT Blesbok originally ranged over entire Highveld, grazing fire-climax grassland. Bontebok inhabited a different Cape fynbos habitat.
FOOD Red oat grass, *Themeda* (at various stages of growth), *Eragrostis* and *Chloromelas* form main part of Blesbok diet. Bontebok also feed on *Eragrostis* species but local dominants, *Bromus* and *Danthonia*, are preferred grasses.
BEHAVIOUR Where pastures in modern enclosures are sufficiently extensive to support them Blesboks still gather in semi-nomadic herds. Even in smaller groups within still smaller enclosures both subspecies retain the habit of circulating around their available range in loose herds. Both subspecies have an 8-month gestation and their young are up and mobile within an hour or two of birth.

TOPI, TIANG, TSESSEBE *Damaliscus lunatus*   see map above

SIZE HB 150–230cm. T 36–42cm. W 75–150kg (female), 120–160kg (male).
DESCRIPTION Large, compact antelope with deep chest, prominently ridged shoulders, rather short neck and long face. Tail narrow and fringed. Horns vary from one region to another but all have backward-curving stems and forward- or inward-curving tips. Body colour varies from rather yellowish bleached brown to red or even purplish brown. Black patches on hindquarters and forelegs above ochre-coloured 'stockings'. Bridge of nose black (very occasionally turning white with maturity).
Subspecies: Tsessebe, *D. l. lunatus* (S Africa); Korrigum, *D. l. korrigum* (Senegal to W Nigeria); Tiang, *D. l. tiang* (NE Nigeria to W Ethiopia); Nyamera, *D. l. jimela* (Great Lakes region); Topi, *D. l. topi* (E African coast). Tsessebe is sometimes treated as a species.
HABITAT Seasonally flooded grasslands. They follow receding waters in the dry season and retreat onto higher ground in the rains or flood season. They favour naturally short or medium-height pastures (such as alkaline pans), regrowth after burns or else concentrate in large herds in tall grass (commonly on wet-season higher ground retreats). Here heavy trampling soon opens up large glades and stimulates continuous regrowth. These annual cycles of movement can involve huge herds of tens of thousands in round journeys of nearly 1,000km, small circuits within closed valleys, or sustained residence on 'permanent' pockets of suitable grassland. The instability and unpredictability of floodplain pastures renders the last group peculiarly vulnerable. The advantages of living in very large, mobile herds include reduced predation, and optimum grazing, partly due to their own trampling. Younger animals benefit from older animals' knowledge of region's pastures.
FOOD Most valley grasses taken. Longer rather than very short leaves are stripped from the stems with a nodding action that finely balances raking wrenches with clipping bites.
BEHAVIOUR Although many Topi live in large migratory herds, they may be neighbours to (or co-exist with) small clusters of residential animals. Residents probably offshoots of larger aggregations but they occupy territories defended by males (also females). Scattered residents less seasonal in their breeding. Large groups have very intense rutting while herds are at their most concentrated. Young are born after an 8-month gestation. The sandy-fawn calf lies up for a few days before joining its mother. Young often gather spontaneously and females may form a defensive ring around them.

Blesbock

Bontebok

Topi

Tsessebe

KONGONI (HARTEBEEST) *Alcelaphus buselaphus* (incl. *lichtensteinii*)

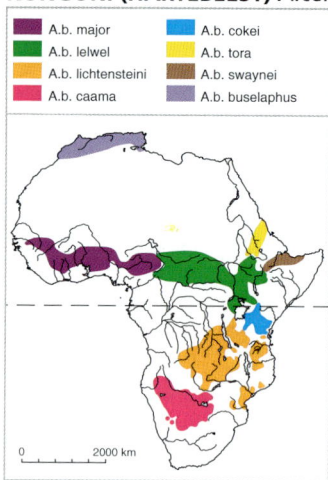

A.b. major	A.b. cokei
A.b. lelwel	A.b. tora
A.b. lichtensteini	A.b. swaynei
A.b. caama	A.b. buselaphus

SIZE HB 160–215cm. T 30–70cm. H 107–150cm. W 116–185kg (female), 125–218kg (male).
DESCRIPTION A large, high-shouldered, deep-chested antelope with long legs, a short neck and a very long, narrow face. The horns are carried on hollow bases, or 'pedicels', and show considerable variation (45–83cm) from individual to individual and from region to region. Coloration also shows considerable regional variation (red and black in the Kalahari, tan in E Africa, golden brown in W Africa) and also individual variation, especially in the Korkay from Ethiopia (*A. b. swaynei*) in which the overall body colour ranges from silvery purplish to red or dark brown and the blotches of black on shoulders and knees vary in shape and extent. The Kongoni has preorbital and pedal (hoof) glands.
Subspecies: Bubal, *A. b. buselaphus* (N Africa), extinct 1925; Tora, *A. b. tora* (E Sudan and N Ethiopia); Korkay, *A. b. swaynei* (Ethiopia); Kongoni, *A. b. cokei* (S Kenya and N Tanzania); Khama, *A. b. caama* (Cape, Kalahari); Kanki, *A. b. major* (W Africa); Lelwel, *A. b. lelwel* (L. Chad to L. Turkana); Nkonzi, *A. b. lichtensteinii* (central and SE Africa).

Note: The 8 subspecies listed above have been generally recognised since 1894. Among some 50 named forms are many collected from interzones between ranges of these populations. Most of these appear to be unstable hybrids rather than graduated intermediate forms, suggesting that former isolation has broken down as two forms, the Lelwel and Nkonzi, expanded their ranges.

HABITAT Formerly distributed in all African grasslands and savannahs (except for a very narrow strip between the R. Juba and R. Tana and the African Highveld). Although regional differences are substantial, Kongonis are consistent everywhere in being grazers that live on boundaries between open grassy plains or glades and parkland, woodland or scrub (often on shallow slopes). They go to water regularly (but territorial males go without for quite long periods). They move down drainage lines for grass and water in the dry season and up onto better drained, thinly grassed woodlands during the rains.

FOOD Grazers, selective of neither species nor component parts of the grass. However, certain species are avoided, notably *Cynodon*, a grass that is readily grazed by other herbivores.

BEHAVIOUR Female Kongonis are gregarious and to variable degrees move up and down shallow grassy valleys in pursuit of the best grass. Males become dispersed along the margins of each drainage line and establish dung-marked territories that embrace all the vegetation types from top to bottom of the slope. Where there is pressure from neighbours, territories may get narrowed but nearly always from the sides and not from above or below. Males waylay female groups as they pass through their territories. In some areas breeding is compressed into a short period during the rains and most males only become territorial at this time. In other areas some breeding continues throughout the year and territories are held more or less continuously. Males mark their territories with dung and posture with the head held upright and the legs placed well back. This is a gesture that suggests ritualised defaecation and may serve to deter neighbouring males and attract passing females. Males fight most intensely in the presence of oestrous females and are especially aggressive towards attendant male offspring. At high densities males are sometimes killed in fights. Females defend their young vigorously and also form temporary all-female hierarchies in which threatening gestures with horns are noticeable. Single young born after 8-month gestation and growth rates strongly influenced by nutrition. Sexual maturity reached in 1 year in some and not until the 4th year in others. Animals live for up to 19 years. Populations crash to very low levels during droughts, disease epidemics or under sustained competitive pressure from cattle. However, they recover quite rapidly when conditions improve. This capacity to build up their numbers is fuelled by subsistence on a normally super-abundant resource. Apart from being easy to hunt, this antelope declines wherever there is competition from intensive cattle-keeping.

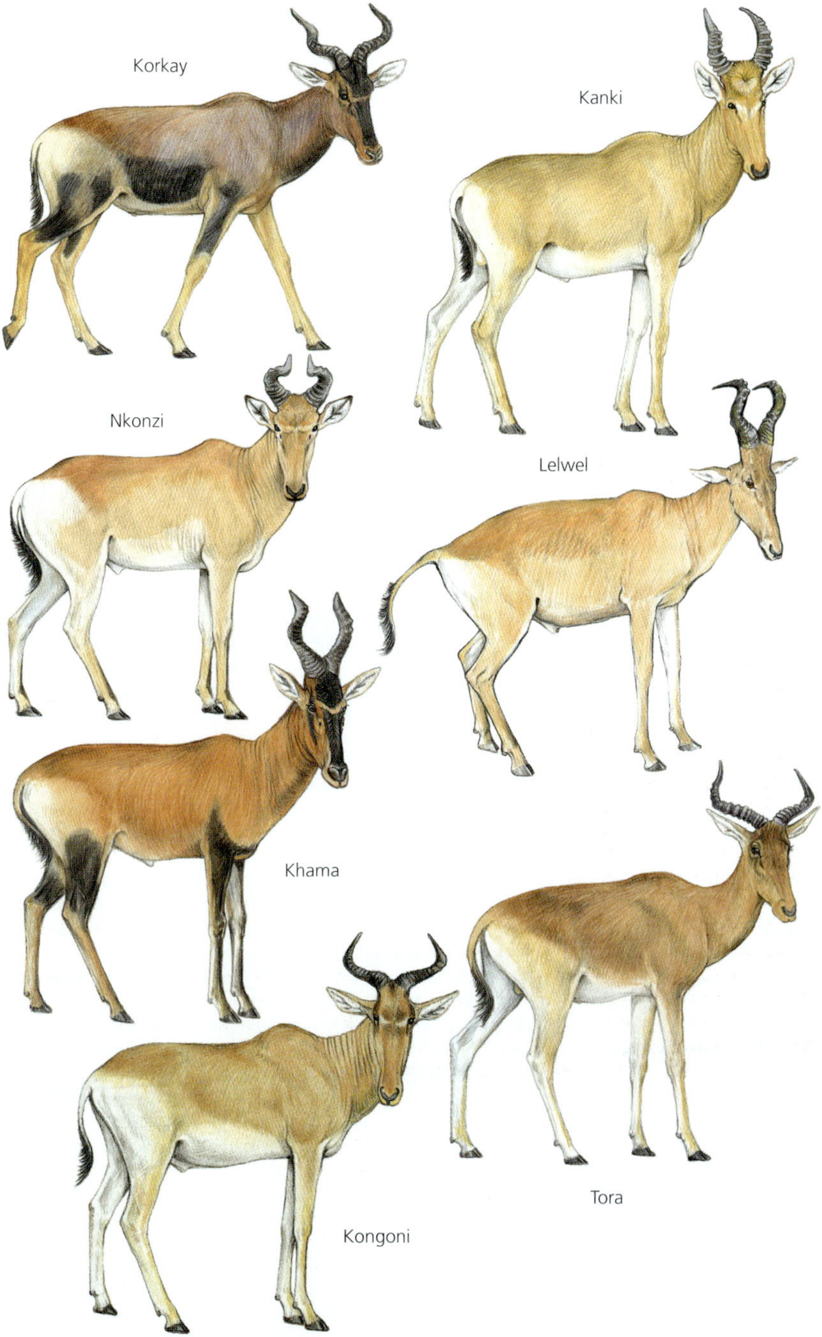
Korkay
Kanki
Nkonzi
Lelwel
Khama
Tora
Kongoni

BRINDLED GNU (BLUE WILDEBEEST) *Connochaetes taurinus*

SIZE HB 170–240cm. T 60–100cm. SH 115–145cm. W 140–260kg (female), 165–290kg (male).
DESCRIPTION Dumpy, thick-necked, long-faced. Horns flare out sideways and then upwards. Flat, rather square nasal plate (with hair-lined, flap-edged nostrils) is bounded by an even broader, grass-nibbling mouth. Muzzle is black in all subspecies, as is the shaggy mane and tail. Body colour of subspecies varies from dark grey-brown to slate blue to pale greyish fawn, with variable degrees of brindling. Neck and chin are bearded in long, black, brown, cream or white hair. Legs short, brown or ochre, with pedal glands between the large true hooves (there are prominent false lateral hooves). Subspecies: Brindled Gnu, *C. t. taurinus* (south of the R. Zambezi, Kalahari); Nyassa Gnu, *C. t. cooksoni* (Luangwa valley); Mozambique Gnu, *C. t. johnstoni* (SE Africa); White-bearded Gnu, *C. t. albojubatus* (S Kenya, N Tanzania).
HABITAT Short grasslands (maintained by fire, shade, rainfall, water table, drainage, soil chemistry, herbivore grazing and trampling) always within about 20km of permanent water. Migration permits gnus to rotate pastures where these requirements are seasonal.
FOOD A wide variety of nutritious grasses that form short swards. At times may be forced to strip leaves from tall stems. Unable to graze persistent rank growth.
BEHAVIOUR Social grazers that congregate in response to the local distribution of short grass pastures and water. Where these are adequate throughout the year, females and their young can remain permanently on home ranges of a few ha. Where their food and water dry out, resident gnus tend to move on to more extensive seasonal pastures. Here they join other gnus, soon losing their local identities in the amalgam of herds. These seasonal aggregations are sometimes quite temporary. Permanent large herds are more continuously nomadic, with females joining up to lead mass movement from one major pasture to another. Males tend to win 'territories' that are simply marked out by their own behaviour. They 'broadcast' sound, scent and eye-catching visual displays in the form of belching grunts and snorts, flurries of scent (transferred from the face to everywhere they can reach) and frantic leaping, cavorting and head-shaking.

WHITE-TAILED GNU (BLACK WILDEBEEST) *Connochaetes gnou*

SIZE HB 170–220cm. T 80–100cm. SH 90–121cm. W 110–160kg (female), 140–180kg (male).
DESCRIPTION A stocky, thick-coated antelope with heavily bossed horns that swing down, forward and upwards in tight angular hooks. Muzzle long, very broad, flat-fronted and covered in dense black fur. Flapped nostrils set above wide rectangular mouth. Body colour dark brown, with black beard and chest tassels. Mane upright, hairs off-white with black tips. Tail long, flowing, white.
HABITAT Temperate grasslands and Karoo shrub lands where it migrated between summer pastures in the Karoo and eastwards to grasslands of the Highveld during the winter. These large-scale movements ceased when European settlement moved into the interior where, by the mid-19th century, this gnu had been brought close to extinction. Now extinct as a wild animal.
FOOD Grazes but supplements grasses with succulents and shrubs, which permits grazing of the arid Karoo without regular water. More continuously active in cool weather but lies up for the heat of the day in summer.
BEHAVIOUR Females wander in groups of up to 60 over home ranges of about 100ha. As they pass through male territories they are inspected and the male attempts to deter them from passing on into the territory of his neighbours. This herding is most intense during the period of female oestrus. Because most females only mate at the end of the hot wet summer (March–April) it would appear that mating used to coincide with a massed eastward shift towards the Highveld winter pastures. This species has evolved particularly dangerous horns and with them elaborate appeasement gestures (including prostration). Very vocal with a metallic snort, a 2-part 'ge-nu' and a very resonant, single 'hick' which is uttered with a violent spasm of the head and neck.

Brindled Gnu

White-tailed Gnu

HORSE-LIKE ANTELOPES Hippotraginae

Large, barrel-bodied antelopes with long, well-annulated horns, long ears and broad hooves. They have sleek coats, striped faces and thick necks with manes. All species are grazers.

ROAN ANTELOPE *Hippotragus equinus*

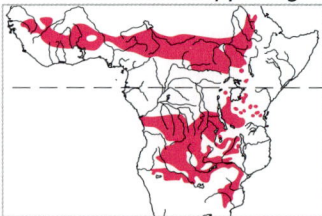

SIZE HB 190–240cm. T 37–48cm. H 126–145cm. W 223–280kg (female), 242–300kg (male).

DESCRIPTION Tall, powerful, with thick neck, robust muzzle, long, droop-tipped ears, and massive, arched horns (50–100cm in males). Coat very coarse, becoming shaggy on the throat; hairs on the upright mane are dark tipped. Face pattern varies individually but also regionally (dark markings more extensive in north, light in south). Body colour also subject to both individual and regional variation (greyish in south, more tawny in north, to reddish in moister parts of range). Two main populations: northern savannahs: *H. e. koba* (Senegal to Nigeria), *H. e. bakeri* (Chad to Ethiopia); and southern savannahs: *H. e. equinus* (S Africa), *H. e. langheldi* (E Africa), *H. e. cottoni* (central Africa).

HABITAT Range from Sahelian steppe (but only within reach of water) and flat floodplains through various woodland and savannah types to montane and plateau grasslands up to 2,400m. Prefer localities in which there are few competitors and carnivores. In many areas have distinct wet- and dry-season ranges.

FOOD Grazers of medium to short grasses belonging to dominant species, such as red oat grass (*Themeda*), thatch grass (*Hyparrhenia*) and couch grass (*Digitaria*). Occasionally browse shrubs or herbs and pick up *Acacia* pods in the dry season. They drink regularly.

BEHAVIOUR Herds totalling 5–35 animals are made up of females and their young attended by a single adult male who excludes other males. Such groups circulate through a well-known and mainly exclusive home range but may converge temporarily on a pasture which is shared with other Roan while grazing.

SABLE ANTELOPE *Hippotragus niger*

SIZE HB 190–255cm. T 40–75cm. SH 117–143cm. W 190–230kg (female), 200–270kg (male).

DESCRIPTION Large, strongly built antelope with thick neck, long, narrow muzzle, pointed ears, large, compact hooves and longish, tufted tail. Arched horns commonly exceed 1m in length and reach over 160cm in the Angolan Giant Sable. The upright mane reaches to behind the shoulders. Infants are dun-coloured and almost without markings. Juveniles and young adults are rich russet, the males maturing to black by 5 years. Females of the southernmost population also turn black. In other populations females blacken more slowly and less completely. Subspecies (under revision): Black Sable, *H. n. niger* (S of Zambezi), Common Sable, *H. n. kirkii* (R Zambezi to R Galana), Giant Sable *H. n. variani* (Angola).

HABITAT Mostly but not wholly confined to Miombo (*Brachystegia*) woodland. They move out as these well-drained and seasonally burnt woodlands begin to dry out. They gather closer to permanent water, in valley-bottom grasslands, or mbugas, for the dry season.

FOOD New grass growth or grasses of medium height belonging to locally dominant types are preferred. Well before the rains begin they leave the valley bottoms (like horses they avoid deep mud if they can) and greatly increase the normally small proportion of woody foliage in their diet.

BEHAVIOUR Females form regional 'clans' of fewer than 100 animals which readily divide up into subgroups of unstable membership. Fission of subgroups may range from a few hours up to a month or more. Females from different clans are hostile to one another. Adult males sometimes follow these herds during their movements, but generally remain on established territories.

Roan Antelope

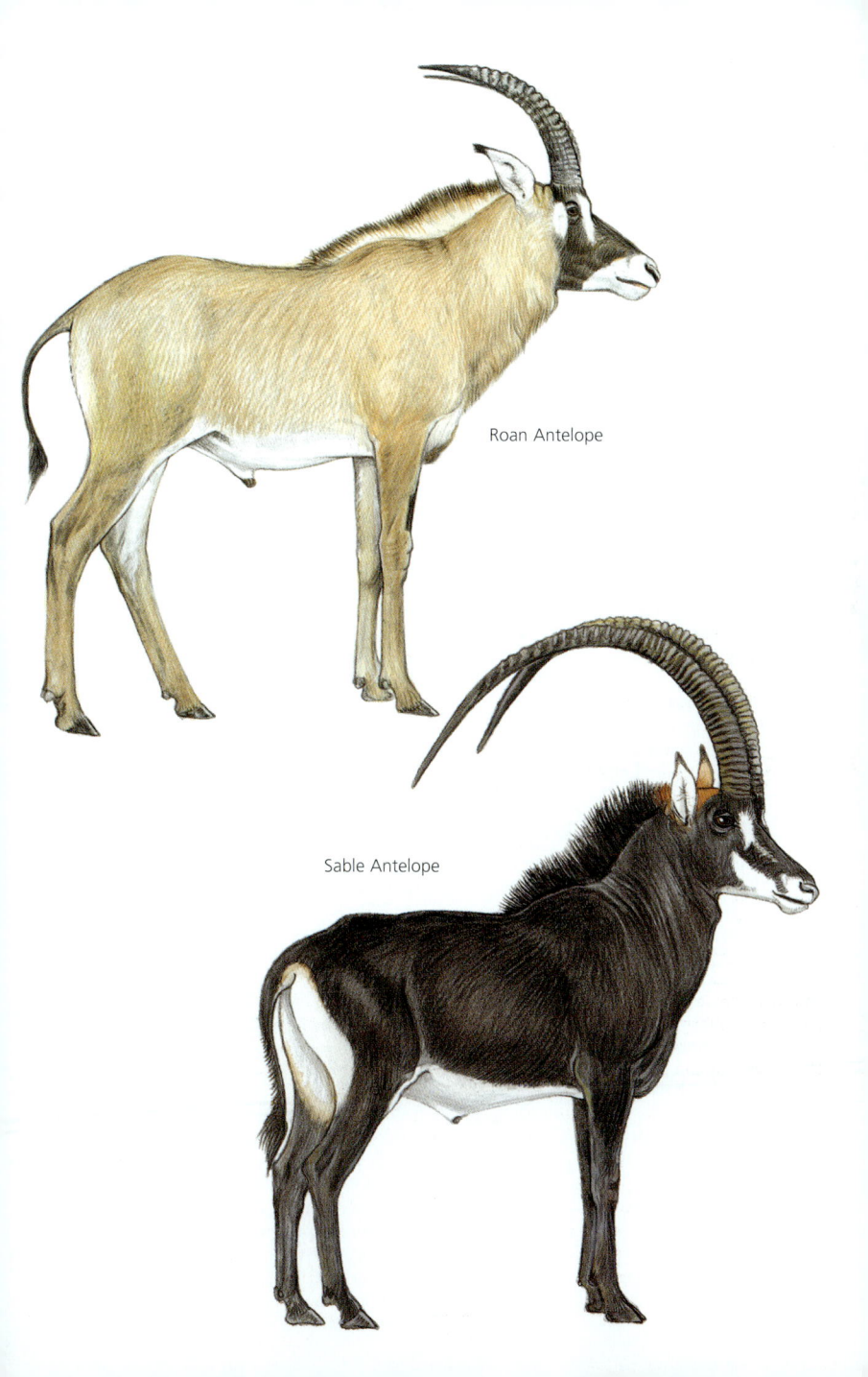

Sable Antelope

PLATE 117 ORYXES AND ADDAX

SCIMITAR-HORNED ORYX *Oryx dammah*

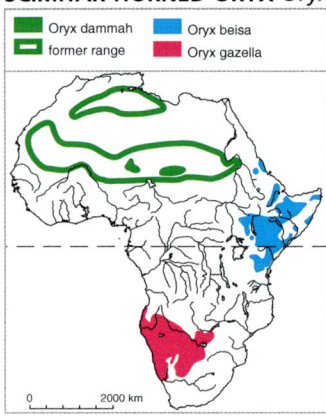

- Oryx dammah
- former range
- Oryx beisa
- Oryx gazella

SIZE HB 190–220cm. T 45–60cm. SH 110–125cm. W 135–140kg.
DESCRIPTION Rotund, with deep chest and relatively short, sturdy legs. Horns long, slender and arched (100–115cm), with many fine annulations. Vestiges of a structured pattern show up as pale apricot-brown tints on a predominantly white animal. Probably extinct in the wild.
HABITAT Semi-desert grasslands of the Sahel and their N Saharan equivalent. Woody plants growing in moisture-retaining troughs between dunes and outcroppings provided some cover and shade but it was flushes of grass that drew the nomadic oryxes back and forth across unknown distances.
FOOD Mostly grasses, also herbs, shrubs and fruits.
BEHAVIOUR Formerly seen in herds of 10 or more. Capable of aggregating and dispersing in response to ephemeral pastures. Reluctant to remain solitary.

BEISA ORYX *Oryx beisa* see map above
SIZE HB 153–170cm. T 45–50cm. SH 110–120cm. W 116–188kg (female), 167–209kg (male).
DESCRIPTION Compact, muscular, with thick neck, long face, long straight horns and distinctive ears. Brownish grey coat is demarcated from black and white facial, flank and foreleg patterns. Line of back-swept straight horns (60–110cm) continues right across the face in the form of a black stripe. Little difference between males and females. Subspecies: Beisa Oryx, *O. b. beisa* (N of R Tana), Fringe-eared Oryx, *O. b. callotis* (S of R Tana).
HABITAT Arid grasslands and bushland but avoids tall grass, also thick bush in dry season.
FOOD Grasses, but will browse *Acacia* and other shrubs. During droughts dig out tubers and roots. Where water is available they drink regularly but can do without.
BEHAVIOUR Mixed herds in which sexes sometimes equally balanced (usually more female). Both sexes establish hierarchies.

SOUTHERN ORYX (GEMSBOK) *Oryx gazella* see map above
SIZE HB 180–195cm. T 40–47cm. SH 117–138cm. W 180–225kg (female), 180–240kg (male).
DESCRIPTION Very thick-necked, with long, straight horns (60–120cm). White muzzle, face stripes, belly and 'stockings' contrast with black markings. Like other oryx, neck and shoulders are enveloped in thick skin. This gives adult bulls a rather 'jacketed' appearance.
HABITAT Wooded grasslands and *Acacia* bush of central Kalahari and Karoo shrublands, entering wetter grasslands and bush along margins of main range.
FOOD A grazer but browses in absence of grass.
BEHAVIOUR Although most female groups nomadic, many males remain in attendance. Old males become more sedentary.

ADDAX *Addax nasomaculatus*

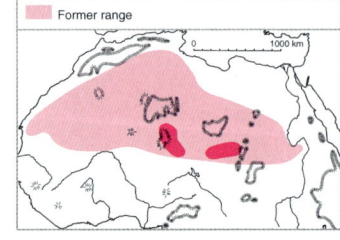

Former range

SIZE HB 120–175cm. T 27–35cm. SH 95–115cm. W 60–90kg (female), 100–135kg (male).
DESCRIPTION Stocky, almost white, with long, annulated horns following loose spirals. Sexes differ very little.
HABITAT Sand-dune deserts (erg). Now extinct except for small pockets in Niger and (possibly) Chad.
FOOD Desert grasses, distinct seasonal preferences.
BEHAVIOUR Formerly travelled in groups of 2–20, sometimes aggregating in larger groups, very occasionally in hordes of many hundreds.

Scimitar-horned Oryx

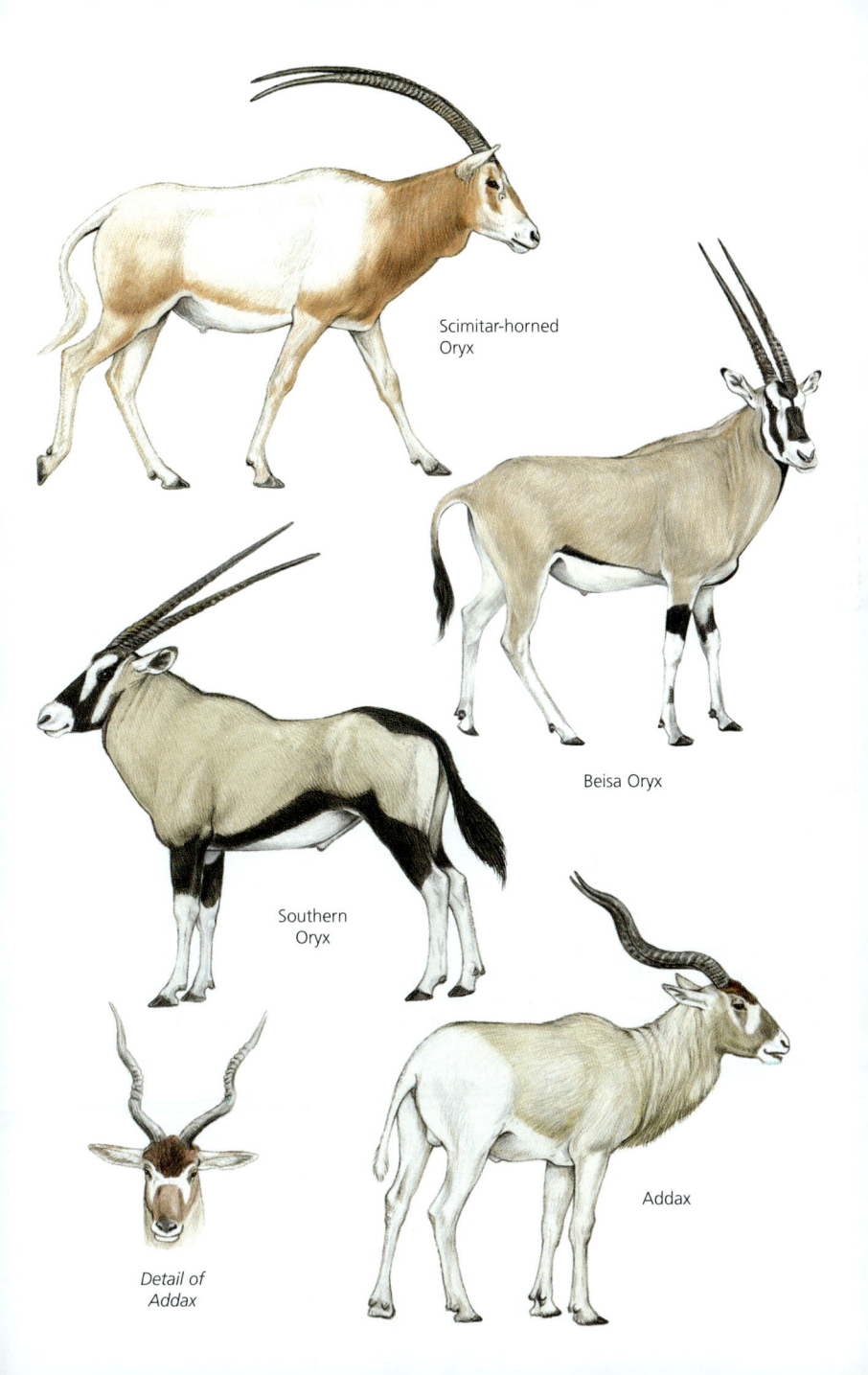

Beisa Oryx

Southern Oryx

Detail of Addax

Addax

SHEEP AND GOATS Caprinae

Medium-sized, thick-legged, compact antelopes with limbs and hooves modified for climbing and leaping over rough ground. Both sexes horned but males have larger ones.

BARBARY SHEEP (AOUDAD) *Ammotragus lervia*

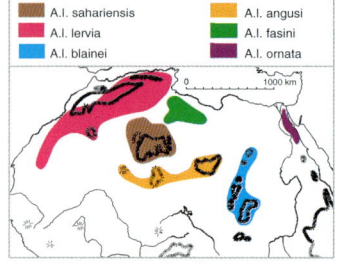

A.l. sahariensis
A.l. lervia
A.l. blainei
A.l. angusi
A.l. fasini
A.l. ornata

SIZE HB 130–165cm. T 15–25cm. SH 75–90cm (female), 90–100cm (male). W 40–55kg (female), 100–140kg (male).
DESCRIPTION Heavily built, thick, short-legged animal, intermediate between a sheep and goat. Outward-arching horns are slender and rounded in females, thick, ridged and much longer in males (which have twice the body weight of females). Face is long and tapered, ears small and white mouth parts contrast with pale tawny-brown coat colour. Fleece woolly in winter, with a harsh texture, but moults to a sleek summer coat. Both sexes have tufts of hair on the upper foreleg and a hanging fringe down the throat but those of males are denser and longer. 6 subspecies (see map).
HABITAT Desert hills and mountains, stony plateaus (hammada) and the slopes of valleys (wadis) well away from mountains. Avoids sand deserts (ergs).
FOOD Grass and herbs; also browse shrubs and trees and will get up onto hindlegs to reach foliage. Prefers to feed at dusk, dawn and during night. Will drink water but can go without.
BEHAVIOUR Forms small family parties in which a single adult male attends several females and their offspring. These tend to remain scattered but have been reported to gather into larger parties (up to 30 members) late in dry season (July). One or 2 young are born in a secluded site where mother and young lie up for a few days before rejoining their group.

NUBIAN/WALIA IBEX *Capra ibex*

SIZE HB 140–170cm. T 15–25cm. SH 65–100cm (female), 75–110cm (male). W 50–100kg (female), 60–125kg (male). Note: Nubian Ibexes average 8cm shorter and about 22kg lighter than Walia.
DESCRIPTION Of all goats, male ibexes have developed the longest and most heavily reinforced horns (100–119cm). They have short ears, a beard on the chin and a mane from nape to tail. There are vestigial stripes on the face, flanks and thighs. The Nubian Ibex is various shades of slaty brown. The Walia Ibex has greyish sides and haunches below a rich russet neck and back. Its horns tend to have fewer knobs on their forward surfaces and average a few cm less in length. Subspecies: Nubian Ibex, *C. i. nubiana* (east of the Nile, formerly from Suez to Massawa); Walia Ibex, *C. i. walie* (Simen Mts, Ethiopia). The two forms are sometimes regarded as separate species.
HABITAT Rocky mountains, gorges and loose stony screes in areas with a sparse cover of trees, scrub and grass. Walia Ibex has moved into a higher, wetter zone (between 2,500 and 4,500m).
FOOD Grass is grazed but main food plants are herbs and shrubs. Leaves, buds, fruits and, in some cases, bark and flowers are eaten from a wide range of desert and montane plants.
BEHAVIOUR Ibexes live in confined ranges of a few km^2, or less. Females may be briefly on their own to give birth but normally have a loose association with other well-known females sharing the home range. Females defend their young and fight strange female Ibexes. Males lead an independent existence until the rut (between September and November) when dominant males seek to exclude all other males from oestrous females. At this time they eat little, fight and chase much, and suffer a marked deterioration in condition.

Barbary Sheep *male*

Barbary Sheep *female*

Nubian Ibex

FURTHER READING

Information on mammals is mostly published in scientific papers. Several of the works mentioned below have extensive bibliographies of such papers which are beyond the scope of this list.

GENERAL ACCOUNTS AND LISTS OF MAMMALS

Duff, A. & Lawson, A. (2004) *Mammals of the World: A Checklist*. London: A&C Black.

Grzimek, B. (ed) (1972) *Animal Life Encyclopaedia*, Vol. 13, *Mammals*. New York: Von Nostrand Reinhold.

Macdonald, D. W. (ed) (1984) *The Encyclopaedia of Mammals*. 2 vols. London: George, Allen & Unwin.

Nowak, R. M. & Paradiso, J. L. (eds) (1983) *Walker's Mammals of the World*. 2 vols. Baltimore: Johns Hopkins University Press.

Wilson, D. E. & Reeder, D. M. (1992) *Mammal Species of the World*. Washington: Smithsonian Institution Press.

BOOKS ON AFRICAN MAMMALS

Allen, G. M. (1939) *A Checklist of African Mammals*. Boston (Mass.): Museum of Comparative Zoology, Harvard.

Dorst, J. & Dandelot, P. (1970) *A Field Guide to the Larger Mammals of Africa*. London: Collins.

Estes, R. D. & Otte, D. (1990) *The Behaviour Guide to African Mammals*. Berkeley: University of California Press.

Haltenorth, T. & Diller, H. (1980) *A Field Guide to the Mammals of Africa*. London: Collins.

Kingdon, J. S. (2003) *The Kingdon Field Guide to African Mammals*. London: A&C Black.

Kingdon, J. S. (1971–1982) *East African Mammals: An Atlas of Evolution in Africa*. 7 parts. London: Academic Press.

Lydekker, R. (1908) *The Game Animals of Africa*. London: Rowland Ward.

Selous, F. C. (1899) *Great and Small Game of Africa*. London: Rowland Ward.

There are many important monographs on regional mammal faunas, individual species, families and orders. Books on evolution that are relevant to an understanding of the importance of mammals (especially African mammals) to humanity and the future of humanity include: Charles Darwin's *Origin of Species*; Richard Dawkins's *The Blind Watchmaker: Why the Evidence of Evolution Reveals a Universe Without Design* and *River Out of Eden: A Darwinian View of Life*; Steven Jones's *The Language of the Genes: Solving the Mysteries of Our Genetic Past, Present and Future*; Jonathan Kingdon's *Self-Made Man: Human Evolution from Eden to Extinction?*, *Lowly Origin: Where, When and Why Our Ancestors First Stood Up*, and *Island Africa: The Evolution of Africa's Rare Animals and Plants*; Christopher Stringer's *African Exodus: The Origins of Modern Humanity*; and Edward Wilson's *The Diversity of Life*.

GLOSSARY

Adult. A physically and reproductively mature individual.

Afrotheria. Ancient radiation of uniquely African mammals that evolved during Africa's continental isolation (100–50MYA). The Aardvark, elephants, sea-cows, hyraxes, elephant shrews, otter shrews and golden moles all share the genetic markers for Afrotheria.

Agouti. Grizzled appearance of the coat resulting from alternating light and dark banding of individual hairs.

Allopatry. Condition in which populations of different species are geographically separated.

Amphibious. Able to live on both land and water.

Anal gland or sac. A gland opening either just inside the anus or on either side of it.

Apocrine glands. Cutaneous scent glands which produce complex and chemically variable secretions.

Aquatic. Applied to animals that live in fresh water. All aquatic mammals move readily on land.

Arboreal. Referring to animals that live in trees.

Arthropod. The largest phylum in the animal kingdom, including insects, spiders, crabs etc.

Artiodactyl. A member of the order Artiodactyla, the even-toed ungulates.

Biome. A major type of ecological community such as savannah or desert.

Biotic community. A naturally occurring group of plants and animals in the same environment.

Bipedal. Two-footed stance or locomotion of four-footed animals.

Bovid. A member of the cow-like artiodactyl family, Bovidae.

Brachydont. Low crowned molars of browsers.

Brindled. Having dark streaks or flecks on a grey or tawny background.

Browser. A herbivore which feeds on shoots and leaves of trees, shrubs and forbs.

Bullae (auditory). Globular, bony capsules housing the middle and inner ear structures. Built onto the underside of the skull.

Callosities. Patches of thickened skin and tissue (as on the hind quarters of monkeys or knees of some ungulates).

Canine teeth. The usually long pointed teeth, one in each quarter of the jaws that are used by animal-eating mammals for killing their prey.

Carnassial teeth. In carnivores, the fourth upper premolar and first lower molar are specialized for shearing meat and sinew.

Carnivore. Any meat-eating organism but also a member of the mammal order Carnivora.

Caudal gland. An enlarged skin gland associated with the root of the tail. (Subcaudal: below the root; supracaudal: above the root.)

Cecum. A blind sac situated at the junction of the small and large intestine, in which digestion of cellulose by bacteria occurs.

Cellulose. Main constituent of the cell walls of plants. Very tough and fibrous, and can be digested only by the intestinal flora in mammalian guts.

Cervid. A member of the deer family (Cervidae), of the Artiodactyla.

Chablis. A tree-fall opening in the forest.

Cheek pouches. A pair of deep pouches extending from the cheeks into the neck skin, present in non-colobid monkeys and some rodents and used for the temporary storage of food.

Cheek teeth. The row of premolars and molars used for chewing food.

Class. A taxonomic category – the mammals, Mammalia, are a class.

Colonial. Living together in colonies. Notably bats and rodents.

Concentrate selector. A herbivore which feeds on those plant parts such as shoots and fruits which are rich in nutrients.

Conspecific. A member of the same species.

Convergence. The evolution of similarities between unrelated species occupying similar ecological niches.

Crepuscular. Active in twilight.

Crustaceans. Members of a class within the phylum Arthropoda typified by crayfish, crabs and shrimps.

Cryptic. Concealing, inconspicuous. Usually referring to colouration and markings.

Cud. Partially digested vegetation that ruminant regurgitates, chews, insalivates and swallows again.

Cursorial. Being adapted for running.

Cusp. A prominence on a cheek-tooth (premolars or molar).

Dental formula. A convention for summarizing the dental arrangement whereby the numbers of each type of tooth in each half of the upper and lower jaw are given; the numbers are always presented in the order: incisor (I), canine (C), premolar (P), molar (M). The final figure is the total number of teeth to be found in the skull. A typical example for Carnivora would be 3 / 3.1 / 1. 4 / 4.3 / 3 = 44.

Dentition. The arrangement of teeth characteristic of particular species.

Dicot. Short for dicotyledon.

Dicotyledon. A plant with two seed leaves; the subclass of angiosperms containing most higher plants.

Digit. Latin for finger or toe.

Digitigrade. Animals that walk on their digits rather than the whole foot.

Dimorphism. Two forms, typically the morphological differences between males and females (sexual dimorphism).

Dispersal. The movements of animals, often as they reach maturity, away from their previous home range (equivalent to emigration).

Display. Any relatively conspicuous pattern of behaviour that conveys specific information to others, usually to members of the same species: can involve visual and or vocal elements, as in threat, courtship or 'greeting' displays. A behaviour pattern that has been modified (ritualized) by evolution to transmit information by a sender to a receiver.

Diurnal. Referring to species that are primarily day-active.

Dorsal. The back or upper surface (opposite of ventral).

Dung midden. Pile of droppings that accumulate through regular deposits, typically in connection with scent-marking (see also latrine).

Ecological niche. The particular combination of adaptations that fits each species to a place different from that filled by any other species within a community of organisms.

Ecology. The scientific study of the interaction of organisms with their environment including both the physical environment and the other organisms that share it.

Ecosystem. A community of organisms together with the physical environment in which they live.

Emigration. Departure of animal(s) usually at or about the time of reaching adulthood, from the group or place of birth. Also of biogeographic exchange between continents or regions.

Endemic. Native plants and animals.

Eocene. Geological epoch 54–38 million years ago.

Epidermis. The outer layer of the skin or surface tissue of a plant.

Equatorial. Geographical region bordering the equator.

False hooves. Vestigal nails (digits 2 and 5) which persist in many ruminants as paired hooves or bumps on the fetlock.

Family. A taxonomic division subordinate to an order and superior to a genus.

Feral. Living in the wild (of domesticated animals, e.g. cat, dog).

Fetlock. Joint above the hooves.

Folivore. An animal whose diet consists mostly of leaves and other foliage.

Forbs. Herbs other than grass which are abundant in grassland, especially during the rains.

Fossorial. Adapted for digging.

Frugivore. An animal that feeds mainly on fruit.

Gallery forest. Trees and other vegetation lining watercourses, thereby extending forested habitat into more open zones.

Generalist. An animal that is not highly specialized. For example, feeding on a variety of foods which require various foraging techniques.

Genotype. The genetic constitution of an organism, determining all aspects of its appearance, structure and function.

Genus. (plural Genera) A taxonomic division superior to species and subordinate to family.

Gestation. The period of development between conception and birth.

Glands. Specialized glandular areas of the skin.

Grazer. A herbivore which feeds upon grasses.

Guard hairs. The outer coat that overlies the shorter, softer hairs of the underfur (underfur is sparse or absent in many tropical mammals, e.g. most ungulates and primates).

Gumivorous. Feeding on gums (plant exudates).

Harem group. A social group consisting of a single adult male, at least two adult females and immature animals.

Herbivore. An animal whose diet consists of plant food.

Herd. A social group, generally applied to gregarious ungulates.

Hindgut fermentation. Process by which breakdown of cellulose occurs in the cecum and large intestine.

Hierarchy. As applied to social groups, a usually linear rank order in which members dominate all those of lower rank and are dominated by all individuals of higher rank.

Home range. The area occupied by an individual or group (usually determined by points where the individual[s] is seen over a period of time and plotting the perimeter).

Hysodont. High crowned characteristic of the molars of grazing mammals (opposite to brachydont).

Hybrid. The offspring of parents of different species.
Inguinal. Pertaining to the groin.
Insectivore. An animal eating mainly arthropods (insects, spiders).
Interdigital. Between the digits; e.g. the interdigital (hoof) glands of many antelopes.
Intestinal flora. Simple plants (e.g. bacteria) which live in the intestines of mammals. They produce enzymes which break down the cellulose in the leaves and stems of green plants and convert it to digestible sugars.
Invertebrate. Animal which lacks backbone (e.g. insects, spiders, crustaceans).
Juvenile. Stage between infant and adult.
Karroo. Arid part of the interior plateau in temperate southern Africa. Dominated by dwarf shrubs and adjoined by Highveld grassland.
Keratin. Tough fibrous substance of which horns, claws, hooves and nails are composed.
Lactation. The secretion of milk from mammory glands.
Larynx. Dilated region of upper part of windpipe, containing vocal chords. Vibration of chords produces vocal sounds.
Latrine. A place where animals regularly deposit their excrement.
Liana, liane. A vine climbing woody plants; major constituents of rain forest.
Mandible. The lower jaw.
Maquis. Dense secondary scrub dominated by heathers and strawberry trees (Mediterranean).
Masseter. A powerful muscle, subdivided into parts, joining the lower and upper jaws, used to bring jaws together when chewing.
Melanism. Darkness of colour due to presence of the black pigment melanin.
Metabolism. The chemical processes occurring within an organism, including the production of protein from amino acids, the exchange of gases in respiration and liberation of energy.
Microhabitat. The particular parts of the habitat that are encountered by an individual in the course of its activities.
Midden. A dunghill or latrine for the regular deposition of faeces by mammals.
Migration. Movement, usually seasonal, from one region or climate to another for purposes of feeding or breeding.
Miocene. A geological epoch 26–7 million years ago.
Montane. Referring to African mountain habitats, including forest, grassland, bamboo zone, moorland etc.
Morphology. Referring to an animal's form and structure.

Mucosa. Mucous membrane; a membrane rich in mucous glands such as the lining of the mouth and nasal passageways.
Mutation. A structural change in a gene which can thus give rise to a new heritable characteristic.
Natural selection. Process whereby the fittest genotypes in a population survive to reproduce; a determinant principle in evolution.
Niche. The role of a species within the community, defined in terms of all aspects of its life history from food, competitors and predators to all its resource requirements.
Nocturnal. Active at night-time.
Nomadic. The wandering habit. Among mammals, species that have no clearly defined residence most of the time; distinct from migratory species, which may be resident except when migrating.
Nose-leaf. Characteristically shaped flaps of skin surrounding the nasal passages of nose-leaf bats. Ultrasonic cries are uttered through the nostrils, with the nose leaves serving to direct the echo-locating pulses forward.
Occipital. Pertaining to the occiput at back of head.
Oestrogen. Hormone produced by ovaries and responsible for expression of many female characteristics.
Oestrus. Behaviour associated with ovulation, being in most mammals the only time when females are sexually receptive ('in heat').
Olfaction, olfactory. The olfactory sense is the sense of smell, depending on receptors located in the epithelium, or membrane lining the nasal cavity.
Oligocene. A geological epoch 38–26 million years ago.
Omnivorous. A mixed diet including both animal and vegetable food.
Opportunistic. Referring to animals which capitalize on opportunities to gain food with the least expenditure of energy.
Order. A taxonomic division subordinate to class and superior to family.
Ovulation. The process of shedding mature ova (eggs) from the ovaries where they are produced.
Paleocene. Geological epoch.
Parturition. The process of giving birth.
Perineal glands. Glandular tissue occurring between the anus and genitalia.
Perissodactyl. Odd-toed ungulate.
Pheromone. Secretions whose odours act as chemical messengers in animal communication.

Phylogenetic. (Of classification or relationship) based on the closeness of evolutionary descent.

Phylogeny. A classification or relationship based on the closeness of evolutionary descent. Often portrayed graphically by a branching tree.

Phylum. A taxonomic division comprising a number of classes.

Physiology. Study of the processes which go on in living organisms.

Pinna. The projecting cartilaginous portion of the external ear (especially in bats).

Placenta. Structure that connects the foetus and the mother's womb to ensure a supply of nutrients to the foetus and removal of its waste products.

Pleistocene. Geological epoch 2–0.01 million years ago.

Pliocene. Geological epoch 7–2 million years ago.

Polymorphism. Occurrence of more than one morphological form of individual in a population.

Population. Members of the same species that are within an area at the same time.

Post-partum oestrus. Renewed ovulation and mating within days or weeks after giving birth.

Predation. The killing and eating of living animal prey.

Predator. Any animal that subsists mainly by eating live animals, usually vertebrates.

Preorbital. In front of the eye (where a gland occurs in many ungulates).

Presenting. The act of directing the hindquarters toward another individual, either in a sexual context or as a gesture of appeasement derived from sexual presenting.

Protein. A complex organic compound made of amino acids. Many different kinds of proteins are present in the muscles and tissues of all mammals.

Proximal. Near to the point of attachment or origin.

Quadrupedal. Walking on all fours.

Race. A subspecies.

Radiation. Speciation by a group of related organisms in the process of adapting to different ecological roles.

Rain forest. Tropical and subtropical forest with abundant and year-round rainfall. Typically species rich and diverse.

Range. (Geographical) area over which an organism is distributed.

Rank order. A hierarchial arrangement of the individuals in a group.

Relict. A persistent remnant population.

Resident. Living within a definite, limited home range, as opposed to being migratory or nomadic.

Reticulum. Second chamber of the ruminant artiodactyl stomach.

Rinderpest. A lethal artiodactyl disease.

Ritualization. Evolutionary modification of a behaviour pattern into a display or other signal, through selection for improved communication.

Ritualized. Referring to behaviour that has been transformed through the process of ritualization.

Rodent. A member of the order Rodentia, the largest mammalian order, which includes rats and mice, squirrels, anomalures and porcupines.

Rumen. First chamber of the ruminant artiodactyl stomach. In the rumen the food is liquefied, kneaded by muscular walls and subjected to fermentation by bacteria.

Ruminant. A mammal with a specialized digestive system typified by the behaviour of chewing the cud. Their stomach is modified so that vegetation is stored, regurgitated for further maceration, then broken down by symbiotic bacteria. The process of rumination is an adaptation to digesting the cellulose walls of plant cells.

Rut. Period of concentrated sexual activity, the mating season.

Savannah. Vegetation characteristic of tropical regions with extended wet and dry seasons. Dominated by grasses and scattered (predominantly leguminous) trees. The trees vary in type and density from broad-leafed, deciduous woodland in the wetter savannah to grassland with scattered thorn trees and acacia bush grading into subdesert.

Scent gland. Area of skin packed with specialized cells that secrete complex chemical compounds which communicate.

Sebaceous glands. The commonest type of cutaneous scent glands, consisting of localized concentrations of flask-shaped follicles that produce volatile fatty acids manufactured by symbiotic bacteria.

Sedentary. Pertaining to mammals which occupy relatively small home ranges.

Selection. Any feature of the environment that results in natural selection, through differential survival and reproductive success of individuals of differing genetic types.

Sexual dimorphism. A condition in which males and females of a species differ consistently in form, size and shape.

Sexual selection. Selection of genotypes through competition between members of the

same sex (usually males) and mating preferences by members of the opposite sex (usually female).
Sinus. A cavity in bone or tissue.
Solitary. Unsocial, referring to animals that do not live in social groups.
Speciation. The process by which new species arise in evolution. Typically occurs when a single species population is divided by some geographical barrier.
Species. Population(s) of closely related and similar organisms which are capable of interbreeding freely with one another, and cannot or normally do not interbreed with members of other species.
Species-specific. Characters that serve to distinguish a species such as its shape, markings or habits.
Spoor. Footprints.
Subadult. No longer an infant or juvenile but not yet fully adult physically and/or socially.
Subdesert. Regions that receive less rainfall than arid zones, but more than true desert.
Subspecies. Population(s) that has been isolated from other populations of the same species long enough to develop genetic differences sufficiently distinctive to be considered a separate race.
Superspecies. A grouping of closely related species.
Swidden. Rotational agriculture in rain forest.
Symbiotic. A mutually dependent relationship between unrelated organisms that are intimately associated, e.g. the symbiosis between a ruminant and the microorganisms that live in its rumen.
Sympatric. Overlapping geographic distribution; applies to related species that coexist without interbreeding (reverse of allopatric).
Systematics. The classification of organisms in an ordered system based on their supposed or known natural relationships.
Tarsal. Pertaining to the tarsus bones in the ankle, articulating between the tibia and fibia of the leg and the metatarsals of the foot (pes).
Termitary. Termite-hill.
Terrestrial. Living on land.
Territoriality. A system of spacing wherein home ranges do not overlap randomly – that is, the location of one individual's or group's home range influences those of others.
Territory. An area defended from intruders by an individual or group.

Testosterone. A male hormone normally synthesised in the testes and responsible for the expression of many male characteristics.
Thermoregulation. The regulation and maintenance of a constant internal body temperature in mammals.
Thoracic. Pertaining to the thorax or chest.
Tooth-comb. A dental modification in which the incisor teeth form a comb-like structure.
Tropical. The climate, flora and fauna of the geograhic region between 23½ degrees N and S of the equator. The latitudes reached by the sun at its maximum declination known respectively as the Tropics of Cancer and Capricorn.
Tsetse fly. Two-winged blood-sucking flies, which transmit 'sleeping sickness' (trypanosomiasis) to man and domestic livestock. The flies' presence in the woodlands of Africa south of the Sahara slowed the pace of settlements and thereby preserved habitats for wild animals which have a natural immunity to tsetse-borne diseases.
Undercoat. The soft insulating underfur beneath the longer, coarser guard hairs of the outer coat.
Ungulate. A member of the orders Artiodactyla (even-toed ungulates), Perissodactyla (odd-toed ungulates), Proboscidea (elephants), Hyracoidea (hyraxes), and Tubulidentata (aardvark), all of which have their feet modified as hooves of various types.
Ventral. The underside, lower surface of an animal, opposite to dorsal.
Vertebrate. An animal with a spinal column and skeleton of bone, including amphibians, reptiles, birds and mammals.
Vestigial. A characteristic with little or no contemporary use, but derived from one which was useful and well developed in an ancestral form.
Vibrissae. Stiff, coarse hairs richly supplied with nerves, found especially around the snout and with a sensory (tactile) function.
Vocalization. Calls or sounds produced by the vocal chords of a mammal, and uttered through the mouth. Vocalizations differ with the age and sex of mammals but are usually similar within a species.
Yearling. A young animal between one and two years of age (referring to species that take at least two years to mature).

Funisciurus congicus 102
Funisciurus isabella 102
Funisciurus lemniscatus 100
Funisciurus leucogenys 100
Funisciurus pyrropus 100
Funisciurus substriatus 102

G

Galago alleni 62
Galago gallarum 64
Galago inustus 64
Galago matschiei 64
Galago moholi 64
Galago senegalensis 64
Galagoides 66
Galagoides demidoff 66
Galagoides granti 66
Galagoides rondoensis 66
Galagoides thomasi 66
Galagoides zanzibaricus 66
Galagonidae 60
Gazella cuvieri 238
Gazella dama 240
Gazella dama dama 240
Gazella dama ruficollis 240
Gazella dorcas 238
Gazella granti granti 240
Gazella granti notata 240
Gazella granti petersi 240
Gazella leptoceros 238
Gazella rufifrons 238
Gazella soemmerringi 240
Gazella soemmerringi berberana 240
Gazella soemmerringi butteri 240
Gazella soemmerringi soemmerringi 240
Gazella spekei 238
Genetta abyssinica 166
Genetta angolensis 164
Genetta genetta 164
Genetta johnstoni 166
Genetta maculata 164
Genetta servalina 164
Genetta thierryi 166
Genetta tigrina 164
Genetta victoriae 164
Georychus capensis 118
Geosciurus inauris 98
Geosciurus princeps 98
Gerbillinae 124
Gerbillurus 126
Gerbillus 124

Giraffa camelopardalis 208
Giraffidae 206
Gliridae 116
Gorilla gorilla 24
Grammomys 136
Graphiurus 116

H

Heimyscus fumosus 134
Heliophobius argenteocinereus 118
Helioscurius gambianus 108
Helioscurius mutabilis 108
Helioscurius punctatus 108
Helioscurius rufobrachium 108
Helioscurius ruwenzori 108
Helioscurius undulatus 108
Helogale hirtula 154
Helogale parvula 154
Hemiechinus aethiopicus 88
Hemiechinus auritus 88
Herpestes ichneumon 156
Herpestes naso 156
Herpestes pulverulenta 156
Herpestes sanguinea 156
Herpestidae 152
Heterocephalus glaber 118
Heterohyrax 188
Hexaprotodon liberiensis 200
Hippopotamidae 200
Hippopotamus amphibius 200
Hipposiderinae 78
Hipposideros 78
Hippotraginae 252
Hippotragus equinus equinus 252
Hippotragus equinus koba 252
Hippotragus niger 252
Hyaena brunnea 162
Hyaenidae 162
Hybomys eisentrauti 138
Hybomys lunaris 138
Hybomys planifrons 138
Hybomys trivirgatus 138
Hybomys univittatus 138
Hyemoschus aquaticus 206
Hyaena hyaena 162
Hylochoerus meinertzhageni 204
Hylomyscus 134
Hypsignathus monstrosus 70
Hyracoidea 188
Hystricidae 120
Hystrix africaeaustralis 120

Hystrix cristata 120

I

Ichneumia albicauda 158
Ictonyx libyca 148
Ictonyx striatus 148
Idiurus macrotis 114
Idiurus zenkeri 114
Insectivora 88

J

Jaculus 122

K

Kerivoula 80
Kobus ellipsiprymnus 236
Kobus kob 236
Kobus leche 236
Kobus megaceros 236
Kobus vardoni 236

L

Laephotis 84
Lagomorpha 94
Lamottemys okuensis 136
Lavia frons 76
Leimacomys buettneri 128
Lemniscomys barbarus 140
Lemniscomys bellieri 140
Lemniscomys griselda 140
Lemniscomys hoogstraali 140
Lemniscomys linulus 140
Lemniscomys macculus 140
Lemniscomys mittendorfi 140
Lemniscomys rosalia 140
Lemniscomys roseveari 140
Lemniscomys striatus 140
Leporidae 94
Lepus capensis 94
Lepus crawshayi 94
Lepus saxatilis 94
Lepus starcki 94
Liberiictis kuhni 152
Lissonycteris angolensis 68
Litocranius walleri 242
Lophiomyinae 122
Lophiomys imhausi 122
Lophocebus albigena 40
Lophocebus aterrimus 40
Lophuromys 132
Loxodonta africana 190
Loxodonta africana africana 190
Loxodonta africana cyclotis 190

Lutra lutra 150
Lutra maculicollis 150
Lutrinae 150
Lycaon pictus 146

M

Macaca sylvanus 40
Macroscelidea 182
Macroscelides proboscideus 182
Madoqua (kirkii) cavendishi 232
Madoqua (kirkii) damarensis 232
Madoqua (kirkii) Somali 232
Madoqua (kirkii) thomasi 232
Madoqua guentheri 232
Madoqua piacentinii 232
Madoqua saltiana 232
Malacomys 132
Malacothrix typica 128
Mandrillus leucophaeus 36
Mandrillus sphinx 36
Manidae 176
Massouteria mzabi 116
Mastomys 134
Megachiroptera 68
Megadendromus nicolausi 128
Megadermatidae 76
Megaloglossus woermanni 72
Mellivora capensis 148
Meriones 124
Mesopotamogale ruwenzorii 186
Microchiroptera 74
Micropotamogale lamottei 186
Micropteropus 70
Mimetillus moloneyi 82
Miniopterus 84
Miopithecus ogouensis 40
Miopithecus talapoin 40
Molossidae 86
Mormopterus 86
Mungos gambianus 152
Mungos mungo 152
Muriculus imberbis 134
Muridae 132
Mus 134
Mustela nivalis 148
Mustela putorius 148
Mustelidae 148
Mustelinae 148
Mylomys dybowski 138
Myomys 134
Myonycteris 70
Myopterus 86
Myosciurus pumilio 102
Myosorex 90
Myotis 80
Myoxidae 116
Mystromyinae 122
Mystromys albicaudatus 122

N

Nandinia binotata 168
Nandinidae 168
Nanonycteris veldkampi 72
Neotragini 228
Neotragus batesi 228
Neotragus moschatus 228
Neotragus pygmaeus 228
Nyctalus 82
Nyctecius schlieffeni 82
Nycteridae 76
Nycteris 76

O

Oenomys 136
Okapia johnstoni 206
Oreotragus oreotragus 230
Orycteropodidae 178
Orycteropus afer 178
Oryctolagus cuniculus 96
Oryx beisa 254
Oryx besia beisa 254
Oryx besia callotis 254
Oryx dammah 254
Oryx gazella 254
Osbornictis piscivora 166
Otocyon megalotis 146
Otolemur argentatus 60
Otolemur crassicaudatus 60
Otolemur garnettii 60
Otolemur sp. nov.? 62
Otomops martiensseni 86
Otomyinae 130
Otomys 130
Otonycteris hemprichii 84
Ourebia ourebi 230

P

Pachyuromys duprasi 124
Pan paniscus 22
Pan troglodytes 22
Panthera leo 174
Panthera pardus 174
Papio anubis 34
Papio cynocephalus 34
Papio hamadryas 34
Papio papio 34
Papio ursinus 34
Paracrocidura 92
Paracynictis selousi 158
Paraxerus alexandri 106
Paraxerus boehmi 106
Paraxerus cepapi 106
Paraxerus cooperi 104
Paraxerus flavovittis 106
Paraxerus lucifer 104
Paraxerus ochraceus 106
Paraxerus palliatus 104
Paraxerus poensis 106
Paraxerus vexillarius 104
Parotomys 130
Pectinator spekei 116
Pedetes capensis 116
Pedetidae 116
Pelea capreolus 234
Pelomys 138
Pelomys campanae 138
Pelomys fallax 138
Pelomys hopkinsi 138
Pelomys isseli 138
Pelomys minor 138
Perissodactyla 192
Perodicticus potto 58
Petrodromus tetradactylus 182
Petromus typicus 122
Petromyscus 130
Phacochoerus aethiopicus 204
Phacochoerus africanus 204
Phataginus tricuspis 176
Pholidota 176
Piliocolobus 26
Piliocolobus badius 26
Piliocolobus gordonorum 28
Piliocolobus kirkii 28
Piliocolobus oustaleti (tephrosceles) 28
Piliocolobus pennanti 26
Piliocolobus preussi 26
Piliocolobus rufomitratus 28
Piliocolobus tholloni 26
Pipistrellus 82
Platymops setiger 86
Plecotus austriacus 84
Plerotes anchietae 72
Poecilogale albinucha 148
Poelagus marjorita 96
Poiana leightoni 166
Poiana richardsoni 166
Potamochoerus larvatus 202
Potamochoerus porcus 202

Potamogale velox 186
Potamogalinae 186
Praomys 134
Prionomys batesi 128
Procavia 188
Procavidae 188
Procolobus verus 26
Pronolagus crassicaudatus 96
Pronolagus randensis 96
Pronolagus rupestris 96
Proteles cristata 162
Protoxerus aubinnii 110
Protoxerus stangeri 110
Psammomys 124
Psuedopotto martini 58
Pteropodidae 68
Pteropus 68

R
Raphicerus campestris 230
Raphicerus melanotis 228
Raphicerus sharpei 228
Redunca arundinum 234
Redunca fulvorufula 234
Redunca redunca 234
Reduncini 234
Rhabdomys pumilio 140
Rhinocerotidae 198
Rhinolophinae 78
Rhinolophus 78
Rhinopoma 74
Rhinopomatidae 74
Rhizomyidae 118
Rhynchocyon chrysopygus 184
Rhynchocyon cirnei 184
Rhynchocyon petersi 184
Rhynchogale melleri 158
Rodentia 98
Rousettus aegyptiacus 68

Ruwenzorisorex suncoides 90

S
Saccolaimus peli 74
Saccostomus 130
Sciuridae 98
Scotoecus 84
Scotophilus 84
Scutisorex somereni 90
Sekeetamys calurus 124
Smutsia gigantea 176
Smutsia temminckii 176
Steatomys 128
Stenocephalemys 134
Stenonycteris lanosus 68
Stochomys longicaudatus 136
Suncus 90
Surdisorex 90
Suricata suricata 152
Sus scrofa 202
Sylvicapra grimmia 220
Sylvisorex 90
Syncerus caffer 210
Syncerus caffer brachyceros 210
Syncerus caffer caffer 210
Syncerus caffer mathewsi 210
Syncerus caffer nanus 210

T
Tachyoryctes 118
Tadarida 86
Taphozous 74
Tatera 126
Taterillus 126
Taurotragus derbianus 218
Taurotragus oryx 218
Tenrecidae 186
Thallomys 136

Thamnomys 136
Theropithecus gelada 36
Thryonomyidae 120
Thryonomys gregorianus 120
Thryonomys swinderianus 120
Tragelaphini 212
Tragelaphus angasi 214
Tragelaphus buxtoni 216
Tragelaphus euryceros 212
Tragelaphus imberbis 214
Tragelaphus scriptus 212
Tragelaphus spekei 212
Tragelaphus strepsiceros 216
Tragulidae 206
Triaenops persicus 78
Tubulidentata 178

U
Uranomys ruddi 132
Uromanis tetradactyla 176

V
Vespertilionidae 80
Viverridae 164
Vulpes cana 146
Vulpes chama 144
Vulpes pallida 144
Vulpes rueppelli 144
Vulpes vulpes 144
Vulpes zerda 146

X
Xerus rutilus 98

Z
Zelotomys 132
Zenkerella insignis 114

ENGLISH NAME INDEX

A
Aardvark 178
Aardwolf 162
Addax 254
Angwantibo, Calabar 58
  Golden 58
Anomalure, Beecroft's 112
  Lesser 112
  Lord Derby's 112
  Pel's 112
Antelope, Dwarf 228
  Roan 252
  Royal 228
  Sable 252
Aoudad 256
Ass, Nubian Wild 196
  Somali Wild 196
  Wild 196

B
Baboon, Chacma 34
  Guinea 34
  Olive 34
  Sacred 34
  Yellow 34
Bat, 'Winged-rat' 86
  African Sheath-tailed 74
  Angola Fruit 68
  Barbastelle 80
  Benguela Fruit 72
  Black Hawk 74
  Butterfly 82
  Collared Fruit 70
  Dwarf Epauletted Fruit 70
  East African Flat-headed 86
  Egyptian Fruit 68
  Epauletted Fruit 70
  Evening 84
  Flat-headed 86
  Flying Calf 72
  Flying Fox 68
  Free-tailed 86
  Fruit 68
  Giant Mastiff 86
  Golden Fruit 72
  Guano 86
  Hairy 80
  Hammer 70
  Heart-nosed 76
  Hempriche's Long-eared 84
  Horseshoe 78
  House 84
  Insect 74
  Large-winged 76
  Leaf-nosed 78
  Long-fingered 84
  Moloney's Flat-headed 82
  Mops 86
  Mountain Fruit 68
  Mouse-tailed 74
  Nectar 72
  Noctules 82
  Northern Long-eared 84
  Percival's Trident 78
  Persian Leaf-nosed 78
  Pipistrelle 82
  Rousette 68
  Schlieffen's Twilight 82
  Serotine 82
  Singing Fruit 70
  Slit-faced 76
  Straw-coloured Fruit 68
  Tear-drop Fruit 72
  Tomb 74
  Trident Leaf-nosed 78
  Tropical Long-eared 84
  Vesper 80
  Winged Rat 86
  Woolly 80
  Wrinkle-lipped 86
  Yellow-winged 76
Beira 230
Blesbok 246
Blesmol, Cape 118
  Common 118
  Dune 118
  Silky 118
Boar, Wild 202
Bongo 212
Bonobo 22
Bontebok 246
Buffalo, African 210
  Savannah 210
Bush-rat 136
Bushbuck 212

C
Cane-rat, Marsh 120
  Savannah 120
Caracal 172
Cat, Black-footed 170
  Golden 172
  Sand 170
  Serval 172
  Swamp 170
  Wild 170
Cheetah 174
Chevrotain, Water 206
Chimpanzee 22
  Pygmy 22
Civet, African 168
  African Palm 168
Colobus, Angola Pied 32
  Black 32
  Geoffroy's Pied 32
  Guereza 32
  Olive 26
  Western Pied 32
Cusimanse, Alexander's 154
  Ansorge's 154
  Common 154
  Flat-headed 154

D
Deer, Red 206
Dibatag 242
Dikdik, Günther's 232
  Kirk's 232
  Salt's 232
  Silver 232
Dog, Wild 146
Dormouse, African 116
  Eastern Orchard 116
Drill 36
Duiker, Abbot's 224
  Ader's 220
  Bay 226
  Black 224
  Black-fronted 222
  Blue 220, 228
  Bush 220
  Harvey's 222
  Jentink's 226
  Maxwell's 220
  Natal 222
  Ogilby's 226
  Peter's 224
  Red-flanked 222
  Ruwenzori Red 222
  White-bellied 224
  Yellow-backed 224
  Zebra 220
Dwarf Galagos 66

E
Eland 218

Derby's 218
Elephant Shrew, Chequered 184
　Four-toed 182
　Golden-rumped 184
　Lesser 182
　Round-eared 182
　Zanj 184
Elephant, African 190
　Bush 190
　Forest 190
　Pygmy 190

F
Flying Calf 72
Flying Fox 68
Fox, Bat-eared 146
　Cape 144
　Fennec 146
　Hoary 146
　Pale 144
　Red 144
　Royal 146
　Ruppell's 144
　Sand 144
　Simien 142

G
Galago, Allen's Squirrel 62
　Demidoff's 66
　Elegant Needle-clawed 62
　Greater 60
　Mozambique 66
　Mwera 62
　Pallid Needle-clawed 62
　Rondo 66
　Senegal 64
　Silver 60
　Small-eared 60
　Somali 64
　South African 64
　Spectacled 64
　Thomas's 66
　Zanzibar 66
Gazelle, Cuvier's 238
　Dama 240
　Dorcas 238
　Grant's 240
　Red-fronted 238
　Rhim 238
　Soemmerring's 240
　Speke's 238
　Thomson's 238
Gedemsa 216

Gelada 36
Gemsbok 254
Genet, Aquatic 166
　Blotched 164
　Common 164
　Ethiopian 166
　Giant 164
　Hausa 166
　Johnston's 166
　Miombo 164
　Servaline 164
Gerbil 124
　Dwarf 126
　Fat-tailed 124
　Hairy-footed 126
　Naked-soled 126
　Namaqua 126
　Tatera 126
　Taterillus 126
Gerenuk 242
Giraffe 208
Gnu, Brindled 250
　Mozambique 250
　Nyassa 250
　White-bearded 250
　White-tailed 250
Gorilla 24
Grass-hare, Uganda 96
Grysbok, Cape 228
　Sharpe's 228
Gundi, Fringe-eared 116
　Senegal 116

H
Hare, Cape 94
　Jameson's Red Rock 96
　Natal Red Rock 96
　Scrub 94
　Smith's Red Rock 96
　Spring 116
　Starck's 94
Hartebeest 248
Hedgehog, African 88
　Long-eared 88
Hippopotamus 200
　Pygmy 200
Hirola 244
Hog, Giant 204
　Red River 202
Honey Badger 148
Hyaena, Brown 162
　Spotted 162
　Striped 162
Hyrax, Bush 188

　Rock 188
　Tree 188

I
Ibex, Nubian 256
　Walia 256
Impala 244
Insectivores 88

J
Jackal, Black-backed 142
　Common (Golden) 142
　Side-striped 142
Jerboa, Four-toed 122
　Desert 122
Jird, Bushy-tailed 124

K
Klipspringer 230
Kob 236
Kongoni 248
Korrigum 246
Kudu, Greater 216
　Lesser 214

L
Lechwe 236
　Nile 236
Leopard 174
Lesser Galagos 64
'Linsang', Central African 166
　West African 166
Lion 174

M
Macaque, Barbary 40
Mandrill 36
Mangabey, Agile 38
　Black 40
　Golden-bellied 38
　Grey-cheeked 40
　Red-capped 38
　Sanje 38
　Sooty 38
　Tana 38
Meerkat 152
Mole, Cape Golden 180
　Cryptic Golden 180
　Desert Golden 180
　Forty-toothed Golden 180
　Giant Golden 180
　Narrow-headed Golden 180
　Yellow Golden 180

Mole-rat, Giant 142
　Naked 118
Mongoose, Banded 152
　Black-legged 160
　Bushy-tailed 160
　Dwarf 154
　Egyptian 156
　Gambian 152
　Ichneumon 156
　Jackson's 160
　Liberian 152
　Long-snouted 156
　Marsh 158
　Meller's 158
　Savannah 152
　Selous's 158
　Slender 156
　Small Grey 156
　Sokoke Dog 160
　Somali Dwarf 154
　White-tailed 158
　Yellow 156
Monkey, Allen's Swamp 40
　Bale 42
　Callithrix 42
　Campbell's 48
　Crowned 48
　de Brazza's 46
　Dent's 48
　Diana 46
　Gentle 50
　Grivet 42
　L'Hoest's 44
　Lesser Spot-nosed 52, 56
　Lowe's 48
　Mona 48
　Moustached 52, 54
　Nigerian White-throated 52, 56
　Owl-faced 46
　Patas 44
　Preuss's 44
　Putty-nosed 50
　Red-eared 52, 54
　Red-tailed 52, 56
　Salonga 46
　Sclater's 52, 54
　Sun-tailed 44
　Tantalus 42
　Vervet 42
　Wolf's 48
Mouse, African wood 134
　Broad-headed Stink 132
　Brush-furred 132
　Climbing 128
　Common 134
　de Balsac's 134
　Delaney's 130
　Dephua 136
　Dollman's Climbing 128
　Fat 128
　Four-striped Grass 140
　Giant Climbing 128
　Hump-nosed 138
　Large-eared 128
　Long-eared Flying 114
　Long-tailed Field 134
　Mount Oku 136
　Narrow-footed Woodland 136
　Pouched 130
　Pygmy rock 130
　Spiny 132
　Togo 128
　Uranomys 132
　Velvet Climbing 128
　White-tailed 122
　Wurch 134
　Zebra 140
　Zenker's Flying 114

N
Nyala 214
　Mountain 216
Nyamera 246

O
Okapi 206
Oribi 230
Oryx, Beisa 254
　Fringe-eared 254
　Scimitar-horned 254
　Southern 254
Otter, African Clawless 150
　Common 150
　Spot-necked 150
　Swamp 150
Oxen 210

P
Pangolin, Giant 176
　Ground 176
　Long-tailed 176
　Tree 176
Pectinator 116
Pig, Bush 202
Polecat 148
Porcupine, Brush-tailed 120
　Crested 120
　South African 120
Potto 58
　Martin's 58
Primates 21
Pseudo-hamster 122
Puku 236

R
Rabbit, Common 96
　Riverine 94
Rat, Acacia 136
　Broad-footed Thicket 136
　Creek 138
　Crested 122
　Dassie 122
　Dega 138
　Ethiopian Meadow 134
　Giant Pouched 130
　Groove-toothed 130
　Lesser Pouched 130
　Link 128
　Long-footed 132
　Maned 122
　Meadow 134
　Mill 138
　Multimammate 134
　Rusty-nosed 136
　Shaggy Swamp 136
　Soft-furred 134
　Target 136
　Unstriped Grass 138
　Velvet 132
　Whistling 130
Ratel 148
Red Colobus 26, 30
　Central African 28
　Iringa 28
　Pennant's 26
　Preuss's 26
　Tana River 28
　Tshuapa 26
　Western 26
　Zanzibar 28
Reedbuck, Bohor 234
　Mountain 234
　Southern 234
Rhebok 234
Rhinoceros, Black 198
　Browse 198
　Grass 198
　White 198
Rodents 98
Root-rat 118

S

Sand-puppy 118
Sand-rat, Fat 124
Scaly-tail, Cameroon 114
Sengi 182
Sheep, Barbary 256
Shrew, Climbing 90
   Congo 90
   Giant Otter 186
   Hero 90
   Mole 90
   Mount Nimba Otter 186
   Mouse 90
   Musk 90
   Rodent 92
   Ruwenzori 90
   Ruwenzori Otter 186
   White-toothed 92
Sitatunga 212
Soricidae 90
Springbuck 242
Squirrel, African Giant 110
   African Pygmy 102
   Alexander's Dwarf 106
   Barbary Ground 98
   Biafran Bight Palm 110
   Boehm's 106
   Bush 104
   Carruther's Mountain 104
   Congo Rope 102
   Cooper's Mountain 104
   Damara Ground 98
   Fire-footed Rope 100
   Gambian Sun 108
   Green 106
   Kintampo Rope 102
   Lady Burton's Rope 102
   Lunda Rope 100
   Lushoto Mountain 104
   Mutable Sun 108
   Ochre Bush 106
   Red-bellied Coast 104
   Red-cheeked Rope 100
   Red-legged Sun 108
   Ribboned Rope 100
   Ruwenzori Sun 108
   Slender-tailed 110
   Smith's Bush 106
   South African Ground 98
   Striped Bush 106
   Striped Ground 98
   Tanganyika Mountain 104
   Thomas's Rope 100
   Unstriped Ground 98
   Western Palm 110
   Zanj Sun 108
Steinbuck 230
Suidae 202
Suni 228
Suricate 152

T

Talapoin, Northern 40
   Southern 40
Tiang 246
Topi 244, 246
Tsessebe 246

W

Walo 126
Warthog, Common 204
   Desert 204
Waterbuck 236
Weasel 148
   Least 148
   Libyan Striped 148
   Striped 148
   White-Naped 148
Wildebeest, Black 250
   Blue 250
Wolf, Ethiopian 142

Z

Zebra, Cape Mountain 194
   Common 192
   Grevy's 196
   Hartmann's Mountain 194
   Mountain 194
Zorilla 148